After Work

AFTER WORK

Japanese Silver Backpackers in Malaysia

Shiori Shakuto

PENN

UNIVERSITY OF PENNSYLVANIA PRESS

PHILADELPHIA

Copyright © 2025 University of Pennsylvania Press

Published by
University of Pennsylvania Press
Philadelphia, Pennsylvania 19104–4112
www.pennpress.org

Printed in the United States of America on acid-free paper

10 9 8 7 6 5 4 3 2 1

A Cataloging-in-Publication record is available from the
Library of Congress.

Hardcover ISBN 978-1-5128-2710-1
Paperback ISBN 978-1-5128-2708-8
Ebook ISBN 978-1-5128-2709-5

To my family

CONTENTS

Preface   ix

Dramatis Personae   xiii

Introduction   1

Chapter 1. Work, Gender, and Lifecourse in Japan   23

Chapter 2. The "Malaysia My Second Home"
Program and Malaysia-Japan Relations   46

Chapter 3. Transnational Negotiation of Normative Aging   71

Chapter 4. Romantic Partnership   95

Chapter 5. Negotiating Families from a Distance   118

Chapter 6. Regeneration, Repair, and Return   141

Conclusion. Beyond Work-Life Balance   158

Glossary   165

Notes   167

References   177

Index   195

Acknowledgments   203

*A*fter *Work* is an ethnography of "silver backpackers" who are pre-dominantly middle-class heterosexual Japanese couples in their mid-fifties to seventies, and who moved to Malaysia for a few years before eventually returning to Japan. When I asked some Japanese silver backpackers why they desired to move to Malaysia, many men cited finding *ikigai* in their second lives. Ikigai has entered popular imagination outside of Japan after the successful publication of Hector Garcia and Francesc Miralles' 2017 bestseller, *Ikigai: The Japanese Secret to a Long and Happy Life.* Although ikigai had been translated by anthropologists of Japan as "what makes life worth living" (e.g., Mathews 1996) or "that which gives a person happiness" (Kavedzija 2019), Garcia and Miralles (2017, 2) translate it as "the happiness of always being busy." They argue that Japanese seniors maintain a happy life by preserving a sense of purpose in their lives. Indeed, lacking a sense of purpose constituted one of the main reasons for silver backpackers' eventual return to Japan. I will begin the account of transnational retirement by talking about a couple who was about to return to Japan. Their stories embody one of the core foci of this book: differences in how women and men viewed their ideal retirement.

A few months after my arrival in Malaysia in 2014, Mr. and Mrs. Yamamoto invited me to their home to meet Mr. and Mrs. Otani.[1] Both couples lived in the same condominium complex, which was popular among Japanese expatriates and retirees. Mr. and Mrs. Otani were about to return to Japan after having spent only a year in Kuala Lumpur.

A tall man in his mid-sixties, Mr. Otani marched into the Yamamotos' living room with his shirt buttoned all the way up. He had worked for a large Japanese trading company for forty years and was an expatriate in the United States before retiring a year prior. His wife followed him into the living room wearing a loose Malaysian batik dress and carrying a bamboo bag on her shoulder.

At their arrival, Mr. Yamamoto asked his wife to prepare tea for the guests. Mr. Otani immediately scorned Mr. Yamamoto for making his wife do the chore. After an awkward moment, Mrs. Yamamoto said she didn't mind and went into the kitchen. Mrs. Otani quickly followed Mrs. Yamamoto into the kitchen to help her prepare tea. Three of us—Mr. Yamamoto, Mr. Otani, and I—sat at the table. I noticed that Mr. Otani had prepared a note for this meeting with a list of points. Ten minutes later, when the tea was served, Mr. Otani thanked Mrs. Yamamoto and began speaking with a clear voice.

> It is not good to just relax in Malaysia. The reason why we decided to leave Malaysia so soon after arriving was that I had failed to come here with a purpose [*mokuteki*], a good sense of what I wanted to do. I did not plan my life course [*jinsei sekkei*] after retirement well.[2]
>
> From what I have observed, I see there are four types of Japanese retirees in Malaysia. The first category is those who left Japan because they saw no future there. Some of them left after the Fukushima nuclear disaster in 2011 to establish a safe haven for themselves and their family in Malaysia, and some were simply disappointed at the state of current politics and economics. The second category is those who wanted to pursue their hobbies like golf. The third category is those who wanted to contribute to the Malaysian community, such as by becoming a Japanese language teacher. These three categories of people all have a clear sense of purpose in Malaysia.
>
> Now, the fourth category is people like me, who came here without any purpose. I didn't do enough planning. Perhaps I am closest to the third category. But I chose the wrong condominium complex. Most residents in this condominium are Japanese; all I hear is the sound of Japanese housewives gossiping around the pool [*shufu ga puru de idobata kaigi shiteiru koe shika kikoenai*]. One needs to become friends with the locals [*rokaru*]. But I couldn't make any local friends here.[3]

Mr. Otani paused to get a glass of water. I turned to his wife, who was playing with the Yamamotos' dog in the living area. Mrs. Yamamoto and Mrs. Otani were good friends because they met daily by the poolside for a chat when Mrs. Yamamoto took her dog for a walk.

Noticing me looking at Mrs. Otani, her husband intervened. "My wife likes it here." Realizing that we were talking about her, Mrs. Otani came and joined our conversation. She said that she enjoyed her time in Malaysia, including the time she spent chatting with other Japanese women in the condominium complex. For her, she said, choosing this condominium was the best decision that they had made in coming to Malaysia. But her husband had already found a reemployment opportunity back in Japan. They soon left the Yamamotos to pack their apartment.

After they left, Mrs. Yamamoto, who had been listening to our conversations quietly, spoke up. "I think what Mr. Otani just said to you, Shiori-san—'we have to have a purpose in Malaysia'—is such a male perspective."

Intrigued by her critique of a man who scorned her husband for making her prepare the tea, I asked Mrs. Yamamoto to elaborate. It would have been disappointing for Mr. Otani, who no doubt thought of himself as a women's ally, perhaps even a feminist, to be told that he was presenting an issue from a male perspective. Mrs. Yamamoto elaborated. "Well, men don't know what to do with freedom and time. It's like our dog. As soon as I unleash her, she gets anxious. She looks at me with a worried look. It's the same for men. A sense of purpose is like a leash. For men, it's less stressful to have a job than to have freedom." Mrs. Yamamoto perceived men's tendencies to seek opportunities for purposeful activities—whether that was a hobby or a job—as a sign of not being able to handle the freedom given to them by their retirement. She continued to mention that she really enjoyed the poolside chat (idobata kaigi); everyday she looked forward to taking her dog for a walk and catching up with her female friends by the swimming pool. Like Mrs. Otani, Mrs. Yamomoto felt that she was lucky to have chosen this condominium complex because of her relations with her Japanese neighbors.

Mrs. Yamamoto's comment pointed to the possibly gendered nature of the desire for a sense of purpose in retirement. Although Hector Garcia and Francesc Miralles placed the sense of purpose and of "always being busy" as the very meaning of ikigai, that might, according to Mrs. Yamamoto, be solely a male perspective.

Pioneering scholarship exploring gender relations in Japan has revealed how the gendered division of labor which had been propagated since the postwar, high-growth period continue to affect the public and intimate lives of young and working-age Japanese people today. In this book, I explore a similar topic, on the emotional consequences of living under a capitalist structure but focus on a population that has received less attention so far—retirees.

After Work explores how gendered values and practices remain or get transformed when one leaves the labor market in times of recession. How do retirees renegotiate personhood and relationships as they face old and new expectations about lifecourses and aging? How do differently positioned Japanese men and women make sense of their "purpose," or the relevance of it at all, in their second life overseas? How does the shifting geopolitical positioning of Japan in the world shape their experiences?

After Work addresses these questions by focusing on retired people who moved transnationally to Malaysia. The impact of transnational retirement on Malaysia is not the main topic of this book, yet the everyday experiences of Japanese transnational retirees both affirmed and shifted the imaginaries of Japan-Malaysia relations. The phenomenon of Japanese transnational retirement in Malaysia cannot be detached from the postcolonial and economic context. Silver backpackers negotiated their post-work personhood, relationality, and their lives from the margins of their own aging temporality and in the spaces of the Global South. It was from these margins that these retirees challenged some of the regulatory forms associated with capitalism. This book is therefore both a study of mobility in later life and a shifting of inter-Asian racial imaginaries. The transnational location provided a productive way to see how historical, cultural, and racialized complexities entangled with the making of intimate relations in increasingly connected Asian countries (Thang et al. 2011). *After Work* highlights the importance of transnational locations in allowing people to creatively enact wellness, achieve respectability, and gain belonging in uncertain times.

DRAMATIS PERSONAE

The descriptions provided here are not a comprehensive ethnographic account of my interlocutors. Rather, this is meant as a reading guide to connect different stories in the book. More comprehensive accounts of each person are provided throughout the book.

Mrs. Aoi	She organized weekly lunch and sewing sessions at her condominium. She brought boxes of cling wrap from Japan to Kuala Lumpur.
Mrs. Hara	Before moving to Malaysia, she got rid of winter clothes and kimonos. She arrived in Malaysia with only two suitcases. Although she initially felt much lighter, she began to feel that her life in Malaysia was *mottainai*, a waste. She and her husband returned to Japan after a few years to look after their grandson.
Martha Hasegawa	A former housewife, she became a conductor for the choir group at the Japan Cultural Center in Kuala Lumpur.
Mrs. Ishida	She was from a small, close-knit community in rural Japan. She felt liberated from social obligations when she came to Malaysia. But she soon found herself tied to social obligations in the Japan Cultural Center.
Mr. and Mrs. Kosaka	Mrs. Kosaka started a yogurt network among female Japanese neighbors in Mont Kiara. She stayed in Kuala Lumpur intermittently because she was looking after the couple's daughter in Japan. Mr. Kosaka volunteered regularly to help newcomers. They returned to Japan together when Mr. Kosaka developed a hearing problem.

Eisaku (Eddie) Kobayashi	He retired from a large trading company where he had a successful career serving as an expatriate in various countries. After retirement, however, he found it hard to connect with his wife and children. He came to Malaysia by himself. He enjoyed attending concerts in Kuala Lumpur.
Ms. Machida	She was a single woman who was part of the yogurt network started by Mrs. Kosaka. Ms. Machida made origami crafts and made friends with the staff of her condominium complex and with Japanese expatriate wives.
Mich	He was a single man who stayed in a hostel in Kuala Lumpur. He took an early retirement and started traveling around the world.
Mrs. Nishiguchi	Mr. Nishiguchi explained the concept of the "give and give" relationship as the accumulation of different layers of colors.
Mrs. Okada	Mrs. Okada had felt that her life was constrained first by her father and then her husband. After five years in Malaysia, Mr. and Mrs. Okada returned to Miyazaki Prefecture, Mrs. Okada's natal home, to look after her mother.
Paul	A former investment banker, he was a flamboyant member of the Art Club. He regularly organized parties for fellow silver backpackers.
Ms. Saito	She was a single mother of three. She moved to Malaysia after she retired in order to learn English.
Mr. and Mrs. Uchida	Mr. and Mrs. Uchida came to Malaysia after his retirement. A natural leader, Mr. Uchida led many activities at the Japan Cultural Center and regularly hosted home parties for his classmates. Mrs. Uchida liked to make patchwork crafts out of fabrics. She spent most of her time in Malaysia sewing at home.

Introduction

Where Do You Want to Be
in Your Retirement?

R elocating to a different city or country for retirement has become a popular choice for many people around the world. Since the early 2000s, Malaysia has emerged as a possible retirement destination for middle- to upper-middle-class Japanese citizens. The number of Japanese residents in Malaysia doubled from 2012 to 2013, and in Kuala Lumpur, the number increased by more than double in the same year (Ministry of Foreign Affairs of Japan 2014). I first encountered some Japanese retirees in Malaysia in 2011 at a late-night food stall in Bangsar, the trendy district of Kuala Lumpur. My friends and I were exchanging stories of our recent lives when I heard the familiar sounds of Japanese behind me. Intrigued by their energetic tones and the frequent outburst of laughter, I turned to find a group of Japanese women and men in their sixties in their T-shirts and shorts with a beer in their hands. They invited us to join the conversation, and they told me that they were "silver backpackers" (*shirubaa bakku pakkaa*).[1] One of them articulated to me what it meant to be a silver backpacker. "Unlike young backpackers, we have no energy, but we have money. So instead of staying in hostels, we rent an apartment in Kuala Lumpur and fly around the world with our handbags."[2]

In their youth, these retirees had read travel novels by Sawaki Kotaro, a backpacker and a writer from the 1970s, and they were inspired to, one day, lead similarly adventurous lives overseas. Having had to work and raise children in their younger years, the opportunity to live adventurous lives overseas finally arose in retirement.[3] Many of them told me that their move to Malaysia was the first chapter in their long retirement life. This first chapter was usually defined by good health and wealth. They possessed good mental and physical capacities to live in a foreign country. Many of their children had left home to go to universities. "The Malaysian chapter of their retirement," as they called it, was a time to live for themselves.

The book is about how silver backpackers navigated this period "after work." Readers seeking the impact of transnational retirement on the receiving country may not get what they were looking for in this book, yet I hope they still take away some of the important insights about aging in an increasingly uncertain and mobile era. Japan offers a helpful case study. In Japan in the early 2010s, the average age up to which one could expect to live without disabilities was seventy years for men and seventy-three for women (Asahi Shimbun 2014). Given that the retirement age for most people was sixty in 2013, many retirees had around an extra ten to fifteen years of temporal extension in which they were neither working nor physically incapacitated. However, the period after retirement from waged labor is one of the least defined periods in one's life. Most silver backpackers in their sixties had lived through a period which was marked by the high rate of employment and lifetime security. Under a grand narrative of postwar recovery and national economic growth, a normative *raihukosu* (lifecourse) marked by productive and reproductive moments—birth, graduation from university, gaining a job, marriage, birth of a child, and retirement—set the momentum of everyday lives (Kelly 1993). Under this lifecourse, there was a clear pathway for "a successful life" which usually meant full-time employment for men and full-time housework for women. Yet there was no normative lifecourse after retirement. In a capitalist society like Japan, perception of one's age is tied to one's productive contributions to society.[4] A person tends to be labeled as "old" especially after retiring from the labor market, highlighting their social and cultural displacement from productivist discourse. In the 1950s, when my interlocutors were born, "the elderly" (*koureisha*) were defined as those above sixty-five, in contrast to those aged between fifteen and sixty-four who were defined as the "productive population" (*seisan nenrei jinkou*) (Cabinet Office 2012b, 14). Now, however, the label "the elderly" does not reflect the improved health of the aging population in contemporary Japan. Increasing longevity meant that many of my interlocutors, whose ages ranged between the late fifties and late seventies, still had, and were caring for, their living parents.

Unlike the working period in which there were clearer goals and a ladder upon which to climb for a lifecourse, what constitutes a good life after work is less clear. Anthony Giddens, a British sociologist who was well-known for his theorizations on modern societies, argued that the concepts of self and identity had become a reflexive project in late modernity. As society moves toward individualization, traditional institutions, which used to offer ritualized rites of passage that had allowed individuals to make transitions in their lives, weakened (Giddens 1991, 33). Instead, the individuals must engage in reflexive processes of creating the narratives of self to mark the transition (Kawashima 2010, 273–74). In other words, as one transitions into "retirement" and eventually into old age, they must shape their own narratives of self and lifecourse after work.

Retirement has thus become a "project" for people to undertake. Terms such as "second life" and "post-retirement" have become buzzwords among retirees in contemporary Japan (Toyota 2006). In Japanese bookshops today one can find a self-help section devoted to titles encouraging older people to fill their time with self-development activities such as craft making, hiking, or volunteering (Mathews 2002). It was in this context that transnational retirement to Malaysia began to attract media attention as providing new opportunities for the realization of an ideal second life (Ono 2009, 615).

After Work offers an examination of one such "retirement project" by Japanese couples and individuals who started their transnational lives in Malaysia. The book deals with the question of retirement as both a self-making project and a relational one for a specific group of Japanese citizens known as the *dankai no sedai* (baby boomers).[5] This generation was born immediately after World War II and worked steadily and industriously to contribute to the high-growth period that began in the 1950s. To what extent do the gendered norms associated with capitalism dictate a good life for women and men after work? For Japanese women and men, most of whom had led very different lives until the men's retirement, the prospect of post-work life posed existential questions around identity and belonging. These questions influenced myriad decisions they had to make, from which activities they would take part in, to where and with whom to do them, and including more complicated issues surrounding gender roles and family relations in retirement.

More often than not, their decisions were characterized by the ambiguities of experiences. The conversations at the Yamamotos' upon which I drew in the preface is just one example of such ambiguities. Mr. Otani called out Mr. Yamamoto for making his wife prepare tea while Mr. Otani himself dismissed his wife's preferences for residence and activities in Malaysia. While Mrs. Yamamoto replied that she didn't mind making tea for everyone, she later made fun of men for not being able to handle freedom. While Mrs. Otani embraced the local material culture and took pleasure in her daily interactions with Japanese neighbors in Malaysia, she followed her husband back to Japan seemingly willingly. Their dialogue and dynamics flag many of the themes and ambiguities discussed in this book. What's at stake is the navigation of life without work.

The consideration of what comes after work is relevant not only for the older population but also for the young who are living through an uncertain economic future in Japan and beyond. After the collapse of the "bubble" economy that began in December 1989, corporations replaced lifetime employment with more contract-based, casual workers to cut costs (Takeyama 2016, 7).[6] The twenty million or so young people who tried to secure jobs after graduation during the recession were called "the lost generation," those for whom lifetime employment was no longer available (Kawashima 2010, 272). The ratio of irregular workers to regular employees had risen from 18.8 percent in 1990 to 38.2 percent in 2012 (Cook 2014, 36). Desperate to secure a job in an era where far fewer jobs were available, they took up positions that were unattractive or nonpermanent (Kawashima 2010, 272). For many of this generation, staying on the expected lifecourse was neither desirable nor achievable. "They had to venture into unknown territory, where past expectations and choices were limited, but patterns regarding new pathways had not yet been established" (Kawashima 2014, 111). Like retirees, youth in contemporary Japan had to pave their own lifecourses after the era of permanent work.

Covid-19 has also called into questions many of the assumptions about how we work and live. For instance, the pandemic has made work-from-home the new normal for many. As is evident from the very term "work-life balance," up to this point, we have treated "work" and "life" as separate aspects and have sought a better balance between the two. In an instant, the coronavirus pandemic tossed the two into a blender. As the boundaries between work and life are ever more blurred in contemporary society, it is time to reconsider the values of life in the aftermath of work. Nowhere is this question considered more thoroughly than among the retired population.

Going overseas has always been a way to depart from the existing social structure, to curve a lifecourse different from the generation before (Kawashima 2010; Kelsky 2001). Long before the pandemic hit, an increasing number of silver backpackers had left the existing structure to explore radically new personhoods, relationalities, and ways of life in their retirement. Just like young backpackers who embark on trips to Southeast Asia in search of freedom, a sense of self, or to reflect on their lives (Casado-Díaz 2006;

Cohen 2003; Riley 1988; Maoz 2007; Vogt 1976, 28), silver backpackers went to Malaysia for a variety of reasons. Initially, I was attracted to these older individuals because of their positivity and energy—their craving for new challenges, which some pursued alone, and others did so as couples. Their lives challenge the common perceptions that older adults and change, or older adults and intimacy, are somewhat incongruent. What about their quest for meanings, recognition, and companionship? How do older adults achieve them transnationally? These are the questions that guided this research about a group of Japanese women and men who moved to Malaysia in their retirement.

Japan, which underwent rapid economic growth followed by a rapid decline in the same century, provides a powerful setting for one of the most critical anthropological questions in contemporary society: how does one navigate life after a long period of secure, permanent work? I use the phrase "after work" to capture this experience and to connect the retirees' later-life negotiations of the meaning of life with their transnational mobility. After work conceptualizes the ambiguities and hope embedded in the silver backpackers' pursuit of meaning in the context of neoliberal aging policies, postcolonial relations, and decades of patriarchal divisions of labor. The term enables a useful analysis of the exercises of mobility, community-making, and modifying and reviving identity after one's working life has finished. Although this work focuses on the experiences of Japanese senior citizens, it also reveals some of the troubling power dynamics of gendered and neoliberal ideals as they take on a new meaning in older age, and in new transnational locations.

Transnational Retirement

Beginning in the late 1990s, there has been an increase in the amount of scholarship focusing on migration in later life. Broadly framed as "international retirement migration" (King, et al. 2000; King, et al. 2021), the literature encompasses a wide range of international mobility by seniors,[7] including the return migration of former labor migrants to their home countries (Bolzman, et al. 2006; Baldassar 2001; Bolognani 2014; Cerase 1974; Hoey 2010), the care migration of older parents to new countries to look after their children's families (Ho and Chiu 2020), and the "lifestyle migration" of those in pursuit of a better quality of life. While the boundaries between these movements are often blurred (Sacramento 2019), silver backpackers would fit best within the last category, although I will show in this book why this term might not readily apply to them either.

Benson and O'Reilly (2009b, 609–10) define lifestyle migration as "the movement of relatively affluent individuals . . . moving either part-time or full-time to places that, for various reasons, signify, for the migrant, a better quality of life."[8] Better quality can include "pleasant climate and natural environment; slower pace of life; lower living costs; social advantages, such as the existence of a community of compatriots; cultural attributes, such as low crime rates and acceptance of older people; health benefits; and ease of travel and proximity to the home country" (O'Reilly and Benson 2015, 421).[9] Studies on transnational retirement were initially conducted among older adults who move within the European and American regions, or those who move from these regions to countries in the Global South (see, for example, Lardiés-Bosque, et al. 2016; Hoggart and Buller 1995; Casado-Díaz 2006; Oliver 2008; King, et al. 2000; A. M. Williams, et al. 1997; Gustafson 2001).[10] Their analyses of transnational retirees have focused largely on two related questions.

First, these scholars focus on the power relations between older adults and the local population in the host community, paying particular attention to postcolonial history (Benson and O'Reilly 2018; Benson 2013). Most host countries of lifestyle migrants were previously colonies of Western countries (Benson 2013; O'Reilly and Benson 2015, 424). This created racialized and classed hierarchies in the destination which placed lifestyle migrants "who are often white, middle-class and in receipt of larger incomes than many within the local population" at the top of the hierarchy (Benson 2013; O'Reilly and Benson 2015, 424). Highlighting the older migrants' power, privilege, and global inequality, scholars point out who has access to wealth and capital to cross borders (B. C. Williams 2018; Hayes 2018; Scuzzarello 2020; Hayes and Pérez-Gañán 2017; Benson 2013).

Second, when scholars focus on the social dynamics within the community of transnational retirees, they often portray middle-class lifestyle migrants as neoliberal subjects who are trying to maximize their quality of life abroad in the context of a wider, successful aging movement (Benson and O'Reilly 2018, 239; Oliver 2008; Hayes 2021).[11] For example, in North America, being busy has become "a badge of honor at any stage," and therefore successful aging promotes a sense of permanent personhood, or agelessness, through one's purpose in life (Lamb 2017, 7).[12] This may partly explain why Hector Garcia and Francesc Miralles, in their bestseller, *Ikigai: The Japanese*

Secret to a Long and Happy Life (García and Miralles 2017, 2), defined *ikigai* as "the happiness of always being busy." Their book's appeal to a global audience may reflect the spread of successful aging discourses across the world.[13] In the context of transnational migration, wealthy retirees from the Global North can pursue their successful aging projects while outsourcing health care and care work to people in the destination countries (O'Reilly and Benson 2015, 424).[14] For this reason, scholars of lifestyle migration have framed those who embark on transnational retirement as both "postcolonial" and "neoliberal," as their practices reflect the rationalization drive for the maximization of quality of life (Benson and O'Reilly 2018, 15).

Transnational retirement is certainly becoming more common, but the motivation of each migrant varies, and when it comes to Japanese retirees in Malaysia, their lives in the destination are shaped by historical and cultural factors distinctive to Japan. Having said that, before I explore these factors in detail in this book, it is important to note the postcolonial and neoliberal tendencies that characterize the positionings of Japanese transnational retirees in Malaysia.

The majority of silver backpackers spent most of their time in the company of other Japanese people, and generally had little interaction with the local people.[15] The very lack of Malaysia in their everyday lives was a sign of postcolonial and racialized relations. Most silver backpackers were born after World War II (1941–1945) where Japan brutally colonized Malaysia, and they had lived through the postwar, high growth era in which Japanese multinational corporations opened branch offices and factories in Malaysia, and in many cases exploitatively extracted resources from the landscape. Given their privilege, it was not necessary for Japanese retirees to integrate with the locals in order to pursue a comfortable life.[16] In this postcolonial landscape, the reference points for many Japanese people were not the locals, but rather the Japanese people in Japan. "If I were in Japan, I would just be sitting at home, quietly sipping tea," male retirees regularly told me. Japanese silver backpackers saw retirees in Japan as either continuing to work beyond retirement age or as being isolated and inactive, having not found anything meaningful to do. In contrast, the postcolonial landscape of Malaysia allowed the silver backpackers to lead a very active lifestyle within the Japanese ethnic bubble. Taking advantage of the lower cost of living and the favorable exchange rate of the Japanese yen against the Malaysian ringgit, Japanese silver backpackers pursued affluent lifestyles in expatriate enclaves less than twenty-minute drive to the Japan Cultural Center, which offered a wide range of activities for the Japanese expatriate population. In many ways, it felt as though the destination, Malaysia, did not matter to the silver backpackers beyond its consumable potentiality, as long as it allowed them to enact their successfully aging lifestyle.

Couplehood in Retirement

The narrative of transnational retirement that I present here is more than a story of a postcolonial, and neoliberal, retirement. It is also a gendered one. In the ethnic bubble they created in Kuala Lumpur, the silver backpackers created another bubble: couplehood. Most Japanese silver backpackers I met came as couples, seemingly enjoying their retirement together with other couples. The image of a couple enjoying retirement together might not be so surprising to many readers of this book, but, in Japan, although trends are shifting rapidly, there is generally less emphasis on couplehood in public spaces, and men and women often socialize separately (Kiyota 2020). The tendency for homosociality is particularly pertinent for the generation of Japanese silver backpackers, retirees from the baby boomer generation.[17] These men and women had lived through a period where Japan's most significant economic activity shifted from agricultural labor to salaried labor, the latter of which was supported by the strict division of labor between women and men as *shufu* (housewife) and *sarariiman* (waged labor). Sarariiman is a term that denotes waged and salaried workers, particularly white-collar office workers who had come to constitute 80 percent of the Japanese labor force by 2005 (Hamada 2005; Brinton 1993, 56). While the (male) sarariiman spent much of their time at work, women were primarily understood through the nurturing and reproducing of male labor power in the postwar capitalist state (Rubin 1997, 162). This strict gendered division of labor separated the husbands and wives' social lives. For instance, one of my female interlocutors had spent almost her entire married life apart from her husband as he had been stationed in China a few years into their marriage. When men were assigned expatriate missions overseas, many of the women stayed in Japan with the children (Goodman 1993). One of the women I spoke with had stayed with her parents in Japan to raise the couple's children, and retirement in Malaysia was the first time that the couple spent a significant amount of time together.

When the baby boomers started to retire in the early 2010s, popular culture began to highlight spousal misrecognition in old age as one of the challenges of that generation. The period that couples had together after men's retirement was almost equivalent to one-third of their total married years (Skolnick 1991). Yet many of the couples faced problems involving intimacy in their retirement as they struggled to form fulfilling relationships with each other. Ryu Murakami (2012), a celebrated Japanese novelist, wrote a collection of short stories exploring love and misrecognition among elderly couples in contemporary Japan. One story, *Campingu Kaa* (Camping Car), is about a man who surprised his wife with a new camper van on the day of his retirement. He thought she would be delighted to start their retirement lives traveling in a camper van, but instead, she seemed upset and asked him to return the van. He couldn't understand why. The popularity of the theme "anxiety among older couples" in popular culture is reinforced by the emerging social phenomenon of later-life divorce (Alexy 2020, 15). The divorce rate for couples married for at least twenty years has been increasing since 1950, and it made up 21.5 percent of divorces in 2020 (Ministry of Health, Labor, and Welfare of Japan 2022). In 2005, a Japanese TV drama series popularized the term *jukunen rikon* (late-life divorce). It told the story of Yoko, a middle-aged housewife who decided to divorce her husband on the day of his retirement. She then embarked on her second life, neither as a wife nor as a mother, but rather as an independent person fulfilling her own dreams later in life.[18]

The anxieties over intimacy and gendered power dynamics in long-married couples are relevant to the lives of retirees in non-Japanese societies. Before publishing this book, I shared my initial observations with audiences in Malaysia, the U.S., Australia, and Singapore. The venues ranged from friendly dinner conversations to academic seminars and conferences. Most often, audiences, particularly women, were intrigued to hear how women and men's views of retirement and companionship in old age differed. There were some vigorous nods when I said that men's affection increased but women didn't necessarily reciprocate. After the seminar, several attendees approached me to share how my talk reminded them of their own parents.

Despite the popular interest, the gender dynamics among older couples are seldom addressed in the literature on later life. Most social scientific studies of aging instead pay attention to the social and political dimensions of aging such as access to health care (Olson 1988). Leading feminist scholars such as Simone de Beauvoir (1972) and Ueno Chizuko (2007) have long argued that aging is a gendered experience. Since the 1980s, a handful of gerontologists have started to study aging and gender (Arber and Ginn 1995b; Browne 1998; Rossi 1985; Arber, et al. 2003), with more recent scholars looking at the intersection of aging, gender, and other regulatory forms such as ethnicity and class (Garner 1999; Calasanti 2004; Freixas, et al. 2012; Lotherington 2019). In talking about gender and aging, however, many scholars tended to treat aging as a problem for women. For instance, one of the more prominent critiques of successful aging is that it perpetuates the gender stereotypes of men's performance and women's beauty (Krekula 2007; Twigg 2004; Pearsall 1997; C. Anderson 2019; Lamb 2017, 16; Calasanti and King 2017, 30). In this approach, older women have been primarily studied through a negative lens, framing aging as a problem (Krekula 2007, 160).

Yet, the capitalist lifecourse, which is often rightly argued as a source of oppression for women (Ueno 1994; Barrett 1989), can be experienced by some women as empowering in older age.[19] As popular culture has already shown, some women use later life as an opportunity for self-actualisation. Despite this, few scholars have explored how the ideals of happiness, including ideas about where and with whom to spend one's remaining life, differ between the genders. This has led feminist gerontologists to describe aging theorists and feminist sociologists as "'diners at separate tables', exchanging glances but without bringing together their conceptual resources" (Krekula 2007, 156). Ignoring gender in the stories of aging prevents us from gaining an adequate understanding of how people age, and as I will show in this book, it leaves out the experiences of women.

Hence, by bringing together the under-investigated links between aging studies and feminist studies, I ask an important question about how people negotiate gender relations in later life. Despite their earlier socialization, silver backpackers seemed to embody and actively promote companionate marriage ideals in Malaysia. One of the best-selling books written by a transnational retiree, who had collected 150 voices of Japanese people who had moved to Malaysia, lists "the liberation of women from domestic duties" as one of the three miracles of overseas retirement (Sakamoto 2011).[20] According to this work, due to the availability of cheap domestic services in Malaysia, Japanese women have more free time. In the freed-up time, the book argues that women and men can enjoy their hobby activities together. Another essay by a retiree in Malaysia mentions that he taught golf to his wife so that they could have a shared hobby in Malaysia (Nagata 2013, 78–85). The man wrote, "I said to my wife, 'let's be healthy and play golf together until at least seventy-five years old!' This is my new goal in life, and until I fall sick, I will live up to the goal" (Nagata 2013, 82).

Yet over the course of my fieldwork, I realized that the "joint retirement project" was often contested by women who had different perceptions of their movement and retirement more generally. Women who had been housewives did not "retire" from domestic work when their male partners retired. This difference impacted their social and spousal well-being in old age. This was reflected, for example, in how women and men referred to their moving abroad. While the majority of husbands called their move *ijuu* (relocation), implying that their move was a permanent or semi-permanent migration from Japan, the majority of women I spoke to referred to it as a *chouki ryokou* (prolonged holiday), with a view to returning to Japan within a few years. A lot of time and energy was spent on negotiating the expectations of mobility between spouses. Most of my interlocutors did end up returning to Japan within a few years of their arrival, often at the insistence of the female spouse, even though the visa would have allowed them to stay in Malaysia for ten years.

One of the core ethnographic observations of my research, therefore, centers on how men and women were situated differently in terms of their paths of belonging in old age, both at home in Japan and in Malaysia. When I looked deeper at the practices and assumptions of companionate marriage ideals, I found it to be not only a particular cultural and political-economic project but oftentimes a counterproductive one, especially for women. This book goes outward from these subtle, often taken-for-granted, differences between women and men to offer a critique of the patriarchal discourses that dominate present narratives of work and retirement.

In doing so, the book highlights the significance of the transnational location for the emotional lives of the group of silver backpackers. Perhaps initially, as many backpackers said, what attracted them to Malaysia was a warmer climate and lower cost of living. But the location seems to have taken on more meaning over time, as many stayed within the Japanese enclave to enact couplehood and other social relations that are increasingly harder to enact in Japan. The concept of "after work" enabled me to answer two central questions. First, how might the desire to retire overseas reflect the political economies of aging and gender in Japan? Second, how are the intimate relationships formed in Malaysia indicative of wider geopolitical relations?

To work through these questions, this book turns to the existing bodies of literature which have offered important insights into the intersection of feminism and transnationalism. A growing number of anthropologists have shown how global geopolitical relations and global capitalist flows manifest themselves in intimate relations, creating racialized and gendered subjectivities (Kelsky 2001; Constable 2003; Stout 2014; B. C. Williams 2018; Yamaura 2020, 8). While these scholars highlight the historical inequality between the migrant-sending countries and the host nations, feminist anthropologists of migration have been very careful not to create a binary image of "rich" hosts and "poor" migrants or of "liberated" hosts and "oppressed" migrants. Instead, scholars have paid nuanced attention to the specific gender contexts in the sending countries. Their research has shown the interconnectedness of gender, class, race, and cultural difference as being central to gendered and racialized subject formation in an increasingly connected world.

I build on these feminist scholars of migration who have facilitated new ways of thinking about cross-border connections through attention to intimacy.[21] I pay attention to intimate relations that are forged and fragmented among the Japanese migrants in the context of their movement to Malaysia. The transnational processes flush out some of the emotional consequences of gendered social relations which have deep roots in national socioeconomic institutions. This book lays out which domestic factors motivate the former elite male corporate workers and their female counterparts, as well as single Japanese women and men, to (temporarily) leave their families, friends, home, communities, and their home country in their old age. At the same time, the book shows that the silver backpackers' subjectivities are deeply shaped by their participation in transnational processes. Instead of conceptualizing gender as a binary between men and women, this book explores how both women and men tried to transcend gendered divisions of labor in their second life abroad, where different gendered subjectivities and relations seemed possible. Their social relations in turn led to the reevaluation of the capitalist framework and the geopolitical imaginaries.

Because silver backpackers' lives demonstrate the dynamism of gender, age, and race and speak to issues of the capitalist lifecourse and postcolonial relations, their experiences are important for understanding the emotional aftermath of the capitalist lifecourse and the associated divisions of labor in an increasingly connected world. The feminist framework allowed me to sharply critique the oppressive nature of some of the seemingly liberatory rhetoric such as "companionship" that became dominant in the transnational location. The finding that migrant women's lives are much more complex than the feminist potential presented in the popular discourse of retirement migration is one of the key outcomes of feminist intervention in this study. The analysis of the Japanese transnational retirement community in Malaysia provided an opportunity for reflection and the provision of a gendered critique about aging and retirement in Japan at a local level, and at a more global level, the capitalist separation of waged and non-waged work and its influence on intimate relations. This ethnography articulates an anthropology of life from the intimate experiences of retired Japanese people who negotiated their lives and relational belonging with fellow Japanese people in Malaysia.

Feminist Methodologies and Theory Building

My research with Japanese transnational retirees in Malaysia started in 2013 when I signed up for an online forum which hosted 2,300 existing and prospective transnational retirees. This forum was a site that many silver backpackers engaged with before, after, and during their relocation to Malaysia. Its many different chat groups ranged from communities discussing Malaysian restaurants and ideas for trips, to visa advice. I wrote to the moderator of the list explaining who I was and the nature of my research. He suggested I create my own profile page and include a detailed introduction. A few retirees, both women and men, offered to meet up right away and help recruit other research participants. Some introduced me to their friends, and others organized meetings at their homes for me to meet their friends, like how Mr. and Mrs. Yamamoto introduced me to Mr. and Mrs. Otani. As my interlocutors integrated their offline and online worlds, my online presence provided me with a relatively seamless entry into the physical world of the Japanese retirees in Malaysia.

Upon arriving in Malaysia in late 2013, I sought permission to access the Japan Cultural Center where many people from the online networks participated in daily activities. As a researcher, I joined some of their daily activities which gave me a systematic entry into the otherwise less defined "field" (Gupta and Ferguson 1997) of Japanese retirees in Kuala Lumpur. Day and night, I trained alongside male and female retirees at the rate of five times a week, assiduously applying myself to every pace of their rigorous routines, from learning the rules of igo (a Japanese board game) to the learning steps of ballroom dancing. In the short span of less than a year, I learned the basics of board games, ballroom dancing, painting, a new language, and choir. Many of my interlocutors likewise were participating in these activities for the first time and became enthusiastic practitioners. Some of them recommended books to read in the Cultural Center's library. For instance, many men were enthusiastic readers of *Tasogare Ryuseigun* (Like Shooting Stars in the Twilight), a popular comic series from 1995–2014 that illustrates middle-aged men's search for romance in later life. It was mostly through sharing these activities that I found the search for purpose and anxiety over one's identity and relationships in the aftermath of work as one of the main animating topics in the emotional lives of silver backpackers.

Half a year quickly passed after I started my fieldwork in Malaysia. My skills in ballroom dancing and igo games were slowly improving, and I became close with some retirees who invited me to their homes. I also spent some days shopping and eating with them in malls and restaurants outside of the cultural center. I also joined two groups on their trips to rural Selangor and Kota Kinabalu. Despite this, I felt that I was not hearing enough female voices. In choosing the interlocutors, I did not consciously single out people with specific markers of identity, such as poor or rich, single or married. Generally speaking, however, men were easier to reach. They readily volunteered to be interviewed and they claimed to speak for both their wives and themselves. "Often women are spoken for or about, but their own perspectives are difficult to discern" (Constable 2003, 5). Japanese women appeared to me to be less well understood, and at a disadvantage in having their voices subsumed under the voices of men. I tried to speak to women in private on several occasions, but the conversation never really touched upon their retirement lives or about Malaysia. Few seemed interested in the topic.

It took me a while to "find women" in the field. One day, unexpectedly, one of my female interlocutors passed me a packet of homemade yogurt. She asked me to use it as a starter and make my own yogurt next time. She had already shared the yogurt with other women, who in turn shared it with their friends. Her passing of yogurt incorporated me into the yogurt network of Japanese women. Following the yogurt network led me to other women, many of whom were, to my surprise, single and not participants in the Japan Cultural Center's activities. The discovery of the women's network outside of the cultural center was crucial in my decentering of discourses such as "activities," "roles," "purpose," and "couplehood" which were dominant in both the Japan Cultural Center and public policies of successful aging in Japan and beyond. By speaking to women in the yogurt network, I finally began to understand the different ways in which women and men produced their values in their second lives abroad.

Reflecting on my research, it was not enough to simply add women to the analysis. As a feminist social gerontologist, Clary Krekula (2007, 160) aptly argues, "adding women" as a variable gives an emphasis on the difference between women and men, which assumes an ideal referent and will likely result in older men being the ideal to which older women are compared. Instead, I should have gone further to question the gendered bias in the theories of successful aging themselves. Men's voices were easier for me to record initially not only because they spoke more or more publicly, but also because their practices and narratives spoke in tandem with the dominant discourse of successful aging that focused on activities in the public domain. It was tempting for me as a researcher to jump onto silver backpackers' active lives in the Japan Cultural Center and start analysing the similarities and gaps between the state discourses and those voices "on the ground." While this perspective is illuminating, it also risks occluding various ethnographic specificities by privileging certain relations (e.g., state-citizen) over others (e.g., gendered personhood, spousal, and familial relations). In the Japanese case, for the reasons I will demonstrate in this book, the focus on active participants in the public domains skewed the observation in favor of men. This might not be limited to Japan; as Krekula (2007) points out, the experiences of older women are seldom addressed in gender theory. By initially looking for women in the Japan Cultural Center and looking for their narratives about their public lives, I was limiting myself to the masculine domain in which men enacted their retirement projects in public. I realized that I was merely "butterfly-collecting" (Geertz 1973) women's voices. I initially missed women because women didn't necessarily speak the language of the dominant discourse that I was trained to observe. On reflection, even the discourse, or the "so what question" that anthropological knowledge tries to answer, is gendered (Ardener 1972; Mohanty 1984).

So where does that leave us in terms of feminist methodologies and theory building? How do we build theories from non-dominant perspectives? Finding women through the yogurt incident, I realized that these conversations about what counts as "activities" in retirement were very similar to the discussion feminist scholars have had about the invisible labor that is performed in domestic spaces. Just as how activities conducted (mostly by women) at home are often not valued or even visible, the activities conducted at home in retirement often are not considered "activities" in the discourse of successful aging. As mentioned before, many male silver backpackers perceived "sitting at home, quietly sipping tea" or "chatting with neighbors by the poolside" as meaningless activities. In fact, all the activities conducted in retirement might not be considered "valuable" under the productivist regime. Silver backpackers were very generous in sharing their stories with me, but they also often questioned the value of my research topic. Many were unconvinced as to why I would want to study them, asking, "What's the value in studying the old who are just playing around in Malaysia?" Some kept saying that I should be studying something "more important," like younger Japanese expatriate communities. The retirees' scepticism no doubt reflected their understandable doubt about my suitability as a researcher both because I was half a century younger than they were and because I had spent almost half of my life outside of Japan. But their scepticism also reflected an internalized ageism which regarded non-waged activities as unimportant.

Feminist economic anthropologists have long reshaped the theories of capitalism by moving beyond the formal spaces of work to highlight other sites, such as the household and the family, that constitute global capitalism (Pollard 2013; McKinnon and Cannell 2013; Yanagisako 2002; Ueno 1994). The decentering of the conceptual separation between waged and non-waged labor is situated in a wider history of feminist anthropological scholarship which has shown how the units of family, care, or love have always been an instrumental part of capitalist processes (Tajima 1992; Allison 1994; Hoang 2015; Osburg 2013; Stout 2014).[22] Their insights can be applied to analyze the period of retirement, a category created by capitalism. This book takes up these feminist critiques of the analytical distinction between productive and reproductive, stretching their analysis to conceptualize some of the ways gender, aging, and transnational mobility complicate our perception of these categories. Few have theorized how these categories change over one's lifecourse in different times and spaces, and the tension that these changes produce. Even in retirement, therefore, we need to continue to mark the unmarked lives of women in order to shape the theory of aging and capitalism. To do so, instead of focusing on activities in the public domain, I treat the anxieties over identity and intimate relations as the very grounds on which my interlocutors encountered aging after work.

Moving beyond public spaces, I try to construct women's social relations by paying particular attention to the cultivation of the home (Weiner 1977; Daniels 2015). Female interlocutors and I cooked Japanese food, watched Japanese news, and did needlework together in their homes. Older Japanese women I met were articulate in general, but they were most delighted when they talked about things that they had brought from Japan. Within the limited space of their suitcases, these women brought to Malaysia surprisingly mundane and ordinary things, such as cling wrap. The conversations about these objects often led to their life histories, which in turn provided important data for an analysis of how the women came to be gendered in Japan and Malaysia. In particular, their stories helped me understand how women's gendered experiences were different from men's experiences of companionship and transnational retirement. Hence, in the later phase of the fieldwork, I decided to go beyond the documentation of discourses and instead pay active attention to objects handled by women, no matter how ephemeral such items appeared to be. This focus opened up the extraordinary world of women's networks and their own value production processes.

Therefore, I present this book as a feminist work, perhaps less in the sense that it highlights women's voices, but rather in the sense that it defamiliarizes men's narratives and larger dominant discourses about work and retirement. The readers will find that descriptions of men and their life worlds often come before those of women in each chapter. Perhaps readers might even find that the descriptions of the former are more detailed than the descriptions of the latter. This partially reflects my own failings in not going beyond the dominant discourse and limitations in documenting the women's worlds. This also mirrors the fact that women's views in general are expressed in much more implicit and nuanced ways than those of men. But I also intentionally placed women's narratives behind those of men to achieve two effects. First, to defamiliarize the familiar. Since men's narratives often speak in tandem with the dominant discourses, I introduced these discourses first through men's voices. I then defamiliarized the discourse by inserting women's perspectives to encourage critical reflection. Second, to replicate my ethnographic observation, that is, to demonstrate how the narratives of men overpower those of women, while all the while the former needs the support of the latter for both legitimacy and survival. In the spirit of feminist collaborative endeavors, I welcome readers to join me in "finding women" in this book.

I chose to focus on the narratives of a dozen or so interlocutors most of whom are marked as dramatis personae in earlier pages. A feminist anthropological approach, especially Black feminist thought, has emphasized narratives and lived experiences as sites of meaning and empowerment (B. C. Williams 2018, 11). By focusing on these selected interlocutors, I seek to show their full selves, stories, and humanity. The stories I will tell through them—how people enacted and experienced transitions from work to post-work—are necessarily partial. But in adopting the narrative style of ethnographic writing, I try to give a fuller and richer context in which the selected narratives were told to me. I also put the retirees' experiences within historical and political-economic contexts so that these silver backpackers emerge also as people "who both exert power and are subject to it" (Constable 2003, 9). Their narratives are neither representational nor entirely atypical but, taken together, their stories and the rest of the book show how each interlocutor was an ambitious and motivated narrator of his or her own life.

Before we go on, I must mention the limitations of this study. While this book explores how Japanese silver backpackers employed transnational strategies to reimagine aging and gender relations, a community I did not address very much was that of the Malaysian locals. I did try to gain the perspectives of local residents separately through a dozen repeated visits to a village which was located next to transnational retirees' condominiums. I went with my Malaysian research assistant, as my Malay language was still too limited to conduct the fieldwork on my own. Yet, after repeated visits, I came to the conclusion that gaining "the local perspective" was beyond my ability as a researcher at that time. The village was occupied by a variety of citizens and migrants, including people with Malay, Indonesian, Nepali, and Indian backgrounds. We could not sufficiently communicate with all of them to understand how their different positions affected their relationships with the Japanese, and even with my research assistant's diligent translation, I could not gain a sense of how my positionality as a Japanese person was affecting their willingness to speak about their Japanese neighbors. I tried on several occasions to visit the local tea shop and "hang out" just to establish a level of trust with my limited language ability, but I was asked a number of times by female villagers not to return without my male assistant. Due to the limited research funds, I decided to forego this aspect of the research and focus instead on Japanese retirees' perceptions of Malaysia. Not all fields are open to everyone, so I decided to focus on what was open to me, and to learn from other scholars about local perspectives (Abdul-Aziz, et al. 2014; Abdul-Aziz et al. 2015).

In this book, I consciously decided to use two specific terminologies. First is the term, "housewife." Most of my female interlocutors referred to themselves as *futsuu no shufu* (ordinary housewives). I pondered over how to translate the term. The word, *sengyo shufu*, had appeared during the early 1970s to denote women who devoted fulltime to domestic work (Ueno 1994, 56). Between 1910 and 1970, more and more women aspired to be housewives in

Japan (Garon 1997, 185; Tsutsui 1998, 237). The term housewife in the Euro-American context has negative connotations of "confinement, provinciality, and absorption in trivialities" (Borovoy 2005, 169) or "a sense of dowdiness, of emptyheaded devotion to daytime television drams, shopping, and trivial gossip" (LeBlanc 1999, 30). The more socially accepted terms in English are "stay-at-home-mom" or "homemakers." But the provincial sound of the term "ordinary" that my female interlocutors used, and the formal sound of "home-makers" didn't seem to fit. Many of my female interlocutors used the phrase, futsuu no shufu as a humble expression. As the reader will see through the coming chapters, many of these women were not ordinary at all. Many were highly aware of the negative connotation of the term shufu yet chose to use it and even own it. Politically active shufu whom LeBlanc (1999, 31) studied explicitly used this terminology to refer to themselves and to describe their social presence to the outside world. Shufu gives those women a public identity precisely because this is how they were understood by the "generalised other" (LeBlanc 1999, 54).[23] Although few of my female interlocutors were po-litically active, they were highly aware of both the constraint and the libera-tion brought by the label. Hutsuu no shufu—to respect the nuance of their expression, I decided to call them "housewives" in this book.

Second, I chose to call their movement "transnational retirement" in con-trast to "lifestyle migration" (Benson and O'Reilly 2009a) or "retirement mi-gration" (Ono 2008), as the trend is more conventionally known by scholars. While both terminologies have been used in nuanced ways to acknowledge the temporality of movement as existing somewhere between migration and tourism, I hesitate to call the movement "migration" for doing so privileges the perspectives of one gender over the other, as I mentioned before. Rather, most Japanese people living in Kuala Lumpur were neither migrants nor tour-ists, and Malaysia was neither wholly homely nor foreign. I thus call the sil-ver backpackers' international movement "transnational retirement" with the hope that this term will accommodate and reflect the shifting natures of their movement as expectations and emotions are transformed in the course of their lives abroad.

Traveling the Book

My interlocutors were avid travelers. They were never stationary; they went from dancing in the Japan Cultural Center to picking up vegetables in a wet market and then to meeting their friends for dinner at home. Their stories, too, went from their childhood to their working lives, to the current adventure in Malaysia and to their return to Japan. The book follows these retirees in diverse locations and temporalities from their gendered lives in Japan (Chapter 1), to their decisions to go to Malaysia (Chapter 2), to their active personhoods in Malaysia (Chapter 3), to their intimate lives (Chapter 4), to relationships with families (Chapter 5), and finally to their eventual returns to Japan (Chapter 6). The book concludes with a critique of the conceptual separation between work and (second) life which lies at the heart of gendered lifecourses and anxieties in retirement. It suggests going beyond the binary and embracing life in its entirety.

Interlude

I t was two in the morning. They couldn't sleep again—preoccupied by that thought, which they had swept under the carpet for a long time. That thought, which they could forget when they were working. That night, it was there to stay. The thought.

Could I have lived my life differently?

Mrs. Okada contemplated her life. She had wanted to study abroad when she was young, but her father didn't let her. After graduating from high school, she sold cosmetics at a department store. She was proud of her job. When she got married, her husband asked her to quit her job and stay at home. "Until our children enter high school," he said. She never returned to work. Their daughter also wanted to study abroad, but her husband didn't let her. Instead, he sent their son to the United States, even though the son wanted to remain in Japan. Mrs. Okada stood alone in an alley of a supermarket. She saw her son's favorite chocolate on the shelf. She missed him.

"Was it my life?"

"But what could I have done?" Mr. Mori contemplated. He had worked for an electric company for forty years. He worked hard to support his family. He bought a house in a suburb. It was two hours away from his workplace, but the suburb had good schools and parks for his children. Every day, he left home before dawn and came back after midnight. When he reached fifty, he knew that his career wouldn't progress further. Many of his peers had gone on to managerial positions, but there were only so many managerial positions. By the time Mr. Mori retired as a mid-level manager of a small branch office, his children barely knew him.

"Was it all a waste?"

"It's not over yet." Mr. Kosaka contemplated. After retirement, he went on a three-month cruise with his wife. Every night, an extravagant dinner was followed by ballroom dancing on a stage. He didn't know how to dance. Enviously, he watched couples dance on the stage. When they returned from the cruise, he asked his wife to join him in ballroom dancing classes.

"If I can choose to be onstage or offstage, I will choose to be onstage."

It was three in the morning. They still couldn't sleep. They switched on the TV. There was an advertisement for a retirement visa for Malaysia.

"This is it." They instinctively knew. They would reenter life onstage in Malaysia.

CHAPTER 1

Work, Gender, and Lifecourse in Japan

The interwoven snippets of lives in the interlude were inspired by some of the common stories told to me by silver backpackers. Reflections on their younger days were often brief, fleetingly mentioned with ambivalence. Many of the retirees had led normative, if not elite, socioeconomical lives before their retirements, yet few talked about those lives in glorious terms. This made their enthusiasm for retirement in Malaysia striking. Perhaps the ambivalence of having had led the normative lifecourse accelerated their hope for a different kind of retirement.

To frame what I explore ethnographically in this book with more macro analytics of retirement for the baby boomers, Chapter 1 analyzes institutions of gender and work that, together, constituted the identity, belonging, and lifecourses of Japanese men and women during the postwar, high-growth period prior to their retirement. Based on their differing lifecourses, the chapter reflects on retirement and how it pertains differently to women and men. The chapter helps to explain why retirement from the workforce carried such high stakes for Japanese men of this generation. It also demonstrates why the impact of retirement on women, who had their own concerns and challenges during their younger days, appeared to be less profound.

I will juxtapose the lived experiences of my interlocutors against the shifting economic regimes present in high-growth era. Three of my interlocutors—Mr. Uchida, Mrs. Okada, and Eddie—are at the center of this chapter. I present their stories as an archetype for the kind of experiences that many others in Malaysia shared. I mainly focus on the experiences of these three in order to decipher what their affective experiences tell us about the emotional conditions and the afterlives of capitalist divisions of labor. By describing the emotional experiences of both women and men as they rode through the high-growth era and into retirement in a post-growth era, I draw attention to the affective costs and benefits of the gendered life-courses, detailing how women and men navigated the personal dimensions of a capitalist political economy. I highlight the strategic and processual aspects of their search for a good life, which came with considerable and continuing sacrifices and efforts in retirement.

Sarariiman and Shufu Lifecourses

A historically specific figure, *dankai no sedai* (baby boomers), emerged in tandem with the birth of the state's ideology of "Japanese-style productivity." Japanese-style productivity entered the popular imagination both in and out of Japan at the height of the Japanese postwar economic recovery. In less than twenty years after World War II, Japan's GNP had grown to rival that of the United Kingdom (Vogel 1979, 10). Products that were "made in Japan," such as cars and electrical products, flooded the American market. Some Japanese manufacturers competed and quickly replaced American and European manufacturers (Vogel 1979, 10). For instance, in 1975 and 1976, Japanese car makers such as Toyota and Nissan produced twice as many cars as European car makers (Vogel 1979, 11–12). In 1987, Honda replaced Volkswagen as the top car exporter to the U.S. market (Vogel 1979, 11). With its unparalleled productivity, the Japanese auto industry was both celebrated and feared as the new global benchmark, replacing the Fordist assembly line model of mass production. This resulted in a plethora of books aiming to uncover the secrets of "Japanese productivity," including Vogel's (1979) best-seller, *Japan as Number One.*

Capitalism during this high-growth period operated through specific forms of gendered relations and aspirations. While *sarariiman* (waged labor) spent much of their time at work, it was mainly through reproducing and then nurturing male labor power that women were articulated into the postwar capitalist state (cf. Rubin 1997, 162). The word *sengyo shufu* (housewife) appeared during the early 1970s to denote women who devoted themselves full-time to domestic work (Ueno 1994, 56). Between 1910 and 1970, more and more women aspired to be housewives (Garon 1997, 185; Tsutsui 1998, 237).

One of the defining features of this generation is the concept of "life-course."[1] Large corporations and public institutions enforced the system of lifelong employment, which resulted in most sarariiman spending, on average, more than thirty-five years in the same workplace (Duke 1986, xvii).

Because their employment was secure with the promise of lifelong employment, a linear conception of "life course" (*jinsei sekkei*) began to shape the public imagination of middle-class life (Kelly 1993, 198). A typical lifecourse started with one's marriage at the age of twenty-five, followed by the birth of a first baby by thirty, the child starting school by thirty-five, higher education by forty-five, and the child's marriage by fifty-five. The graph ended with the parents' retirement at the age of sixty (Kelly 1993, 201; Plath 1980, 89). Kelly (1993) observes that in the eyes of the state, this sequence of socio-economically "productive" moments was what it meant to have a life at all. Elizabeth Freeman (2010) theorizes what she calls a "chrononormativity" in which bodies are bound into socially meaningful embodiments through the temporal regulation of individual human bodies toward maximum productivity. The temporality of lifecourse appears governed by "reproductive futurism," the sense of hope that hard work today would yield a better tomorrow (Edelman 2004). The security of lifelong employment enabled the articulation of these life events with the progressive attainment of middle-class status. The objectives of the state and the personal goals of individuals came together in a mass utopia of high-growth Japan.

The institution of marriage embodies the convergence of personal desires and state goals (Friedman 2005, 312). One of the key defining moments in the Japanese baby boomer's lifecourse was marriage (Rosenberger 2001).[2] In high-growth Japan, the boundaries between marriage and work were constantly blurred as the event of marriage was conflated with the sign of social maturity, and oftentimes company arranged a marriage for their male employees (Tokuhiro 2010, 19; Suzuki 2002; Edwards 1989).[3] For instance, unmarried men, categorized as *seinen* (youth), were often grouped with women and excluded from important decision-making in the company (Suzuki 2002).[4] Just as marriage was important for men in their lifecourses, marriage played a vital role in women's lifecourses. In what follows, I will show how the gendered lifecourse was experienced by both women and men through the life histories of my interlocutors in Malaysia.

Shufu Lifecourse: Securing Good Marriage and Becoming a Good Wife, a Wise Mother

Mrs. Okada was in her early sixties when I met her in Kuala Lumpur in 2014. She always looked radiantly beautiful. One day, as we were walking through a mall, I asked her which cosmetic products she was using. "Oh, I use Clinique. My daughter works for Clinique so I get free samples." She smiled proudly.

Mrs. Okada herself used to work in a department store before she got married in the early 1970s. As a salesperson for a well-known cosmetic company, she would commute every morning to the department store, and carefully put on makeup before the store opened its door to its first customer. She liked to be looked at by customers in the store. Young women dressed up in trendy clothes glanced at her as they walked past the store. From nine in the morning to five in the evening, as she stood in the well-lit store, she was the face of the cosmetic brand. The lights, smells, and colors of the department store made her feel confident.

Before she started working at the department store, Mrs. Okada had felt as though her life was only designed to secure a good marriage. Mrs. Okada was the eldest daughter of a middle-class family in Miyazaki Prefecture on southern Japan's Kyushu Island. When she began school, the mandatory separation of boys and girls' education had just been abolished, and Mrs. Okada enjoyed going to school with boys.[5] Since 1965, almost equal numbers of men and women—around 95 percent for both—have graduated from high school. The baby boomer generation is typically distinguished from earlier generations by their high educational attainment. Yet, after high school, men were far more likely to receive tertiary education than women (Brinton 1993, 190). In 1935, only 3 percent of elementary school graduates went to university (Brinton 1993, 191). In the 1970s, around 35 percent of men attended universities whereas only 8 percent of women did so (Brinton 1993, 200). Instead of going to university, around 13 percent of women attended a junior college, which offered courses shorter than four years.

Mrs. Okada had wanted to study at a university instead of the junior college, but higher education was considered a liability in *omiai*, the arranged marriage market (Brinton 1993, 211). Love marriage remained a relatively rare phenomenon for the baby boomer generation.[6] The practice of omiai has evolved since the 1890s from alliance-making between households to a formal blind date, set up by a respected member of the community.[7] Omiai for many baby boomers came to mean an arrangement by a matchmaker who could be a friend, a neighbor, or a colleague (Tokuhiro 2010, 99). During omiai, the prospective partner was selected by parents in consultation with relatives (Tokuhiro 2010, 93). Matchmakers would typically ask for a photograph and a brief personal history from the young person to show to interested families

(Hendry 1981a, 122). If both parties were interested, the matchmaker would formally introduce potential marriage partners and their families to each other. The potential couple would then be given a short time to speak to each other alone. If there was a mutual attraction, the matchmaker would carry follow-up messages between the parties (Tokuhiro 2010, 99). After a few dates, a decision of marriage would be made.

Because women were encouraged to marry up, a university degree hindered their chances in the omiai market. Instead, attendance at junior college was seen to better women's chances for a match with a highly educated man, who would likely succeed in their career (Brinton 1993, 199). Mrs. Okada reluctantly had agreed to attend junior college.

During her junior college years, Mrs. Okada wanted to go and study abroad. But her father was adamantly against it. In the omiai market, women who had lived at home under the protection of the patriarch were considered more desirable than those who had lived independently away from their parents (Brinton 1993, 199). Because of this, most women lived at home and commuted to nearby schools or workplaces.

Soon after taking on a job as a salesperson in a department store near her parents' home, Mrs. Okada turned twenty-four. Between 1960 and 1975, most women were married by the age of twenty-five and most men by twenty-eight (Tokuhiro 2010, 3). Mrs. Okada's parents urged her to get married and set up numerous omiai dates for her. Thanks to meticulous planning aimed at increasing her desirability in the omiai market, Mrs. Okada was soon matched with a promising young employee at a leading car manufacturing company. Her future husband proposed to her and simultaneously asked her to resign from her job. She was devastated by the prospect of quitting the job she loved, but Mrs. Okada also knew what was expected of her: to become a full-time housewife. She did not consider working part-time, because she knew what people said about married part-time workers. Because of the high emphasis on women's role in child rearing, those who chose to continue working after childbirth were criticized for being "selfish" (Rosenberger 2001, 120; Dales 2009, 21). In fact, a book, *Working Mothers and Lonely Children,* had just become a best seller (Dales 2009, 21). The middle-class ideal was the woman as "a mistress without a job" (Ueno 1987, 80).

Sensing her disappointment, Mrs. Okada's future husband suggested that she could go back to work after their children grew up, but it was not financially or socially viable to do so. The gendered division of labor was supported by various state mechanisms including the systems of taxation (Osawa 2002).[8]

To benefit fully from the taxation and welfare system, women could not earn more than a certain amount a year. In other words, the taxation system made it financially disadvantageous for married women to have full-time jobs (Mackie 2003, 9). This created a situation where married women had to justify why they wanted to pursue a full-time career.

Even if Mrs. Okada were to go back to work, only part-time jobs were available for women without a skill, experience, or qualification (Hamada 2005). Generally speaking, Japanese women were more likely than women in other industrialized nations such as the United States to have blue-collar jobs because the former possessed fewer skills and lower educational qualifications. Many worked as "office ladies" (OL) who were mainly in charge of menial work in offices (Ogasawara 1998), on the shop floor, in a factory, or in a family-run enterprise (Roberts 1994; Brinton 1993). In 1987, at the height of the high-growth era, only 8 percent of managers were women and the male-to-female wage gap was far wider in Japan than in other industrialized nations (Brinton 1993, 7). By being employed on a casual, part-time basis, women contributed to the Japanese economy by providing inexpensive labor while nurturing a higher-priced male worker (Brinton 1993, 12; Kimoto 2005). Part-time work did not reduce women's share of household tasks (Ueno 1994, 57). In exchange for giving up her spare time, wives got "pin money" (Ueno 1994, 57). "Then what is the point?" Mrs. Okada thought to herself. Many women thus made the conscious decision not to work, which perpetuated their financial dependency on men (Izuhara 2006, 166). Mrs. Okada accepted the proposal and never went back to work.

After marriage, Mrs. Okada took on her husband's surname as required by law. Despite the egalitarian emphasis of the postwar Constitution and the revised Civil Code,[9] laws relating to the family continue to have patriarchal characteristics (Mackie 2003, 130). Mrs. Okada left her father's household registration system (*koseki*) in order to be subsumed under her husband's, with the latter as the head of the family (Mackie 2003, 130).

Mrs. Okada also moved to live with her parents-in-law and looked after them in their old age before coming to Malaysia. Before the oil shock in 1974, the 1970s saw an expansion of welfare policies (R. Goodman 1996). The state declared 1973 as *Fukushi Gannen* (Year One of the Welfare Era) and introduced a range of policies aimed at supporting the older generation, including an increase in the benefit level of pensions and the introduction of free medical care for people over seventy. But the welfare era was short-lived. After the oil crisis, between 1975 and 1985, the unemployment rate rose threefold,

resulting in increased welfare expenditure (R. Goodman 1996). Social security expenditure rose about sevenfold between 1970 and 1980, from JPY 3.5
billion to JPY 24.8 billion (Peng 2002). Social security expenditure as a portion of GNP rose from 3.5 percent in 1960 to 11 percent in 1984 (Ferries 1996,
236). The government responded to the crisis by proposing a new political
language, *Fukushi Minaoshi* (Reconsideration of Welfare), and introduced a
range of new policies that curtailed welfare services for seniors, including the
abolition of free medical care for senior citizens over seventy. The government stressed that continuing welfare expansion would be dangerous for investment in a competitive economy and decried the the expansion in 1970s
as a "Western-style" welfare system.[10] Instead, the Japanese state evoked a rhetoric of a "Japanese-style welfare system" that sought to restore the pre-war
Confucian and Buddhist values of filial piety (R. Goodman 1996; Traphagan
2003; Osawa 2011). The Confucius ideology of filial piety (*oya koko*) came to
espouse a practice in which adult children, particularly the eldest son and
his wife, resided with his parents and cared for them in their old age (Lock
2002, 202). The Confucian narrative of filial piety shifted a greater part of the
burden of social welfare to the family members, particularly to daughters-
in-law (R. Goodman 1996, 112; Peng 2002). The wartime terminology of "good
wife, wise mother" was also re-popularized during the high-growth period
with a new emphasis promoting women's contribution as providing welfare
at home (Uno 1993, 293).[11] Through the manipulation of these discourses, the
Japanese state narrated family care responsibilities in moral terms and thereby
naturalized its welfare cuts.[12] By 1980, nearly 70 percent of seniors were living with their children. For many women, the experience of co-residency was
emotionally constraining as their ability to control the household was limited
by the authority of the in-laws.

Within the confines of the home, women were also the primary carers of
children (Hamada 2005, 131–32).[13] Soon after marriage Mrs. Okada had a son
and a daughter. When the daughter entered university, she, like Mrs. Okada,
had wanted to study abroad, but her father would not let her go. Instead,
Mr. Okada decided to send their son to Canada, even though the son hadn't
wanted to leave Japan. Just as Mrs. Okada moved her home and official registration record from her father to her husband, the patriarch had also shifted
from her father to her husband.

Mrs. Okada was an ambitious woman whose aspirations to attend a university, study abroad, and work were prevented by her marriage. Mrs. Okada's
life story shows how marriage shaped women's lifecourses, even if they tried

to resist. Japanese marriage practices kept women in the domains of home and reproduction (Ueno and Tabusa 2020). Yet women continue to have aspirations. After I introduce the affective lives of sarariiman in the next section, I will show how women cultivated distinct values and attributes in domestic spaces.

Sarariiman Lifecourse: How to be a Company Warrior

The male counterpart to the female shufu, sarariiman came into popular imagination in the high-growth era. These men are often depicted as almost non-human in popular culture. For instance, Jun Tomizawa's comic series, *Kigyou Senshi Yamazaki* (Company Warrior Yamazaki), features a man called Yamazaki, who, after his death from overwork, was resurrected as a company cyborg. Yamazaki possessed a robotic efficiency and capacity to work and solve the company's problems. While the cyborg Yamazaki epitomized the Japanese workers' productivity, overseas musicians and popular media alike mocked the Japanese sarariiman's seemingly single-minded dedication to work. Styx, an American rock band from the 1980s, released a single album *Mr. Roboto* which featured a mindless samurai robot working on the assembly line.

Yet despite the plethora of scholarly and pop cultural work on sarariiman, the lives of these men are often misunderstood. Unlike the image of a heartless robot painted by both Japanese and overseas popular culture, my male interlocutors' lifecourses were shaped and motivated by complex emotions. In his book, *It's Hard to be Men* (original: *Otokoga Tsuraiyo*), sociologist Toshiyuki Tanaka (2015) outlines various forms of anxiety and difficulties experienced by men in contemporary Japan, including pressures around supporting one's family financially, and exhaustion from long hours. Tanaka (2015, 82) argues that underlying these anxieties is a culture which encourages the single-minded dedication to work as a reflection of the highest moral standards. Such a system values employees' abilities to sacrifice things and people for work, including relationships with family and friends. A good sarariiman has the ability to respond flexibly to the company's various demands and to accept them without considering their own needs (Tanaka 2015, 82). Such extraordinary virtue is not cultivated overnight. Mr. Uchida's story shows how such flexibility was cultivated throughout a man's lifecourse, from school to work, and importantly, in conjunction with their sentiments.

Mr. Uchida grew up in a small town in the countryside of Okayama Prefecture. From an early age, he was talented at sports. He was trained as a swimmer in school and went on to win various national titles in his youth. At his peak, he placed fifth nationally. Mr. Uchida wouldn't talk much about these past achievements, but if pressed, he would say ever so shyly that he would have qualified for the Olympics if they were held during his peak.

Mr. Uchida's childhood dream was to become a pilot and fly around the world, but he failed the eye test. He thought to himself that, even if he might not have had eyesight for flying, he had eyes for detail. If he couldn't manoeuvre the plane from behind the wheel, he could still manoeuvre it in other ways. He thus decided to become an aviation engineer and work in civil service.

The entry into the national civil service was exclusive to graduates from public universities and top private universities like Waseda University and Keio University. Because of the limited number of places at top universities, competition was intense (Brinton 1993, 190). Mr. Uchida studied hard and gained entrance into a top national university. His experience with team sports was looked upon favorably during the graduate recruitment as it was perceived to lay the basis for his future employer-employee relations (Duke 1986, 25).[14] It was commonplace for companies to set a recruitment examination that tested, not the candidates' skills, but rather their aptitude to work (Brinton 1993, 194). Companies expected employees to give their best. (Duke 1986, 145). Through sports, Mr. Uchida had learned to appreciate the value of perseverance. He was offered a job at his top choice.

The university qualification continued to matter after one started working. Although the seniority system meant that promotions were based primarily on years of service in the company, as one got older, a small minority of sarariiman climbed the corporate ladder to become managers, or *bijiness-man*, in their fifties. A bijinesuman remained in a main office in a big city to oversee the management of the corporation as a whole while a sarariiman was promoted to become manager of a smaller branch office in a country area and retired there. More often than not, those who made it to the rank of bijinesuman were graduates from elite universities. They guarded their elite status in the company by establishing an *OB-kai* (alumni network) among the graduates of the same universities. They socialized with each other through informal events outside the company, such as gatherings at golf clubs.

Many sarariiman, therefore, sensed intense anxiety as they entered their fifties and started to wonder about their future in the company. In ways that resonated with the experience of many sarariiman in their late forties to mid-fifties, one of my male interlocutors, Mr. Akiyama, related to me how he started thinking about Malaysia when he was transferred from the main office of a large electric company to a smaller branch office in a rural part of Japan:

> When you reach around forty-five, you more or less foresee your future in the company. Around the age of fifty, 90 percent of workers will be transferred to smaller branch offices. Only 10 percent can stay and climb up a corporate ladder in the main office. I was among the 90 percent. Most people would continue to persevere in branch offices. But I had no patience for that [*iikagen na ningen dakara*]. My wife and I did not have any children. I could have stayed in the company and worked until sixty-five, but I could only be healthy for so long. I didn't want to waste my life on a dead cause any longer [*mottainai desho*]. My interest in the company diminished, and I began to think about the next project in life.

When Mr. Akiyama realized that his career would not progress further, his motivation to stay in the company diminished. He decided to take early retirement and left for Malaysia at the age of fifty-three.

Besides the competitiveness of corporate progression, there was another source of anxiety in the sarariiman lifecourse: the long working hours. In return for financial security, sarariiman were expected to work long hours. Once Mr. Uchida became an aviation engineer, for example, he worked day and night, leaving home early in the morning and coming home after dinner. In 1986, when most of my interlocutors were in their thirties, the average Japanese worker worked for fifty to sixty hours a week while the average American worker worked for just under thirty-six (Duke 1986, 48). Some Japanese workers literally died of overwork. The 1980s saw the emergence of a societal phenomenon called *karoushi* (death by overwork); there was an epidemic of sudden deaths among corporate workers. The problem of karoushi continues today.[15]

Yet for sarariiman in the 1980s, overwork was not necessarily perceived as exploitation; rather, hard work was seen as a sign of high morality and often justified as being rewarding to the individual worker (Mathews 2002; Rohlen 1973; Okamoto 2018a, 28). Confucian ideologies are said to have influenced the emergence of the Japanese management system which was highly conscious of quality (Dore and Dore 2000). For instance, Toyota executives developed their own production method known as the lean model of production or, more popularly, "Toyotism," in contrast to its counterpart, Fordism (Tsutsui 1998, 185). While Ford focused on machine technology in determining the pace of factory work, Toyota engineers sought to optimise the productivity of the individual workers themselves (Tsutsui 1998, 186). Compared with the rigidity of the assembly line, the lean model of production was said to promise superior quality (Tsutsui 1998, 3). Corporate employees went through quality-control training programs to build a consensus on quality in Japanese industries. This employee involvement in the continuous process of quality improvement marked one of the distinct features of the "total quality control" found in the Japanese industry (Hamada 2005, 137). Ronald Dore (2000) writes that the Japanese regularly emphasized that they made "things," not "money" (*mono dukuri*). Sarariiman viewed the making of things, specifically of high-quality products, as a moral duty to one's fellow citizens (Dore 2000). The devotion to work reflected one's morality and became the source of one's pride.

For Mr. Uchida, his devotion to work was also shaped by his moral duty to his colleagues. One of the things he had learned through sports was to respect hierarchy and value his teammates. He applied this spirit to his work. Mr. Uchida was a natural leader. He was liked by his bosses and respected by his junior members. He regularly went drinking with his colleagues after work to listen to their personal stories and to offer advice. It was on these occasions involving drinking that sarariiman like Mr. Uchida shared with colleagues the most private details of their lives, from their upbringing to family life. Many sarariiman went on company-paid holidays together and played golf on weekends, too (Allison 1994). Nightclubs also played a large role in sarariimans' socialization. In the 1980s, women from other Asian nations, such as South Korea, the Philippines, and Thailand entertained men in those nightclubs (Douglass 2000; Mackie 2003, 205). By participating in this socializing, male colleagues built a strong bond of solidarity beyond the profit-driven nature of the corporations. The more one invested in social relations at work, the more one was rewarded emotionally.

However, because sarariiman spent so much time at work, there was little time left for their families or for themselves.[16] Feminist writers such as Sayoko Nobuta (2013) and Eiko Tabusa (2020) point out the lack of emotional presence of fathers at home. When a mother and a daughter are quarrelling, for instance, a father would become "a rock" and disengage completely (Ueno and Tabusa 2020, 44–45). An activist and writer, Karin Amamiya, called the emotional absence of fathers a type of emotional violence (Ueno and Tabusa 2020, 45). Becoming "absent fathers" at home, it was the men's wages that materialized their ties to the family.

With a strict division of labor within the conjugal relationship, the sentiment felt by the partners in marriage was that of obligation to the relationship rather than a positive feeling about the partner (Tokuhiro 2010, 19; Borovoy 2005). A survey conducted by the Asahi Shimbun in 1998 asked people about their image of marriage. The most popular keyword among men was *sekinin* (responsibility), while for women it was *nintai* (patience) (Tokuhiro 2010, 19). Many men said that they found a space of belonging (*ibasho*) at the workplace, not at home.

Mr. Uchida stayed with his job until his retirement. On the day of his retirement, Mr. Uchida's colleagues organized a farewell party at his favourite *izakaya* (Japanese pub) to send him off. They delivered speeches about funny and touching moments that they had gone through together over the past forty years. Over bottles of sake, Mr. Uchida laughed and cried with them about memories of his first sake with his boss, of comforting his junior colleagues, and of numerous welcome and farewell parties that they all had attended together. He finally went home when the morning sun shone through the windows. As he said his last goodbyes, Mr. Uchida's heart ached a little. "This is the last time I drink with my friends." He had not had time to build friendship networks outside of work.

The stories of Mrs. Okada and Mr. Uchida illustrate how the gendered divisions of labor and the temporalized narrative of lifecourse together homogenized and standardized middle-class expectations for both women and men in postwar Japan. Women and men accrued their own roles and networks through complementary but different ways as they progressed through their lifecourses. Progression demanded sacrifices and efforts on both parts, as marriage culled some women's aspirations for higher education and career, and work demanded a total sacrifice of men's family and social relations. In making these sacrifices, both groups were called to foster the progress of something greater than themselves, such as their family, company, and their nation. At the same time, these individuals were motivated by distinct aspirations, including the attainment of career goals, material comforts, and spaces of belonging. This integration of productive and reproductive work with gender ideals and class consciousness made it difficult for both women and men to derail from the temporality and the morality of the productive lifecourse. The system of lifelong employment and divisions of labor offered a secure and comfortable future on the one hand but demanded a lifelong commitment to the productivist lifecourse on the other.

Retirement for Women

Women who had been housewives did not necessarily "retire" from their domestic work or have a clear start date for their "second life." Although state policies and popular writings on aging seldom differentiate the definitions of aging or retirement for women and men, the exchange at the Yamamotos' recounted in the Preface made it abundantly clear that Japanese women and men of the baby boomer generation did not "retire" in the same way. The rest of the chapter will contrast the gendered experiences of second life.

Despite the constricted nature of their domestic lives, women are generally said to have better support networks in later life than men (Okamoto 2018a, 51). Women's lives as managers of a home environment were shaped by their participation in the community and the neighborhood (Borovoy 2005, 5–7; Sasagawa 2006). Many mothers were involved in children's activities, such as the Parents and Teachers Association (PTA), and in neighborhood associations, such as the Housewives' Association (*fujinkai*) (Sasagawa 2006, 136; Hendry 1981a, 61). As members of the Housewives' Association, women regularly cleaned the neighborhood halls and other public areas, and, in return, they received funds to organize events, such as demonstrations of craft work or a day's outing to places of interest (Hendry 1981, 61). This deployment of women to clean public spaces no doubt had the objective of minimizing the welfare costs for the government (Garon 1997, 164–65). At the same time, however, it provided wives with an avenue to escape the domesticity and the power of their in-laws. Some women even pursued these activities to have a sense of purpose wider than domestic duties (LeBlanc 1999, 43). The state in turn utilized such sentiments to inculcate the spirits of social solidarity and mutual assistance among women.

As with any social relations, the ties of solidarity among women were both liberating and constraining. Community ties produced *shigarami* (social obligation) from which many women wanted to be liberated. Mrs. Ishida, a woman I met in Kuala Lumpur, expressed the constraints of living in a close-knit community back in Japan: "I used to live in a village in Yamaguchi Prefecture. It was a close-knit community with both good and bad qualities.

Neighbors cared for each other, but there was also a sense that I was constantly watched. I couldn't play all day, otherwise, the neighbors would think that I was lazy. If I didn't take care of the garden, the neighbors would comment on it. If I left home too often, they would ask me where I was going to have a good time." As women entered later life, there were more avenues to temporarily leave their houses and neighbors' watchful eyes. In a lifecourse in which one was expected to be married and give birth to children by the age of thirty, women in their thirties began to have more spare time as their youngest children started school. Extra time was further made available by the availability of new household products, such as refrigerators and rice cookers, which drastically shortened the time required to complete domestic tasks (Ueno 1994, 180). The amount of free time further increased after children left home or in-laws passed away (Moore 2010; Thang et al. 2011, 244). Many Japanese women turned to self-development in their spare time. In general, women who belonged to higher socio-economic classes had more time and financial resources to take up artistic pursuits, such as music, calligraphy, and flower arrangement (Ueno 1994, 58). Although women generally did not work outside of the home, the teaching of these artistic pursuits was considered an exception and was generally regarded as a female profession (Saso 1990, 9). Some of my female interlocutors had taught these courses when they were in Japan, and others enjoyed participating in them.

These interest groups were not restricted to neighborhood communities. In Japan, most women freely moved around using various transportation systems, from walks to buses, bikes, and cars, to access different hobby groups. The women's ties created through these external activities were distinct from the ties men created within companies. A leading Japanese feminist, Chizuko Ueno (1994), describes the networks of women and men as *sentaku en* (choice network) and *sha en* (corporate network), respectively. As the name suggests, the former is a network based on choice. These women's groups often did not have a defined leadership structure or rules (Ueno 1994, 293). In contrast, men's sha en was hierarchically organized (Ueno 1994, 298). Ueno (1994, 294–95) further observes that unlike corporate networks, the membership of women's choice networks seldom overlapped. She introduces an example of a woman in her fifties who belonged to a cultural school. The woman was also a leader of a civic movement. But she never disclosed her civic identity to her female friends at the cultural school. Her friends at the school only discovered her other identity when she was featured in a newspaper. Katrina Moore (2013, 265), an anthropologist who studied amateur female Noh performers in Japan, similarly observes that her female interlocutors did not see the sentaku en activities as loci for accumulating public recognition. Rather, these activities allowed female participants to peel off their identities and allow the emergence of new states of self. In this way, women could manage multiple identities, and the possible number increased even more in women's old age.

Retirement for Men

Men, many of whom had worked in a highly stressful and competitive corporate environment, may have imagined home as a refuge which finally offered them love and healing at the end of work (Ueno 1994, 77). However, decades of strict gendered divisions of labor made the fulfilment of men's desire for familial intimacy not a straightforward process. One of the emotional consequences of the capitalist lifecourse was that sarariiman from the baby boomer generation did not particularly feel relaxed or welcomed at home (Borovoy 2005, 90). The story of Eisaku Kobayashi, or Eddie as he was commonly known to his friends in Malaysia, illustrates this.[17]

Eddie retired at the age of sixty from a large trading company in Fukuoka, Japan. He was a successful bijinesuman; he had held various managerial positions as an expatriate around the world. He fondly recalled his time as an expatriate in Argentina and Canada. He was mostly alone during his expatriate missions; his wife stayed in Japan to raise their children as she was worried about the disruption moving might cause to the children. Eddie bought a house in a suburb of Nagoya so that his children had a good school. The location significantly increased his commuting time and reduced his time spent with his children, but it was his sacrificial act for them. Daily, he left early in the morning and came back late at night. On weekends, he went on golf tours with his clients. Eddie barely had time to make friends outside of work or to spend time with his family.

When Eddie retired, he intended to spend the rest of his life with his family for whom he felt that he had made a lot of sacrifices. But "the sacrificial contract" (Sennett and Cobb 1977) did not yield the promised result. He quickly noticed the disjuncture when he realized that he and his family didn't have any common topics of conversation. Through the decades of separated spaces of socialization, his wife had established a daily routine that did not include him. Eddie's retirement also coincided with the marriages of his children and the passing of his parents. His wife was finally liberated from these reproductive duties and she preferred to spend her newly gained leisure time, not with Eddie, but with her friends. In 2010, 78.8 percent of men said that they drew emotional support from their spouse, while only 54 percent of women answered the same, revealing the men's reliance on their wives (Okamoto 2018b, 51). In 2012, the Cabinet Office conducted a survey which revealed that 36 percent of older men experienced *ikigai*, "that which gives a person happiness" (Kavedzija 2019), while spending time with their spouse. However, only 29 percent of women felt the same way (Cabinet Office 2012b, 23). Instead, 43.4 percent of women felt ikigai when spending time with their friends, compared to only 27.4 percent of men.

"I became a *nureochiba*," Eddie lamented. Nureochiba refers literally to the wet fallen leaves that stick around and are hard to remove (Mathews 1996, 15). The term is popularly used to describe retired husbands with no friends or hobbies who stick with their wives wherever they go. Social isolation among Japanese men was the highest among the Organisation for Economic Cooperation and Development (OECD) nations in 2005 (Okamoto 2018, 68). Neither working nor participating in community or family life, retirement brought with it a great deal of boredom for many ex-sarariiman. In Japan, retired men typically experienced their later life as one of "existential immobility" (Lems and Moderbacher 2016) or as "stuckedness" (Hage 2009) in space and time—*doko he mo ikutokoro ga nai* (having nowhere to go to) and *nani mo suru koto ga nai* (having nothing to do).

Eddie spent the first few months of his retirement reading books and browsing the Internet. After a while, he felt increasingly judged by his wife and neighbors for doing nothing productive or useful. Eddie's lack of social networks, in contrast to his wife's abundance, affected his morale and gender positioning at home. Eddie felt *katami ga semai*, which literally means, "constricted shoulders," an idiom referring to a state in which one finds no place of belonging. He constricted his shoulders to occupy as little space as possible in his own home.

Beyond metaphor, this sense of stagnancy was painfully internalized by some of my male interlocutors who became self-conscious of their "aging body odor" (*kareishuu*) (Bardsley 2011, 116). Though none of my interlocutors could explain what an "aging body odour" was, Bardsley (2011, 116) mentions the liberal use of pomade by Japanese men. Perhaps, perhaps not. But the odor was certainly felt by the older men. One of the male interlocutors confided to me that he took a thirty-minute shower before going out of his house. He was worried that his scruffy old-man smell would offend the public.[18]

Smell constructs power relations in our society as the center governs from a position of olfactory neutrality and those on the periphery are classified as odorous (Classen et al. 1994, 161). In the early twentieth century, George Orwell highlighted the interrelationship between the olfactory and the political with the famous line: "the lower classes smell" (Classen et al. 1994, 8). Even though the middle-class corporate workers had worked in the capitalist lifecourse and the associated division of labor, in the absence of work, their strained relationships with family members in retirement made the men feel anxious and marginalized at home.

Many retired people in Japan, hence, continue to search for reemployment opportunities. Part of it is personal, but it is also financial.[19] The Japanese government's pension funds only allow one to receive a full pension from the age of sixty-five, yet the mandatory retirement age for most people from the baby boomer generation was sixty in early 2010s.[20] In order to fill in the income gap from retirement to pensionable age, the government revised a law (Act on Stabilization of Employment of Elderly Persons) to make it possible for people to stay employed until the age of sixty-five, but at a lower position and lower salary.[21] In 2018, 65 percent of those hired under the reemployment scheme worked at reduced hours, between fifteen and thirty-one hours a week. They saw their income reduced by 50–60 percent (Japan Times 2017). Even then, from 2005 to 2010, the employment rate of people aged between sixty and sixty-four increased from 52 to 57 percent. Many seniors were also choosing to work even after reaching the pensionable age in order to supplement their pensions. In 2015, the average monthly public pension for a couple aged over sixty was JPY 177,970 (around USD 1,600).[22] In the same year, the average monthly spending of a couple over sixty was JPY 247,815 (around USD 2,260). The public pension scheme covered, at most, only 70 percent of the average living costs for a couple. The revelation by the government's Financial Services Agency in 2019 that retired couples would need at least twenty million yen (around USD 184,000) in savings to supplement their pension shocked the nation as it went against the long-held belief that the public pension was sufficient for old age. Except for those with additional income from investments, many seniors decided to continue working even after they started to receive their pension. In 2016, 31 percent of men and 16 percent of women over sixty-five were still employed (Statistics Japan 2016).[23] In a 2015 survey, 28.9 percent of Japanese people over sixty answered that they wanted to keep working until they were physically unable to do so (Cabinet Office 2016, 21).

However, the search for reemployment opportunities posed distinct challenges to former elite sarariiman who used to lead successful lives. The story of Mr. Uchida's retirement demonstrates this. Before Mr. Uchida retired, there had been a talk of a reemployment opportunity at a lower position and at a reduced salary. Many of his former senior colleagues and his friends had taken up the reemployment offers. Mr. Uchida initially contemplated working for at least another five years like his friends, but those who had taken the reemployment package warned him. They said that they felt continuous pressure to resign so that the organization could hire younger employees. They told Mr. Uchida, "As it turned out, they were just waiting for me to retire. My work was seen as too old-fashioned."

Mr. Yamamoto, an interlocutor who used to work as a human resource manager of a major electric company, explained to me the reason for this pressure using the same principles of productivity and redundancy that he previous had used for his job. He drew a chart to explain the principle to me. (See Figure 1).The chart divided people into four categories according to two criteria: motivation and productivity. Category One contained those who had high motivation and high productivity. In contrast, Category Four consisted of those who had low motivation and low productivity. Mr. Yamamoto asked me to guess which group of people would be fired first. I guessed people in category four. They had low motivation and low productivity. But he said that the people he would cut first were in category three. He explained to me, "People in Category Four still have the potential to improve their productivity if I manage to increase their motivation." He continued, "but people in category three are already so motivated. Yet their productivity is so low. They are the lost cause." He told me that as employees got older, many slowly transitioned from category one to category three. Their productivity gradually dropped due to their physical and mental decline, and more recently, the introduction of new digital technologies.

Mr. Uchida did not want to be a burden to his organization and so he took the retirement package and moved from Tokyo back to his childhood home in Okayama Prefecture with his wife. Back in Okayama, he immediately looked for a job. It wasn't his nature to be idle. Neither did he have any local friends to spend time with; most of his childhood friends had left the rural

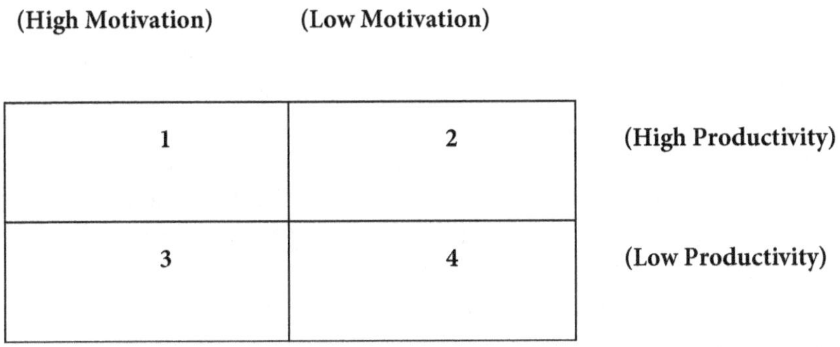

(High Motivation)   (Low Motivation)

1	2	(High Productivity)
3	4	(Low Productivity)

Figure 1. The Productivity and Redundancy Chart by Mr. Yamamoto.

town for larger cities. It would have been too costly for Mr. Uchida to travel to visit them frequently, and even if he did, he couldn't spend as much money on drinking as his friends who were still working.

Mr. Uchida soon realized that there were not many jobs that suited his professional experience in Okayama. Many of male silver backpackers retired at the managerial level or higher. When they wanted to reenter the employment market, however, only menial jobs were available. Mr. Uchida took almost a year to find a job as an insurance salesperson. He lasted in the job for a year.

Ryu Murakami (2012), a Japanese novelist, published a collection of short stories illuminating the emotional conditions of male retirees in contemporary Japan. One of them is about a retired man who used to work as a sales manager at a renowned company. During his working life, the man had made many friends and built a good reputation. Reemployment should have been easy. But when he called his old friends to arrange a retirement job, he was rejected by all of them. Other retired colleagues started working as office cleaners and cashiers at supermarkets. The reality dawned on him: "After retirement, I am nothing but 'an old man'" (Shakuto 2018b, 191).

But not one of my interlocutors saw themselves as "an old man." Some local governments established a *Roujin Daigaku* (University for the Aged) or several *Shougai Gakushuu Daigaku* (Lifelong Learning Universities) in the 1990s to encourage seniors' lifelong learning.[24] Similar to the University of Third Age established in the U.K. by Peter Laslett in the 1980s, the Japanese school offers classes from history to computers to arts. In a focus group interview at the Japan Cultural Center in Kuala Lumpur, I asked my interlocutors if they had considered attending the University for the Aged in Japan. "No way!" they all responded at once. "We are not *roujin* [elderly] yet, please!" (Shakuto 2018b, 191). Indeed, in response to the question "who are the elderly," most people in their sixties responded by referring to people over seventy years old (Cabinet Office 2013, 7). The Japanese Gerontological Society and the Japan Geriatrics Society proposed to redefine "the elderly" as seventy-five or older (The Japan Times 2017). In a society that boasts one of the world's highest longevities, those who just retired might well have another twenty to thirty years to live. In such a temporal framework, it is understandable that people in their sixties might not yet have felt "old."[25]

Mr. Uchida began to feel agitated soon after his retirement. Up to that point, he had known how to succeed. He was a top athlete in school. He graduated from a top university. He gained a prestigious job in a large city and he was well liked by his colleagues. But good education and good work didn't seem to guarantee a "good" retirement. Most male silver backpackers had typically led elite, successful lives under the postwar, capitalist lifecourse. Yet because of their success under this lifecourse, the dislocation that the retired men felt in their retirement affected them severely. In contemporary Japanese society, male retirees who used to lead normative lifecourses seem to be "less melancholic than ontologically at odds" (Allison 2013, 114). Going to University for the Aged? Work as an office cleaner? None of these registered, "existentially, affectively, subjectively" (Allison 2013, 114). For many Japanese ex-corporate sarariiman who lived on the linear lifecourse of the high-growth era, the sense of not being able to move forward on the new second life lifecourse was experienced as the ultimate form of dislocation from where they comfortably belonged. One of my male interlocutors described the transition as "having been taken off stage to be hidden away from public view." He repeated to me throughout my fieldwork, almost as if to remind himself of who he really was: "I am an on-stage person, not an off-stage person" (Shakuto 2018b, 191).

These conditions of retirement, and the anxious sentiment over spousal relations, made some retired ex-sarariiman seriously rethink their lives after work. They could no longer assume that one way of life—that which was governed by work and its associated moral and gendered practices—was possible. Yet it was difficult to make new friends or establish new communities.

Who am I after retirement? What is next in life? Although retirement arrived in an instant in the capitalist lifecourse, its consequences unfolded slowly as retired men began to ponder and transform the meanings of who they were, who they wanted to be, and with whom.

Conclusion

This chapter examined multiple ways the political economy of the state and the individual emotions contributed to the creation of particular affective states in one's later life in Japan. The chapter exposed the historical process behind the creation of such sentiments, showing that "matters of emotion are social and political" (Williams 2018, 33), and that they are embedded in histories of gendered divisions of labor. The emotional consequences of the capitalist lifecourses and gendered divisions of labor in later life set the scene for the next chapter, which will discuss the emergence of Malaysia as a utopic landscape which allows Japanese seniors to make a transition into "successful retirement." I will juxtapose these sentiments against the postcolonial history of inequality between Japan and Malaysia, and the perceptions of international mobility by older Japanese women who did not necessarily have similar existential immobility, at least in their later life in Japan.

Interlude

"Do you feel it?" Mr. Watase turned to me, and then back to the window of his spacious condominium. "You can feel the sea breeze here." He closed his eyes and inhaled a deep breath as if to catch the presence of the ocean in the room. I could hear the sound of waves hitting the rocks and I smelled the warm salty air. "Every afternoon I lie here and read a book until I fall asleep."

I met Mr. and Mrs. Watase, who had relocated to the island of Penang, Malaysia, after Mr. Watase's retirement from a mining company. As part of its national economic strategies, the Malaysian government had been issuing long-term visas to affluent foreign retirees since 2002. Penang experienced a real estate boom with foreign investors and retirees coming to buy or rent properties by the beach. Mr. and Mrs. Watase were among them. Wearing a bright orange Jim Thompson T-shirt, Mr. Watase told me, "We play golf three times a week. I taught golf to my wife just before my retirement so that we could play it together in Malaysia."

As her husband finished showing me the rooms in their luxurious condominium, Mrs. Watase appeared from the kitchen where she was preparing coffee and snacks. She served us two sets of coffee and mangosteen, one for me and another for her husband, but none for herself. Instead, she crossed her fingers in front of her.

Mrs. Watase was in her early sixties and had a gentle demeanor. She told me that she had been a housewife until their children left home, after which she started to help with a relative's business before moving to Malaysia. In contrast to her energetic husband in his bright orange T-shirt, she wore a blouse in a muted color.

"How do you like Malaysia?" I asked Mrs. Watase. "Well," she said, pausing to glance at her husband. He was busy reaching for the mangosteen. She chuckled nervously and gave me an unexpected answer. "Going to Southeast Asia was like *shimanagashi* [banishment]. It was embarrassing to tell my friends and neighbors that I was going to live in Southeast Asia." Shimana-gashi refers to a feudal punishment in which a political offender was banished to a small, isolated island. Mrs. Watase's description stood in stark contrast to her husband's enthusiastic narration of their leisured lifestyle.

"I am fine now," Mrs. Watase continued, but her smile faded. "I partici-pate in volunteer activities and have made some new friends in Penang. But I still like to go back to Japan at least a few times a year to see my family and friends."

"I don't," her husband immediately interjected. "I much prefer it here. After a week in Japan, I would start missing Penang. It's so expensive to do anything in Japan. I only go back to Japan once a year for medical check-ups and my tax returns. When my wife is away in Japan, I'd rather go to Cebu in the Philippines with my friends to go diving. I started diving at the age of sixty-two, you know!" He smiled at me with his tanned face.

I saw Mrs. Watase gripping her fingers tighter. She persisted, "For me, home is still Japan. Life in Penang is at most an extension of tourism."

"I disagree," Mr. Watase said, not backing down. "I feel relieved when I come back from Japan to this condominium in Penang. I'd say, *tadaima!*" (Tadaima is a greeting one says when entering a place regarded as one's home).

The room fell silent for several seconds. Awkwardly I reached for a man-gosteen. Then suddenly Mr. Watase turned to me and asked a question. "So, why did you decide to study in Australia?"

I was caught off guard. "Well . . . my partner was working in Australia and . . ."

Mr. Watase quickly finished the sentence for me. "I see. Since you needed to follow him to Australia anyway, you must have thought that you might as well study there."

"Of course not!"

Mrs. Watase interrupted firmly. I almost choked on the mangosteen. "Shiori-san has her own dream and goals in life!"

Mr. Watase kept quiet. The tension in the room was palpable.[1]

CHAPTER 2

The "Malaysia My Second Home" Program and Malaysia-Japan Relations

A t the Shinagawa station, located in one of the wealthier suburbs of Tokyo, a large picture of a tropical rainforest and orangutans appeared on a major notice board with a catchphrase, "Malaysia, Truly Asia." I was often surprised by the apparent spontaneity with which most silver backpackers had moved to Malaysia. In lifestyle migration elsewhere, scholars have observed that older travelers tend to have prior connections to the destination country through family, work, or tourism (Benson 2015, 421). This was rarely the case for Japanese silver backpackers. Few could speak English or Malay. Even fewer had any experience of living in Malaysia, or in any other foreign country. But they were devout believers that a better life awaited them—and their spouses—in Malaysia. While this sentiment was expressed among both women and men, it was not uncommon to witness some resistance from women like Mrs. Watase, who described their move to Malaysia as shimanagashi, punishment. What historical or political conditions had led to this mixed characterisation of the inter-Asian movement? Why does the divergent characterization seem to follow the gendered line? And why do people like Mrs. Watase still move with their husbands to Malaysia despite their own reluctance?

In exploring these questions, this chapter will answer a set of questions that I often receive from people: "Why Malaysia? Why not Australia or Hawaii?" The chapter explores what made transnational retirement to Malaysia a conceivable idea for the group of former corporate workers, their spouses, and some single people. In the first part, the chapter follows the journey of Mr. and Mrs. Uchida, who had just arrived in Malaysia. Their passage through the postcolonial landscape of Malaysia shows how Malaysia's national project to develop itself into a moral nation through tourism went hand in hand with the affective conditions of middle-class, male, Japanese seniors who sought to maintain respectability in retirement. Malaysia's national development strategy corresponded with the postwar policies of the Japanese government which in turn instilled a certain postcolonial affect on Japanese retirees in Malaysia. At the same time, these national and transnational projects were enacted upon the lives of Malaysian residents in the periphery. I will explore the symbolic juxtaposition of one street in Kuala Lumpur, which was progressively cleared to make way for the privileged existence of silver backpackers and other wealthy expatriates in the exclusive enclave. The final part of this chapter will take the readers into Mrs. Aoi's kitchen to contrast the male experiences of Japan-Malaysia relations with those of their female counterparts. Attention to the domestic material culture will show how the postwar gendered socialization led women to enact the geopolitical relations between Malaysia and Japan differently.

Tourism as a Site of Nation-Building in Malaysia

Around the same time that Japanese sarariiman from the baby boomer generation started contemplating their retirement, the Malaysian government embarked on an economic campaign to make itself a tourist destination for rich foreign tourists. Tourism has been an important locus of the Malaysian state's articulation of its development goals. The inclusion of tourism as part of the national strategy has a long history in Malaysia. The 8th Malaysia Plan (8MP) (2001–2005) mentioned tourism broadly in relation to foreign exchange earnings (8MP, 8). The 9th Malaysia Plan (9MP) (2006–2010) was much more specific as it spelled out an aspiration to develop Malaysia as a regional center for health tourism in both traditional and modern health treatments. Health tourism was targeted at wealthy patients from nearby Southeast Asian and Middle Eastern countries (9MP, 15–16). The result made Kuala Lumpur the center of medical tourism in the region. The 10th Malaysia Plan (10MP) (2011–2015) added a new aspiration: to make the country "a premier destination for tourists, particularly for eco and heritage tourism" (10MP, 120). It targeted families seeking nature adventure and cultural diversity, and businesses interested in hosting meetings and conferences (10MP, 128).[1] The 11th Malaysia plan (11MP) (2016–2020) continued to mention the importance of medical tourism and ecotourism (11MP, 241–255). As can be seen from the promotion of medical tourism and ecotourism, Malaysia's tourism strategy has targeted two specific kinds of tourists: wealthy medical patients from neighboring countries, and family-oriented and well-educated ecotourists.

The targeting of wealthy patients, families, and well-educated tourists went hand in hand with the Malaysian state's development plan which centered on creating an Islamic world class city. After the Asian financial crisis of 1998, the influential Prime Minister Mohamad Mahathir wanted to find a niche within the global economy for Malaysia to thrive, but he also recognized a need to create an alternative to the conventional financial system (Rudnyckyj 2019, 7, 16). In the 10th Malaysia Plan (2011–2015), he announced that they would make Malaysia into a center of Islamic finance. The aspiration shifted the center of global finance from New York, London, and Tokyo to the network of Islamic finance, such as Kuala Lumpur, Dubai, and Istanbul (Rudnyckyj 2019, 16). Daromir Rudnyckyj (2019), an anthropologist of Islamic finance in Malaysia, discusses Islamic finance as an economic and political strategy for nation-building. In a country with a majority Muslim population, the Islamic finance project represented the interpretation of religion as broadly complicit with modernity and capitalist development (Rudnyckyj 2019, 29).[2] Under this framework, the targeting of wealthy travelers through medical and ecotourism allowed Malaysia to differentiate itself from other Southeast Asian countries which had become popular destinations for backpackers and sex tourists.

The building of an Islamic world-class city and its associated tourism strategies targeting wealthy tourists from neighboring countries was also in line with Mahathir's commitment to shifting the conventional colonial networks around Western nations to new inter-Asian networks around the Middle East and Asia (Rudnyckyj 2019, 51). Since gaining independence from Britain in 1957, Malaysia's relationship with Britain has deteriorated. For instance, after Britain tightened some investment rules in the aftermath of the Malaysian government successfully taking control of a British plantation company, the Malaysian government launched the "Buy British Last" campaign (Furuoka 2007, 508).

When Mahathir became prime minister in 1981, he sought to counter the assumption that the West was the universal model for developing countries to follow. Instead, in 1982, he launched a "Look East" policy which evoked Japan as an alternative model of development and promoted robust economic ties between Malaysia and Japan (Rudnyckyj 2019, 29; Furuoka 2007, 506). The announcement of the "look east" policy was carefully timed to coincide with the British foreign minister's visit to Kuala Lumpur, signalling the growing disenchantment with Britain and the newfound ties with Japan (Furuoka 2007, 508).

Malaysia's new alignment with Japan took place despite the legacies of Japanese atrocities during World War II. The Japanese occupied Malaysia from February 1941 to August 1945. During the occupation, the Japanese were brutal. The large-scale massacre and torture of the civilian population took place in many parts of Malaysia and Singapore through *sook ching* (cleansing massacres) of those who were deemed anti-Japanese (Blackburn 2009; Tay 2015, 221). Many Malay and Chinese women were forcibly taken from their villages to serve the Japanese soldiers as comfort women (Nakahara 2001). Parents who begged the Japanese soldiers not to take their daughters were killed or raped and then killed (Nakahara 2001, 584). The memory of cruel occupation had created resentment against Japanese among the local population.

In the post-World War II 1950s, the Japanese government started pouring foreign aid into Malaysia as part of the postwar repatriation program. It was not all out of remorse, however. Japan's postwar aid programs to Malaysia aimed at furthering Japan's economic interests at the cost of Malaysia's (Khong 1987). According to Dauvergne's research on Japanese aid policies in Asia, Japan's aid program became part of its national efforts and foreign policies aimed at securing resources, especially in the aftermath of the 1973 Oil Shock (Dauvergne 1997, 22). In 1994, 57.3 percent of bilateral aid went to Asia, and 19.5 percent to countries in the Association of Southeast Asian Nations (ASEAN) (Dauvergne 1997, 22). The Japanese government's Overseas Economic Cooperation Fund and the Japan International Cooperation Agency provided loans to Japanese companies seeking to invest in the Global South, usually at very low-interest rates (Dauvergne 1997, 24). Japanese multinational corporations were lobbied to set up overseas offices and factories in Malaysia in the name of "technology transfer" (Furuoka 2007, 506). These concessional loans comprised almost half of the Japanese aid program, and they placed heavy pressure on ASEAN governments to exploit natural resources in order to repay their debts (Dauvergne 1997, 24). Since the 1960s, Japan has been the world's largest tropical timber importer. Between 1964 and 1980, "Japan imported over half of the total log production from Indonesia, East Malaysia, and the Philippines" (Dauvergne 1997, 2), leaving the greatest indirect impact on Southeast Asia's commercial forests. Dauvergne (1997) uses the concept of "shadow ecology" to "evaluate the environnemental impact of one country's economy on resource management in another country or area." The ecological shadows are caused by the tactics and economic function of Japan's sixteen general trading companies (*sogo shosha*).[3] Some of the silver backpackers had served as expatriates in one of these companies in Malaysia in the late 1980s to mid-1990s. While these companies propelled Japan's high-growth economy, they also caused widespread environmental degradation in the resource-rich countries of the Global South (Dauvergne 1997, 6).

While the Malaysian government encouraged the opening of Japanese factories in Malaysia to promote its economic development under the "look east" policy, it faced resistance by the Malay-Muslim voters who insisted on the "priority of 'spiritual' over industrial development" (Ong 2010, 149). To legitimize the presence of Japanese companies in the eyes of the Malay-Muslim voters, Prime Minister Mahathir emphasized the perceived similarities of Japanese culture with Islam. He argued that, although Japan was not a religious country, its "cultural values" were akin to "the kind of morals and ethics" that he wanted the Malaysian citizens to emulate (Ong 2010, 149). The shared values, such as efficiency, cleanliness, and trust, were, in turn, configured into a vocabulary of moral responsibility as a means to manage Malay workers working in Japanese factories (Ong 2010, 149).

The "look east" policy's emphasis on cultural values went hand in hand with the Japanese government's soft power campaign which relied on the cultural constructions of proximity and sameness among Asians (Iwabuchi 2002; Watanabe 2019, 74). Japanese popular culture, including TV dramas and anime series, quickly spread among Malaysian youth in the 1980s and 1990s.

Educational exchange programs also fostered the sharing of cultural values. Part of the Japanese aid program was to fund scholarships for Malaysian students to study for engineering and science degrees in Japan (Furuoka 2007, 510).[4] Many bright young Malaysian students were sent to Japanese universities to learn and then serve their home country upon their return (Furuoka 2007, 509).

The decades of the "look east" policy, together with Japan's soft power policy through popular culture, created a political and social effect in Malaysia (Iwabuchi 2002). By the 1980s, the anti-Japanese sentiment witnessed in the 1970s was slowly being replaced with a view that Japanese multinational corporations could stimulate the local economy (Furuoka 2007, 514).

It was in these contexts of the Malaysian state's development programs around Islamic morality and the fostering of greater ties with Japan that the Malaysian government introduced a retirement visa program targeting wealthy Japanese retirees in 1996. Called the "Silver Hair Program," it exclusively targeted retired people above the age of fifty, and it was only open to nationals of Japan and Western Europe. The retirement visa holders were not allowed to work in Malaysia but they were encouraged to spend foreign money and thus stimulate the local economy.[5]

A year after the Silver Hair Program started, the Asian financial crisis hit Malaysia and other countries in Southeast Asia. The high-end condominiums and other services that had been popular among the wealthy local middle class suddenly lost their clientele because of the dramatic reduction of their income levels. In this economic condition, foreign retirees were imagined as the saviours of a dire situation, as those who could fill in the oversupply of these high-end commodities (Toyota and Thang 2017a, 561). To bring in more overseas retirees, in 2002 the Malaysian government renamed the program "Malaysia My Second Home" (MM2H) and opened its doors to citizens of all countries regardless of age.

The MM2H program kept the theme of Malaysia's original development goals in two ways. First, it encourages wealthy migrants by imposing a high financial requirement. Although the rules are constantly revised, as of 2014, applicants had to meet the following financial requirements to qualify for the MM2H program. At the time of application, an individual must be at least fifty, must show assets over MYR 350,000 (approximately USD 84,860), and must have a monthly income of at least MYR 10,000 (approximately USD 2,500). Once they are in Malaysia, the visa holders must open a bank account with a fixed-term deposit of MYR 150,000 (approximately USD 36,350) or more. Overall, MM2H visa holders were expected to live in high-end condominiums, use high-end services, and contribute to sustaining the consumption level (Toyota and Thang 2017a, 561).

Second, MM2H encourages family migration, as the program allows applicants to bring their spouse and children under twenty-one years of age. This contrasts with a retirement visa in neighboring Thailand, where each spouse has to meet the conditions of the retirement visa. By 2018, the MM2H program had attracted over 40,000 applications from 130 countries. Japanese have remained the second largest recipient of MM2H visas, after the Chinese (12,881); in total, 4,778 visas were issued to Japanese applicants between 2002–2018.[6]

The Promotion of Transnational Retirement
as a Site of Japan's Nation-Building

Postcolonial relations and geopolitical inequality also shaped the policy land-scape of Japanese transnational retirement. In 1956, the Japanese govern-ment proclaimed that the postwar period was over. By then, basic needs had been met, and high-level production and consumption became the new goals of the state's postwar recovery efforts (Ivy 1995, 247). Particularly illustrative was the appropriation of three sacred imperial symbols (mirror, sword, and jewel) by postwar mass media to signify a variety of consumer desires (Kelly 1993, 195). For instance, in the 1950s, when most of my interlocutors were born, the media promoted the three S's—*senpuki*, *sentakki*, and *suihanki* (fan, washing machine, and rice cooker). In the 1960s, when my interlocutors were growing up, the three K's were promoted—*kaa*, *kuura*, and *kara terebi* (car, air conditioner, and color television).

Among these material objects of desire, television in particular had an important role to play in the creation of an "imagined community" (B. An-derson 2016). Following its introduction in 1953, a television became one of the most desired objects for consumers. Sales skyrocketed in 1959 when the crown prince's wedding was broadcast (Ivy 1993, 248). The whole country watched the first Tokyo Olympics in 1964, becoming witnesses to the coun-try's postwar recovery and progress. Television promoted a sense of cohesion and belonging to postwar, high-growth Japan.

In promoting a sense of cohesion, television also played a significant role in creating a sense of the hierarchy of nation-states. While television articu-lated a sense of national belonging, it also broadcast images of the West as the idealized future (Creighton 1995). American serials such as *I Love Lucy* and *Father Knows Best* played major roles in invoking certain material de-sires and aspirations among the viewers, especially among female audiences (Tsutsui 1998, 134–38; Rosenberger 2001, 148–153). Most of my interlocutors grew up with the image of "typical" American families as one surrounded by consumer luxuries and electric appliances such as refrigerators, vacuum cleaners, and washing machines. My female interlocutors regularly told me that life in the United States was their *akogare* (dream, yearning) when they were growing up. The middle-class "American way of life" became the utopian goal for many Japanese people who were born in the 1950s (Ivy 1993, 249).

Hawaii, in particular, caught people's imagination as the dream island. By the mid-1970s, many people from Japan had become affluent enough to travel overseas (Mackie 2003, 178). In the 1970s, Japanese expected to attain the three J's: *jueru, jetto,* and *jutaku* (jewels, overseas vacation, and a house) (Kelly 1993, 195). The Nomura Investment Bank had a catchy advertisement in 1969: "Lady, you can take a trip to Hawaii out of your 25,000-yen salary." The advertisement encouraged young working women to save so that they could embark on a holiday in Hawaii. Fukushima Prefecture created an artificial tourist facility named the Joban Hawaiian Center in 1966 so that domestic tourists who missed out on overseas travel could swim at artificial indoor beaches and watch a hula dance to experience Hawaiian culture.[7] By the end of the 1980s, many five-star hotels, golf courses, and luxury apartments on the Gold Coast, in Australia, and in Hawaii were in Japanese hands.

In this context of a bubble economy and an overseas travel boom, the Ministry of International Trade and Industry (MITI) developed the "Silver Columbia Plan 92: A Project to Support Overseas Residency for the Fulfilling Second Life" (*Shiruba Coronbia Keikaku 92: Yutakana Daini no Jinsei wo Kaigai de Sugosutame no Kaigai Kyojuu Shien Jigyou*) which aimed at building high-tech resort facilities to accommodate groups of Japanese retirees in Australia (McCormack 1998). The plan was developed under the Comprehensive Resort Region Provision Law of 1987, which had been enacted to address the social need for rest, recuperation, and return to nature. Shimizu Kensetsu, one of the largest construction firms in Japan, was heavily involved in the planning of the retirement resort in Australia. Gavan McCormack, a historian of Japan based in Australia, argues that the emphasis on leisure during the late 1980s was due in part to lobbying activities by Shimizu Kensetsu and other large construction companies, all of which benefited from the construction of the resort facilities (personal communication with McCormack 2013). The next step was to build a retirement resort for Japanese retirees. However, the Silver Columbia Plan was abandoned before its launch in 1992 due to protests by local Australian residents. Australian protestors feared that the development would increase land prices and criticized Japan for dumping old people out of sight (Toyota 2006; Ono 2008).

After the Silver Columbia Plan 92 was abandoned, MITI established the Long Stay Foundation to continue promoting overseas retirement, or what they called "the long stay" (*rongusutei*). The foundation defines long stay as "a long-term holiday abroad, where the travelers interact with the local people, and thereby contribute to the friendly relations between Japan and the recipient countries" (Long Stay Foundation 2022). The definition inherited the initial ideologies of the bilateral project between Australia and Japan. The foundation has maintained ties with the MITI (now called the Ministry of Economy, Trade, and Industry) by having two former public servants from the ministry as its executive committee members.

Since its inception in 1992, the Long Stay Foundation has promoted transnational retirement in Southeast Asia, Europe, Australia, and North America by organising promotional sessions and experimental tours. The tours usually take between three days and two weeks. During that time, potential applicants inspect condominium units, supermarkets, restaurants, and local Japanese community groups.

The Long Stay Foundation actively promotes Malaysia as a retirement destination due to the relatively affordable cost of the MM2H program visa. This is the case even though the general public ranked the places they want to live in their retirement in the following order: Australia, New Zealand, Hawaii, Canada, and the mainland United States. Malaysia was ranked sixteenth (Yamada 2013; Ono 2015b, 617).[8] When I started my research, I asked Japanese retirees why they chose Malaysia as opposed to other popular destinations for Japanese tourists such as Hawaii or Australia. Many of my interlocutors answered that they started off by exploring retirement options in Australia or Hawaii. This was no surprise given the aspiration for the Western lifestyle that had been cultivated throughout their lifecourses. But they soon noticed several barriers imposed by financial and racialized hurdles.

Financially, my middle-class interlocutors found that the retirement visas in Australia and Hawaii were not affordable. To apply for an Australian retirement visa, for example, one needs to have assets of at least AUD 750,000 (USD 542,000), and be willing to invest at least AUD 750,000 (USD 542,000) in Australia. In addition to this, one must have an annual income of at least AUD 65,000 (USD 47,000) in retirement. Given that the average annual pension for an ex-sarariiman today is around JPY 2,500,000 (about AUD 30,600), these were difficult conditions to satisfy. In contrast, for an MM2H visa, an applicant must have a monthly income of at least MYR 10,000 (about USD 2,300) *at the time of application*. Applicants can apply for the visa during their working lives, and, indeed, most apply for it when they are between fifty and sixty years of age before their retirement. According to the National Tax Agency of Japan (2015), in 2014, the average monthly income of a Japanese worker was JPY 360,000 (about MYR 12,809 / USD 2,370). The average income among those who worked in a large company (more than 5,000 employees) was even higher at JPY 423,000 per month (about MYR 16,560 / USD2,790). Furthermore, male employees aged between fifty and sixty enjoyed the highest average income of JPY 540,000 per month (about MYR 20,000 / USD3,560).[9] Hence, sarariiman in their fifties could apply for the MM2H visa for themselves and their partners with relative ease.

Racially, many transnational retirees in Malaysia found that the emotional hurdle of going to Western countries was too high (*haadoru ga takai*). They felt uncomfortable speaking in English to native speakers in Australia (Ono 2008). Existing research on Japanese retirement communities in Australia shows that even those who actively participated in local activities through schools and volunteer groups felt uncomfortable speaking to the Australian locals in English (Thang et al. 2012a, 251; Nagatomo 2014, 147). This did not necessarily reflect the Japanese retirees' English levels, as those who had been overseas for a long time, or had been English teachers before, felt equally uncomfortable (Thang, Sone, and Toyota 2012b, 253). Being older Asian people in Australia, they had internalized a double discrimination based on race and age.

In contrast, Southeast Asia, or the rest of Asia in general, had a negative image among Japanese consumers, especially the baby boomer generation. Mrs. Watase's opening remarks which described her move to Malaysia as shimanagashi, a punishment, illustrate this negative image. This aversion reflects longstanding Japanese ideologies about racial differences that posit Japan as more developed than other Asian nations. The high growth period witnessed Japanese media comparing Japan with the rest of Asia. At the height of economic nationalism, media and newspaper reports portrayed Asian people as materially deprived; there were many news reports describing Asian tourists buying Japanese electric products to bring home (Mackie 2003, 210). By portraying non-Japanese tourists as materially deprived the media depicted Asia as less developed than Japan and placed those countries in the temporal past from which Japan could measure its advancement. This patronizing portrayal of Asia is hardly a thing of the past. Even today, major newspapers use the word *bakugai* (explosive buying) to describe the "insatiable desire for consumption" by Chinese tourists in Japan (Bofulin and Coates 2017). The word "Asia" was denigrated to such an extent that, when the blockbuster film *Crazy Rich Asians* was introduced into Japanese cinemas, the title was changed to "Crazy Rich." Crazy rich Asians, in the Japanese media's imagination, was an oxymoron. While the West was placed in a temporal future through its material abundance as shown on TV screens, the rest of Asia was placed in a temporal past with material scarcity.

When some of the interlocutors visited Malaysia on their experimental tours, therefore, they were not very surprised to witness the great selections of Japanese supermarkets (e.g., Aeon, Isetan, and Daiso) and restaurants in major shopping malls, and the enthusiastic uptake of Japanese popular culture (e.g., anime, comic books, and TV drama series) by the Malaysian locals. Kuala Lumpur's most exclusive mall has dedicated an entire floor to "Little Tokyo," an area featuring Japanese brands and eateries (Shakuto 2019a). Ono's (2008) research shows that due to privilege, many Japanese transnational retirees in Malaysia felt comfortable speaking and even making mistakes in English. One of my interlocutors expressed the racialized sentiment particularly clearly. "When I went to Australia, I was seen as an Asian. Here, I am seen as Japanese. I feel comfortable in Malaysia because the locals are friendly towards Japanese people." In contrast to the double marginalization that they experienced in Australia, Japanese retirees became visible as Japanese people in the postcolonial landscape of Malaysia.

In this way, Malaysia emerged as an affordable place with a friendly affect for Japanese retirees who were seeking to retire overseas. The silver backpackers perceived living among the locals in places like Australia and Europe as desirable but unattainable. In Malaysia, in contrast, they felt that they were part of a privileged group, as opposed to being an Asian in Australia where they were part of a racially discriminated group. At the same time, both the affordability of Malaysian visas and the friendly atmosphere were created because of the unequal postcolonial relations in which the Japanese government and corporations exploited both the natural and human resources of Malaysia. From wartime occupation to imports of Malaysian timber to exports of Japanese retirees, which in turn are supported by the Malaysian government's nation-building strategies and the real estate industry's corporate interests, the apparently spontaneous decisions made by the Japanese retirees to move to Malaysia build upon a long history of unequal geopolitical relations between Japan and Malaysia.

The First Impression and the Cost of Nation-Building

Mr. Uchida decided to go on a trial visit to Kuala Lumpur after seeing a TV program about Japanese retirees in Malaysia. The program featured Mr. and Mrs. Komura, who had been living in Malaysia for five years. The camera followed the couple from their lavish home in the heart of Kuala Lumpur to an affordable outdoor restaurant where they took their daily breakfast. Mr. Komura exchanged pleasantries with the restaurant owner in fluent English. The camera then switched to the couple's favourite activities at the Japan Cultural Center in Kuala Lumpur; there, they took part in karaoke sessions every Saturday with fellow Japanese retirees. Thirty or so women and men of the couple's age dressed up in various colors and sang many songs from their youth.

Mr. Uchida switched off the TV. He had never been to Malaysia or Southeast Asia, but the faces of those people singing karaoke in Malaysia looked much brighter than those he saw in Okayama. He didn't see himself in the latter, but he saw himself among Mr. Komura and the other singing faces in the Japan Cultural Center of Kuala Lumpur. There, no one was working. He too could speak English. He too could sing and even dance to the music.

Mr. Uchida bought a guidebook to transnational retirement written by Mr. Komura himself. The book listed numerous benefits of moving to Malaysia. "A warm climate will improve your health." "The cheaper cost of living will stretch your pension funds." Mr. Uchida continued flipping pages. Then he stopped as words jumped out of one page. "The availability of tasty Malaysian food in hawker stalls and affordable domestic services would liberate your wife from her household tasks and you can enjoy the free time together." Mr. Uchida imagined travelling around the world with his wife from Malaysia. His wife liked watching American TV dramas and had always said that she dreamed of one day living overseas. When he shared the idea of transnational retirement to Malaysia with her, Mrs. Uchida's response was that she preferred Paris to Kuala Lumpur. But he promised her that they could travel to Paris from Kuala Lumpur because of affordable flights by AirAsia. She finally agreed, and he signed up for a trial visit. He wrote to Mr. Kosaka, a transnational retiree who had moved to Malaysia in the early 2010s.

Mr. Kosaka was part of the MM2H Club at the Japan Cultural Center. The MM2H Club had an online forum which connected prospective migrants with existing expats. In 2014, the online forum boasted 2,300 members, 20 percent of whom lived in Malaysia and the rest were nearing retirement in Japan. The online forum often became a source of contacts for the prospective migrants' experimental trips to Malaysia, and Mr. Kosaka regularly chatted with prospective migrants online and volunteered to show them around Kuala Lumpur if they came on trial visits.

One day, Mr. Kosaka received an email from Mr. Uchida requesting to meet up in Kuala Lumpur. In early 2012, Mr. Kosaka picked up Mr. and Mrs. Uchida from the Kuala Lumpur International Airport. Mr. Kosaka immediately recognized the couple even though they had never met each other. The husband was dressed in a cream-colored shirt tightly tucked into long gray pants. The wife wore a cream-colored summer shirt with a light-colored yellow jacket and long white pants. Both wore white hats. They stood out in the Kuala Lumpur International Airport where posters, shops, and dresses were beaming with vivid colors.

Mr. Kosaka first brought the couple to the expatriate district of Mont Kiara where he lived. "This area houses many expatriate families from Europe and Japan," Mr. Kosaka told them. As a newly developed expatriate enclave, Mont Kiara was popular with Japanese families and upper-middle-class retirees.[10] Although there were more than a dozen condominiums in the suburb, most retirees concentrated in one or two condominium complexes. There were two Japanese-speaking real estate agents who monopolized the Japanese retirement market, and they mainly introduced retirees to these two condominium complexes. Newcomers, in turn, gained information about these condominiums through existing residents like Mr. Kosaka.

Mr. Kosaka drove Mr. and Mrs. Uchida through Kiara Street which was lined with tall leafy trees. The shade and breeze from the trees made it a pleasant drive. There was an international school there, and Mr. Uchida saw European children rushing out of it to be picked up by their parents in luxury cars. There was even a group of young Japanese mothers chatting in front of the school while waiting for their children.

Halfway through the street of Mont Kiara, Mr. Kosaka shut the window. "This is a local area," Mr. Kosaka said. Mr. Uchida saw a wooden signboard pinned to a tire by the side of the road. "Welcome to Segambut Village." He noticed that the street that he had been on had changed its name from Kiara Street to Segambut Street. The Mont Kiara district was connected to Segambut Village by one street with two different names.

From behind the shut window, Mr. Uchida saw a dramatically different landscape from the manicured neighborhood of Mont Kiara (Figure 2). Seven-Eleven convenience stores and Gloria Jeans coffee shops were replaced with roadside *warung* (small eateries); Italian restaurants replaced with *restoran* (local restaurants) and international schools with *sekolah* (local schools). Honda and Toyota cars replaced with motorbikes with leafy vegetables strapped on their riders' back. The two neighborhoods were physically

Figure 2. Segambut Village next to Mont Kiara. The high-rise condominiums on the left belong to the Mont Kiara district, while the single-story households at the front belong to Segambut Village. Photograph by the author.

connected, but materially, they were marked by differences in the types of residents, lifestyles, healthcare services, and education available.

Despite the bright new rhetoric around the Islamic world class city, the lived reality in Malaysia is stratified along race, class, and citizenship (Mayaram 2009; Butcher and Velayutham 2009). As part of the making of Kuala Lumpur into this idealized image, urban villages and squatter settlements were demolished to make way for the construction of gentrified townships for the urban rich and expatriates.[11] The real estate sector has been redeveloping land to create high end, gated residential communities (Toyota and Thang 2017b, 561). In these redeveloped areas, there are dramatic differences and lifestyle and income inequalities between local populations and affluent expatriates (see, for instance, Torres and Momsen 2005).[12] The rapid increase in land and property prices has meant that local people have been priced out of their places of residence (see, for instance, McWatters 2008; Zoomers 2010).

Formerly a Malay reserve, the Segambut Village was no exception to the spread of redevelopment and displacement. The presence of wealthier foreign retirees in gated communities has led to the gentrification of the neighborhood (Hayes 2018). Around the area marking the transition from Kiara Street to Segambut Street, there was a new bakery called "The Bakery." It seemed that the owner of one of the warung had renovated a vendor into a bakery reminiscent of hipster cafes. The shop lined up drinks in the style of a Segambut warung, but the bakery painted its stylishly simple name using microbrew fonts. This symbolic vendor marked the blurred boundaries between the two areas. Some complexes of condominiums from Mont Kiara were indeed spilling over to Segambut Village. One gated condominium community in the heart of Segambut Village was called, for example, *Impian Kiara* (The Dream of Kiara). With the spread of this "dream," Segambut Village was slowly but surely disappearing.

There was also visible environmental degradation in the rapidly redeveloping areas (Spalding 2020; Spalding 2013). As a result of rushed developments in Mont Kiara, for example, there were swamps and holes amidst the shacks and half-demolished houses. Rubbish was thrown into vacant land to fill the space. Environmental degradation included disease; there was an outbreak of dengue fever in the Mont Kiara/Segambut districts in 2014. When I visited Segambut Village between 2014 and 2015, a rotten smell regularly permeated the air.

The present lived experience of the world class city is equally shaped by the colonial and postcolonial history of Japan and Malaysia. According to the residents of Segambut, the area was a site of wartime atrocities during World War II. When I conducted fieldwork among the residents of Segambut, one of the residents took my research assistant and me on a small hike up a hill where he and his family had lived for over three generations. On top there was a settlement of five of his relatives who all lived in makeshift shacks made of rubbles our guide had collected from construction sites in Mont Kiara. His grandparents had migrated from Aceh, Indonesia, to Kuala Lumpur. "Most of my neighbors had fled the hill to other parts of town when the Japanese soldiers established a helicopter launching site near our settlement," he told me. Our guide brought us to an area which had significantly less growth than other parts of the hill. He said that the Japanese soldiers had cleared the area for their helicopters. He continued to explain that, even though Japanese soldiers had executed many villagers, his grandfather and his neighbors cremated the bodies of dead Japanese soldiers in this hill.[13] Our guide's stories evoked how the land and the residents of Segambut had long been subjected to a form of Japanese presence. The locals had few choices but to accommodate the Japanese, either through burial or redevelopment.

The Temporality of Nostalgia and Progress

I have so far outlined how the development strategy of the Malaysian state together with the postcolonial relations between Japan and Malaysia gave rise to the popularity of the transnational retirement of middle-class Japanese people to Malaysia. Readers might still wonder though, what made retirement in Malaysia so appealing? This section will examine one of many answers silver backpackers provided—that of temporality.

When I asked my interlocutors the above question about Malaysia versus Japan, they often emphasized that they felt younger in Malaysia (*wakagaeru*). They then redirected the conversation to praise Malaysia for its vibrant economy (*genkiga aru*). Retirees regularly compared Japanese youth with Malaysian youth: "Malaysian children's eyes are beaming with hope [*me ga kira-kira shiteru*] whereas Japanese children's eyes are dead [*me ga shinderu*]." The silver backpackers described Japanese children in Japan as living in a country with neither hope nor a future. Once, as we were finishing up an interview, one of my interlocutors said, "In Malaysia, I can be hopeful about tomorrow."

Contrary to what Mr. Uchida had imagined, Malaysia was much more cosmopolitan and technologically advanced than Japan. The internet speed was fast; the public transportation system was efficient; and shopping malls sold many international brands, including Japanese ones. After the trial visit, Mr. Uchida couldn't help but wonder about the future of Japan. Despite the stark contrast between the cosmopolitan landscape of Mont Kiara and the rundown Segambut Village, Mr. Uchida was taken in by the latter's landscape. On the wall of one of the village houses, he saw a picture of Ultraman, a Japanese cartoon that his son used to watch. The occupants must have painted the image for their children. Outside the house, the residents had set up a round dining table facing the road. Four male villagers around his age gathered on the table and chatted away over coffee while looking at passing motorbikes. The child for whom the picture of Ultraman must have been drawn was sitting by the adults listening to the conversation. The village reminded Mr. Uchida of his own childhood and the neighborhood he grew up in Okayama. "Malaysia is like Japan's younger brother," he said to himself.

The utopian project of postwar miraculous growth in Japan had created a nightmare not only for retirees like himself but also for the Japanese state itself. Japan had not recovered from the recession of the 1990s, and its trade deficit reached a record high in 2014. At that point, it was not merely retirees who had stopped progressing on the capitalist lifecourse. So did Japan as a whole. With the international media reporting the rise of China and the decline of Japan, many retirees mourned the death of Japan, Inc. (Ivy 1995). Some even anticipated an apocalypse: Mr. Kawata, a wealthy former electrical engineer who had moved to Kuala Lumpur with his wife in 2014, was convinced that Japan would default in a few years' time. He had shifted all his assets to Malaysia. Unlike many other retirees, Mr. Kawata had no intention of returning to Japan, and he had even convinced his only daughter to quit her teaching job in Japan and move to Malaysia with them. People like Mr. Kawata saw a future in Malaysia. Many interlocutors expressed their admiration for the speed with which Malaysia progressed before their eyes (Shakuto 2017, 166).

Anthropologists have long documented the projection of a romantic vision of "the Other" as a society copes with the negative effect of social and economic changes (Moeran 1998; Ball and Nozawa 2016). The experience of Mr. Uchida as he visited Malaysia illustrates how Malaysia became a nostalgic site in which many male Japanese retirees could see what they had lost: the temporality of progress (Shakuto 2017, 162). Yet this romantic projection hinges on perceiving Malaysia as "the Other." Male Japanese retirees regularly called Malaysia "a promising younger brother" in relation to the decrepit, older brother that was Japan. The image of Malaysia as a younger brother reflected the negative historical stereotype held by Japanese people of other Asian countries, and, as a result, Malaysia was regularly subjected to scorn from male silver backpackers. One day, for instance, as as our group was walking in Mont Kiara, one male interlocutor spotted rubbish on the road. "Why can't they do something about rubbish? It is such a beautiful country except for the rubbish issues." The speaker said he had even contemplated starting an NGO to clean the streets. When prompted by others that perhaps he should do as the Romans do, he replied that it was his responsibility as a resident to take an interest in the affairs of the country and to impart his skills for the benefit of the community. He distinguished himself from fleeting tourists and demonstrated his commitment to the place through his scorning. Yet the man's commitment to the place as a privileged foreign retiree in an expatriate enclave in fact demonstrated the contradiction of "imperialist nostalgia" which Rosaldo (1989, 108) describes as a paradoxical condition in which "a person kills somebody and then mourns his or her victim."

In such a context, the term "silver backpacker" embodies the contradicting narratives of the transnational retirement of many Japanese men and women. On one hand, the term appears to signal the desire to engage with the locals in order to gain new relationships and perspectives in a new country. However, actual engagement with locals and other expatriate groups was sparse and rare. Other than a few exceptional cases,[14] the migrant-local interactions were usually restricted to the discourse level, such as those cultural commentaries (usually negative) about Malaysian infrastructures, hygiene, and safety standards.

At the same time, precisely because of its position as a younger brother, Malaysia was perceived by male Japanese retirees as having a full future ahead of itself, unlike Japan. In Malaysia, the temporality which stagnated in Japan (see Chapter 1) started to progress again. Some retirees narrated their progressive temporality in Malaysia through the metaphors of school. Newcomers referred to themselves as Kuala Lumpur *ichi nensei*, which translated to "Kuala Lumpur freshman." They then progressed to Kuala Lumpur *ni nensei* (sophomore) and Kuala Lumpur *san nensei* (junior).

During his trial tour, Mr. Uchida became increasingly thrilled to be part of the temporality of progress in Malaysia. "I am going to challenge myself like I used to; I am going to live overseas for the next ten years. This is my new goal in life!" He and his wife sold their house in Okayama and signed a three-year lease for a two-bedroom condominium unit in Mont Kiara. Mr. Uchida enrolled himself in the Malaysian Language Club at the Japan Cultural Center. Within a year, he was venturing out alone to Segambut Village. He walked around the village with his freshly learned Malay and successfully bought some fruits and drinks. He felt alive.

Malaysia, therefore, seemed to be governed by two contradictory modes of time in relation to Japan: that of a nostalgic past and that of a progressive future. The effect of this sociocultural representation of progress was the emergence of a utopian landscape in which lives that had once lost momentum could be rejuvenated. Retirees reflected and at the same time contested the nation-state's ideologies which simultaneously reflected the hierarchy of nation-states (Roy and Ong 2011).

Cling Wrap: Enacting Geopolitical
Relations from the Kitchen

Many women who had been homemakers had different retirement lives from
their male counterparts in Japan (see Chapter 1). These differences seem to
have continued in the women's lives in Malaysia. The interlude to this chapter illustrates the awkward conversations between Mr. and Mrs. Watase, who
seem to have had different views of Malaysia and the nature of their stay there.
While Mr. Watase enjoyed his active life in Malaysia, Mrs. Watase seemed,
at least initially, to perceive her movement to Malaysia as a punishment, and
made trips back to Japan more often than her partner. While Mr. Watase perceived Malaysia as his new home, Mrs. Watase insisted that her home was still
Japan, and life in Penang was at most an extension of tourism. Do the gendered divisions of labor affect the visions of geopolitical relations? How does
gender affect the way men and women reflect on, and enact, these geopolitical
relations in Malaysia? The following sections will focus on the experiences of
women, both in Japan and Malaysia, to answer these questions.

The perceived material scarcity, or the potential inferiority of non-
Japanese products, in Southeast Asia was a real concern for many women,
who had supported the high-growth economy through their roles as consumers and household financial managers (Garon 1997). As electrical products
became the objects of desire and the signs of middle-class inclusion in the
postwar era (Ivy 1993, 249), the images of women as frugal homemakers began to circulate in housewives' magazines and posters (Garon 1997, 185).[15] A
"good wife, wise mother" made solid decisions about financial investments
ranging from purchasing insurance to managing loan repayments (Borovoy
2005, 105). The aptitude for saving was associated with being a modern
woman. Oku Mumeo, a feminist who led the Housewives Association (*shu-
furen*),[16] encouraged women to keep a household account book called *kakeibo*
so that they could handle household accounts properly and confidently (Garon 1997, 275).[17] It became the norm for husbands to tender their monthly
earnings to their wives, who would then determine how much they would
give back to the husbands for their monthly pocket money (Garon 1997, 274).[18]
By the mid-1970s, the Japanese household savings rate rose to 23 percent and
Japan quickly developed a reputation for high rates of personal savings (Garon 1997, 21, 268). By promoting a desire for products with the dual virtues
of frugality and savings, Japan in the high-growth period made its citizen,
and especially its women, extremely quality conscious. Female consumers

became de facto officers of quality control, ensuring that the things they bought were of the highest quality (Tsutsui 1998). Women as consumers, in turn, enjoyed distinguishing themselves by their consumption of carefully chosen, high-quality, domestic products (Rosenberger 2001, 150). The quality of a home came to symbolize femininity. In these ways, women took charge of household finances and organized themselves to create and maintain the high qualities of the home.

It is in these cultural and historical contexts that Mrs. Watase's initial unwillingness to come to Malaysia should be understood. Female Japanese retirees entered Malaysia with a combination of two racialized and gendered imaginaries. The postcolonial geopolitical imaginary placed Malaysia as materially deprived, while the gendered imaginary placed the responsibility of securing quality products for households on women. Acquiring quality products in a country that they had perceived as materiality deprived would indeed be a difficult task, leading the women to call the move a punishment. I will end this chapter with a story of how some Japanese women coped with this task, thereby enacting and materializing the geopolitical relations between Malaysia and Japan from their kitchens.

Many Japanese women in their fifties and sixties gathered regularly in each other's homes in Kuala Lumpur to chat over hobby activities, such as sewing and origami-making. Mrs. Aoi hosted weekly sewing sessions in her condominium unit in Mont Kiara. A group of three to four Japanese women in their gathered around noon at her home to have lunch and sew together. When I asked if I could join her sewing classes, Mrs. Aoi replied kindly with a broad smile, "Of course! It is not a class. If done alone, sewing can be a chore. But done with friends, it's so much fun. I am just providing my home for it." I felt immediately at ease with her friendly persona. For the remainder of my fieldwork, the weekly lunch and sewing session at Mrs. Aoi's became an activity that I looked forward to in Malaysia. As part of the sewing sessions, we often prepared lunch together. As we cooked, we would talk freely about anything that came to our minds. One conversation stayed with me, and I returned to it many times after leaving the field.

One dish required us to wrap rice balls with salmon and shiso leaves in plastic wrap. Mrs. Aoi provided us with imported Japanese wrap for this. The women carefully measured the wrap so as not to waste any. Mrs. Aoi encouraged us to use it liberally because she had just returned from Japan with more boxes of plastic wrap. The women became animated upon hearing this. One of them exclaimed, "I must restock mine when I go back next month!"

Bewildered, I asked Mrs. Aoi. "Why did you bring the wrap [from Japan] when you could easily buy it here?" "Oh, no! No! No!" She seemed offended by my ignorance. "Japanese wrap tears better! It's sturdier, and it doesn't cling to itself easily. The local wrap is sticky and doesn't make a sharp sound as it tears, and it frustrates me." She took one box of wrap from the cabinet. "It feels so good when the wrap tears in a clean slice" (*patto kiretara kimochi iidesho*). Mrs. Aoi then demonstrated the tearing in front of me. Her motion, from rolling the layer of film out of the container to tearing it against the sharp edges, was so slow that I could see her indulging in the whole experience. As she finished her performance, she looked at me and smiled. "See?" Mrs. Aoi could feel the tactility of tearing.

The physical material—polyvinylidene chloride (PVDC)—from which the Malaysian and Japanese wrap was made, was identical. But female retirees were very excited and comforted by their perceptions of the sight, sound, and tactility of the Japanese wrap. They started to list other products that they had brought from Japan, from dishwashing liquids to tablecloths and laundry detergents. The discussion was mostly light-hearted with humour and laughter. One of the women told the group that she even brought rolls of toilet paper from Japan. "Whenever I have a Japanese guest, I switch the local toilet paper to soft and silky Japanese toilet paper to show my hospitality" (*yawarakai toiretto pepa de omotenashi*). I could never tell if I was treated with Japanese toilet paper when I visited my interlocutors' homes, but true enough, I was always served tea and snacks that they had brought from Japan.

At first I was puzzled by the significance of these seemingly mundane Japanese products for female seniors. When a couple made the decision to move to Malaysia, women were often tasked with packing the suitcases. My female interlocutors had thrown away many of their personal items before coming to Malaysia, but they chose to bring box loads of plastic wrap. In Kurotani's (2005) ethnography of Japanese expatriate wives in the United States, she documented many of these wives bringing daily consumables in their first shipment to the foreign country. But later, the women restocked these items from the local supermarket. The elder Japanese women in Malaysia, however, continued to bring these domestic products to Malaysia, even years after they first arrived.[19] In the literature on migrant objects, scholars have observed that migrants tend to bring "personal effects of little or no utilitarian or market value" (Parkin 1999), such as a landscape painting of home (Walsh 2006) or photographs of distant loved ones (Law 2001, 279). But Japanese women packed their suitcases, not with pictures of their loved ones,

but with disposables. Typical migrant objects tend to be displayed promi-
nently on the walls of their new homes. Plastic wrap, on the other hand, was
kept in the cupboard most of the time and got disposed of after its use.

Over the course of my fieldwork, I encountered many occasions where
my female interlocutors gathered in their kitchens and humorously shared
the sensuous comforts of Japanese domestic products. In most of the cases
that I observed, men did not touch or use these domestic products. The
men would stay in the living rooms while women prepared the meals. It
was women who were listening to each other, and women who were respond-
ing with glee to those appraisals and joining in to praise Japanese domestic
products. These exchanges often accompanied light-hearted banter about
their husbands.

Japanese women's negative perception of Malaysian domestic products no
doubt reflected the negative stereotype of Asian people as materially deprived.
After spending more time with women in their kitchens and listening to their
life narratives, however, I came to understand that the social performance
around Japanese wrap was also a form of individual and collective release
that was connected to the larger stories that the women told about the contradictory perceptions of transnational retirement between their husbands
and themselves. For many men, a retirement in Malaysia presented an entrepreneurial opportunity to reimagine their post-work lives. In doing so,
men blurred the boundaries of home between Japan and Malaysia. At the
same time, the gendered labor in the domestic contexts and the fact that
women's labor was meant to produce a homely atmosphere—whether that be
in Japan or Malaysia—remained unchanged for many women in their retirement. By insisting on using plastic wrap from Japan, female silver backpackers drew a distinct boundary between Japan and Malaysia, a boundary that
would require a change of toilet paper to cross. The social performance made
the racial distinction seem real, so real in fact that the women brought boxes
of cling wrap with them in their suitcases (Harms 2010, 58). The Japanese
plastic wrap's symbolism rested on both the continuity of unequal race relations between Malaysia and Japan and the continuity of unequal spousal relations in which women were be expected to follow their husbands' decisions
regarding their place of living. When I asked the women why they agreed to
come to Malaysia, which they clearly saw as shimanagashi, most shrugged
their shoulders and merely answered that their husbands wanted to come.
Most women worked within this heteronormative inequality without overtly
challenging it. Women hung out with each other to create women's networks

around Japanese domestic products in Malaysia. Though this did not solve inequality in terms of gender or geopolitical racial relations, it did provide a way to deal with the emotional consequences of a movement from Japan to Malaysia.

Conclusion

This chapter evoked how the large-scale national and bilateral projects became entangled with the affective conditions of residents—both local and foreign. It has shown how the Malaysian state's development goals, the geopolitical relations between Malaysia and Japan, and the individual retirees' aspirations came together to transform Japanese transnational retirement in Malaysia as a social phenomenon. The Malaysian state's policies aimed at making the country a moral nation and its promotion of itself as such to respectable tourists from overseas went hand in hand with the anxious desire of former elite corporate workers from Japan to make themselves respectable again. Their experiences were situated within the complex postcolonial and temporal conditions that reflected the hierarchies of nation-states (Harms 2016, 2; Sun 2021). At the same time, those experiences also went beyond the unequal geopolitical imaginaries between Japan and Malaysia. Many former (male) sarariiman who had felt a sense of stagnation in Japan saw a future, a life post-work and post-growth, in Malaysia. Women, on the other hand, enacted the geopolitical imaginaries between Malaysia and Japan through their migrant objects in the kitchens. While many women would have preferred an overseas life in the West and or to stay in Japan rather than go to Malaysia, they still followed their husbands to pursue the latter's after-work projects in Malaysia. In doing so, the women made sure to maintain their quality of domestic life by bringing what were perceived to be superior Japanese products. This chapter has started to bring out subtle differences in women and men's experiences of transnational retirement and the interpretations of geopolitical relations. I will unwrap these layered stories and boundaries more in the coming chapters.

Interlude

D ancing onto the stage with a microphone, Paul introduced the band. Paul's real name was Toshihiko Yoshioka, but he liked people to call him Paul. "Let me introduce you to the Deviants! They flew all the way from Tokyo to be with us tonight!"

The crowd cheered with excitement. The band was comprised of four Japanese men and Paul's wife, Yasuko. Paul continued, "Despite the name of their band, they are not deviants in their real lives. They are all *eriito sarari-iman* [elite salaried men] who work for big companies. They formed the Deviants when they were students at Keio University, back in . . . well, some time ago!"

The concert was held in a cozy British-style pub in a residential suburb of Kuala Lumpur, which Paul preferred to the plusher, more touristy suburb of Bukit Bintang. "An oldies club," the locals would call the pub, for it played songs from the sixties. That night, the pub was packed with fifty or so Japanese people in their late fifties to seventies. One man wore a kimono, some wore bright colored dresses, and others wore casual clothes in subdued colors. At five in the evening, the night was just beginning but the crowd was already in high spirits. The band sang a few Japanese and American pop songs from the 1960s and 1970s, including "Top of the World" by the Carpenters.[1] A few couples went on stage to dance along, while others gently swayed at their tables. Claire, a close female friend of Paul, leaned toward my ear as she tried to speak over the music. "These are songs I grew up with. This is so exciting!" She stood up and danced away, waving her hand to Paul.

Almost sixty-five years old, Paul had come to Malaysia five years earlier, shortly after retiring from an investment company in China. I first met Paul in January 2014 at an art session in the Japan Cultural Center. He was painting alone at the back of the class but he stood out with his wavy gray hair, colorful glasses, and bright red T-shirt. I soon learned that Paul was the author of a famous online blog about retirement lives in Malaysia read by many of the Japanese retirees in Kuala Lumpur. Paul spent most of his time socializing with other Japanese retirees, painting, playing golf, and occasionally organizing parties.

Paul came to talk to me. "People usually host parties at the Japan Cultural Center. But this is more my vibe." Paul looked around the pub. His glasses reflected the multiple lights on the disco floor. He wore different glasses every day. That day, he wore a red pair. I noticed over the following months that he wore red whenever he was in good mood. "If I were in Japan, I would just sit at home, quietly sipping tea. But this is the kind of life that I like, and I can make."

As he finished the sentence, Paul jumped onto the center of the stage to start a drinking game with the crowd. He invited three people onto the stage and passed them cups of clear liquid; two had water, and one had vodka. The three people swallowed the liquid and maintained their poker faces while the crowd had to guess who had vodka. The prize for guessing the right one was a bottle of sake and a brain exercise game.

CHAPTER 3

Transnational Negotiation
of Normative Aging

In the previous chapters, I discussed how the Malaysian state's development strategy, as well as racialized, gendered, and postcolonial relations led to the middle-class Japanese people favoring transnational retirement. But readers might still be wondering, why not just stay in Japan? After all, as Paul mentioned during the party, many retirees spent most of their time at the Japan Cultural Center.

"That's because we are deviants," many silver backpackers probably answered. Just as the band of elite sararriman had named themselves "The Deviants," in Kuala Lumpur some male retirees seemed to have labeled themselves as the delinquent elderly—and they wore it as a badge of pride (Shakuto 2017, 161). These men explained that they were delinquent because, compared to many of their former colleagues who had stayed in Japan to continue working after retirement, they were devoting their time to leisure activities in Malaysia.

Despite the label, there was something earnest about the way these silver backpackers conducted themselves in Malaysia. While they seemed to enjoy dancing and playing drinking games, they also kept themselves in check (half-jokingly) through brain exercise games. The expectations for baby boomers were different compared to previous generations. At the turn of the century, policies and laws regarding the welfare of senior citizens had shifted, swinging in focus from familial care to individual responsibility. In Kuala Lumpur, there seemed to be a reenactment of some of these new aging ideals.

This chapter will focus on the more personal aspects of transnational retirement by looking at individual motivations and activities, and how they are given meaning in Malaysia. I will first introduce the Japan Cultural

Center in Kuala Lumpur as one of the key sites of transnational retirement. For many retired sarariiman, this transnational location enabled them to find purposeful activities with more ease. Some women, on the other hand, expressed their desire for transnational retirement as a liberation from the gendered lifecourse. This chapter will show how transnational retirees—both women and men—are adhering to, and at the same time deviating from, the normative aging ideals. In doing so, I will nuance the ideas of successful aging as they are enacted and, at the same time, contested in transnational locations.

Japan Cultural Center in Kuala Lumpur

Japan Cultural Center, formerly a Japanese school, is situated in the heart of Kuala Lumpur, only about a seven-minute drive or thirty-minute walk from the Kuala Lumpur Central Station. The Japan Cultural Center was a simulated Japan, in the Baudrillardian sense. Once past the guard house, one would enter the center, which was equipped with everything "Japanese." It had a Japanese grocery shop, a Japanese restaurant, a Japanese bookshop, a Japanese library, a Japanese DVD rental shop, a Japanese tourist agency, a Japanese massage service, a Japanese kindergarten, and even a Japanese souvenir shop selling things to take home to Japan. Non-visual sensations also evoked Japan. The temperature in the Japan Cultural Center was maintained at 27°C, the common temperature setting in Japanese homes in summer. This was in contrast to chilly Malaysian shopping centers, where air-conditioners were set at 18°C. The large TV screen in the center's lobby area broadcast Japanese entertainment programs and dramas, and I could hear the chattering voices from the screen whenever I entered the lobby area. Through its appeal to the eye, skin, and ears, the Japan Cultural Center replicated Japan for the Japanese residents of Kuala Lumpur. The Japan Cultural Center felt like an extension of their Japanese middle-class suburbs rather than an overseas location.

Japan Cultural Center of Kuala Lumpur is considered one of the largest Japanese organizations outside of Japan. In 2015, it boasted 4,000 members. The members of the Japan Cultural Center were mostly Japanese expatriates, Japanese retirees, and Malaysian students who took lessons in Japanese martial arts and language. For a nominal fee of MYR 40 (USD 10) a month, members could enjoy over seventy-five activities ranging from language classes to sports, cooking, and crafts and have access to the center's facilities.[2] In addition to offering activities and classes for its members, the Japan Cultural Center was responsible for managing a Japanese cemetery in Malaysia. The cemetery is the final resting place of Japanese residents who migrated to Malaysia, including former sex workers known as *karayuki-san*. These women were sold by their families to work overseas during the late 1800s (Morisaki, 2016). The center also hosted one of the largest Bon-Odori festivals, a Japanese summertime dance festival, outside of Japan, and an annual charity bazaar for both Japanese and local residents in Kuala Lumpur.

The center's membership of Japanese retirees has been steadily increasing since the mass retirement of the baby-boomer generation in 2012. Although the overwhelming majority of its 4,000 members were expatriates, during the weekdays, retirees dominated the activities offered by the center. Most of the seventy-five activities offered by the Cultural Center were comprised of the retired Japanese people. I regularly saw a dozen retired Japanese men in the lobby reading Japanese newspapers or watching Japanese morning TV series. Retirees routinely displayed self-deprecatory humor, saying that the Japan Cultural Center had become the Japanese "Seniors" Center (*Roujin Kurabu*).

Although the Japan Cultural Center hosted Japanese language classes for local residents, it was rare to see Japanese residents and the local residents intermingle at the center. Two entrances symbolically divided the two populations. While the Japanese residents entered from the front of the building which was located deep inside the compound, the entrance to the Japanese language classes, the entrance used by the local students, was placed at the back of the building, just after the gate. This latter entrance was referred to by the staff as "the backdoor." The students did not need to travel far into the compound to use this "backdoor" entrance to the center. The structure of the building was designed in such a way that the local students could enter the building and finish their classes without meeting any Japanese people.[3] The Japan Cultural Center evoked Japan by creating sensorial and demographic bubbles.

Becoming Ageless in Malaysia

At the Japan Cultural Center, silver backpackers kept a busy weekly schedule filled with activities. A typical schedule looked like this:

Monday	Golf
Tuesday	Ballroom Dancing Practice
Wednesday	Igo Practice
Thursday	Language Lesson
Friday	Ballroom Dancing Practice
Saturday	Karaoke
Sunday	Japanese Language Volunteering

The retirees pursued their hobby activities in Malaysia with a strong will to improve. For instance, during the ballroom dancing lessons, dancers were divided into beginner, intermediate, and advanced levels. Beginners were asked to step aside while the coach taught the advanced and intermediate dancers. Beginners zealously made video recordings of the advanced dancers' movements to practice by themselves at home.

Hisashi Toyotomi, one of the transnational retirees, wrote in a promotional book about the importance of challenging oneself in old age (Nagata 2013, 84): "When I was young, I was improving my life every day. Things I couldn't do one day, I could learn to do the next day. But now, as I become older, things I could do the day before, I can't do today. The physical decay is beyond my control, but coming to Malaysia, I realized that with a will to improve, I can, at least, maintain my emotional youth." He started learning English to improve his communication with the locals. Toyotomi concluded his chapter with, "The secret to maintaining our health is to challenge ourselves constantly no matter how old one becomes!"[4]

The constant challenging of their minds and bodies was in turn understood to improve the silver backpackers' health. According to Ono's research (2012), in recent years, the Long Stay Foundation has emphasized the health benefits of transnational movements. Ono (2012) has shown that the word "health" appeared on the Long Stay Foundation's website for the first time in 2006: "You may get healthier through the long stay." By 2009, the wording had become more affirmative: "You *will* become healthier (my emphasis)" (Ono 2012). In 2015, the foundation's website featured a story of a man whose sickness was miraculously cured in Malaysia: "After an accident seven years before, I had given up playing golf. But here in Ipoh, I started playing again. I have lost weight and feel healthy . . . Malaysian weather has healed my body and soul."[5] I argue that at the heart of the retirees' bodily rejuvenation was their engagement with the morality and temporality of the new aging society in Japan (Shakuto 2017, 167, 168). To contextualize the transnational retirees' narratives within these larger political-economic discourses in Japan, the rest of this section will explore the government policies regarding aging in Japan and beyond.

Independence and Mutual Support as a Twenty-First Century Aging Ideal

In 2012, the Cabinet Office of Japan released a report entitled, "Towards Dignified Independence and Mutual Support" (*Songen aru jiritsu to sasaeai wo mezashite*) (Cabinet Office 2012a). The cover page included a picture of Shima Kousaku, the main character in a popular comic widely read by male baby boomers. Starting in 1983, the long-running series tracked the life of Shima Kousaku, who embodied the successful sarariiman lifecourse. He climbed up a corporate ladder from being an ordinary sarariiman to a bijinesuman and then to being the chairperson of a major electric company. Many readers lived through the same events covered in the series, from the period of high growth to the bubble burst and then the tsunami disaster in 2011. Shima retired in the last episode in 2016. The cover of the report went further than the final episode. In the report, Shima was seventy-five, and he was sharing his expertise on corporate social responsibility with younger employees. The report states, "It is important to instill the understanding among the citizens that one is as much a giver as a recipient of a social welfare system" (Cabinet Office 2012a, 9).

Since Shima was an inspirational character for many sarariiman, the use of his image on the cover of the cabinet report seems strategic. The cabinet report calls for a shift in the public perception of seniors from "those who need support" to "those who can support themselves and others" (Cabinet Office 2012a). This ideal has been legally entrenched in the Basic Law on Measures for the Aging Society (Law No. 129 1995). The word "independence" appears four times in this short act of only fifteen articles. For instance, Article 12 states, "to enable the elderly to maintain independence in their daily lives, the government shall adopt measures necessary for promoting the construction of appropriate housing etc. for the elderly." Article 11 further outlines measures to ensure the senior's lifelong learning and social involvement in the local community through volunteer services. The 2012 report similarly suggests that both work and volunteering activities will create a space of belonging for senior citizens and thus allow them to play a greater role in society (Cabinet Office 2012a, 16). To this end, the Ministry of Labor provides voluntary and temporary part-time work opportunities for seniors through its Silver Human Resource Centers (Roberts 1996).

The seniors under this model of an aging society are represented as responsible subjects who could look after themselves and each other. The report goes on to draw on the experience of the 2011 tsunami, where people offered mutual support (*gojo*) within their local communities to navigate through the hardships. Calling such spirit "the pride of Japan," the report calls for a similar spirit of mutual support in the aging society (Cabinet Office 2012a, 25).

By describing the principle of mutual support as the pride of Japan, the cabinet report evokes Confucian notions of the individual as a member of a community (Long 2005, 106). In the Confucian framework, individual concerns and interests are generally understood to be suppressed for the sake of society (Lock 2002, 194). Although the new aging discourse placed "an independent self" at the center of the ideologies, the report's authors positioned attention to self as an act of care for the other, and particularly for the precarious youth in Japan, which I will discuss more in Chapter 5 (Shea 2014). These ideologies have had particular traction in contemporary Japanese society in which the sentiment of not causing trouble (*meiwaku*) or not wanting to ask for assistance is widespread (Long 2005; Kavedzija 2015, 143). The report further cultivates that nationalist sentiment as it notes that this new model of an aging society will offer a model for other Asian nations that will soon have their own increasingly aged population (Cabinet Office 2012a, 1).

Although the new aging ideologies have been naturalized as inherent qualities of Japanese people, similar rhetoric is echoed in the aging ideologies across the world. Anthropologists have documented a desire among seniors in industrialized nations to maintain their membership in society through work (Lynch 2013). Greenberg and Muehlebach (2007), for instance, observed that many seniors in Western European nations—specifically, Germany, Britain, Italy, and Switzerland—found themselves "unemployed" rather than being in the "Third Age" of leisure, a term coined by Peter Laslett (1989) to denote a period after retirement but before chronic illness. Seniors in this age were supposed to be filled with energy and to have the time and resources to enjoy their lives. However, the researchers found that the seniors in these countries were called upon to provide labor for societies facing a demographic crisis (Greenberg and Muehlebach 2007). Yet the exploitation of the seniors' labor is masked by a seemingly positive moral imperative of social engagement by the elderly and wide public recognition (Muehlebach

2009). Self-responsibility and mutual support—these two performative cultural productions have become the mutually constitutive regulatory forms for older citizens in Japan and beyond.

To live up to these new aging ideals, the cabinet report suggests that seniors need to possess three set of skills (*ryoku*): skills to look after self (self skill—*jiko ryoku*), skills to have friends (friendship-skill—*nakama ryoku*), and skills to be part of a local community (community skill—*chiiki ryoku*).[6] Self skill is premised on the principle of self-responsibility in which one is to realize one's full potential until the very end, by oneself. Someone with self skills is independent and contributes to society with dignity. The seniors should also draw support from their friends (friendship skill) given the increasing difficulty of supporting the elderly within the family, more on this in Chapter 5. Community skill refers to the ability of a local community to support the seniors' self-actualization (Cabinet Office 2012a, 10). The ideal community is one in which members, both young and old, support each other through intergenerational interactions (Cabinet Office 2012a, 24). The report also expects that participation by the seniors will, in turn, improve the local communities, which have been in decline in the postwar period (Thang 2001).

To reinforce these skills, the Cabinet Office established two new national awards in 2006 to recognize individuals and groups who are leading and encouraging others to have a fulfilled life using their "skills." The first award is given to Ageless Life Cases recognizing independent individuals who are leading a free and fulfilled life using their skills mentioned above. The second award is given to "Community Participation Cases" (*shakai sanka katsudou jirei*), that is, groups which encourage seniors to participate in their local communities. In the year 2016, a total of fifty-five individuals and fifty-five groups were honored with the award. For instance, Tomie Ishikawa (aged ninety-four), a former nurse, was honored with the "Ageless Life Award" (*eiji resu raifu jissen jirei*) for her support of other seniors who needed care. The Male Choir Golden Age Fukui (*dansei gasshoudan gouruden eiji Fukui*), a senior male choir group, received the Community Participation Award for providing seniors with a space for social participation and for volunteering to sing at a local welfare center. These awardees served as role models of the new aging ideals.

To prepare for a successful retirement under this new model, the report encourages those who are currently in the workforce to start acquiring these three skills before they retire (Cabinet Office 2012a, 12–13). For instance, to enhance one's self skill, youth are encouraged to save during their working days to financially prepare for their retirement. To enhance one's "friendship skill" and "community skill," the report emphasizes the importance of "work-life balance" (*waaku raifu barannsu*) which will enable working persons to actively participate in family, hobbies, and volunteer activities in preparation for their retirement (Cabinet Office 2012a, 24–25).

In this way, the ideologies of independent and mutually supportive retirement make self-responsibility a central mandate in retirement. In contemporary Japan, by narrating the attainment of these aging skills in relation to the lifecourse, the state reframes the period of retirement from one merely of "comfortable retirement" to one in which people can use their savings and the life skills that they have accumulated over their working lives to realize their "second lives" (Cabinet Office 2012a, 13). In this way, the Cabinet Report notes, there will be a cycle of investment (Cabinet Office 2012a, 13). The workers' lifecourses, which were to end with retirement, would resume moving forward into their second lives. The use of the term "skill," coupled with the idea of investing financially and socially for retirement throughout the lifecourse, points to the neoliberal nature of the new aging ideologies. In particular, the use of the term makes each component—self, friends, and community—a standard against which one is evaluated.

This has given rise to a new class structure (*kaikyu*) among retired people in Japan. In Jan Bardsley's (2011, 118) research on trends and fashions among older Japanese men, she quotes Makoto Obuse, a famous writer of self-help books for retired men; he divides older men into upper and lower classes. Makoto Obuse's classification is not based on financial or academic backgrounds; instead, it is based on one's attitude to life (Bardsley 2011, 118). The upper-class men are those who "make an effort to live youthfully by having a positive attitude, are willing to try new things, exhibit kindness and empathy toward others, maintain their curiosity, and can look at themselves objectively" (Bardsley 2011, 118). In contrast, the lower-class men "have lost interest in everything, become crabby, and give in to a wretched old age" (Bardsley 2011, 118). The anthropologist Takeyama also notes that, in millennial Japan, hopes and dreams are no longer simply a personal state of mind. Rather, they are "rearticulated as individual self-improvement projects that all citizens are equally eligible to undertake for a better future" (Takeyama 2016, 9). Moreover, "Hopes and dreams have become classification markers of the social winners, who have (and will potentially have) realized their dreams, and the losers, who have given up hope, shaping a new class consciousness" (Takeyama 2016, 9).

By integrating the attainment of social distinction with one's attitudes, these narratives encourage seniors to become neoliberal subjects working towards self-improvement along the new aging ideals. Whether it was through providing care to other seniors or singing in a choir, the ideologies of independent and mutually supportive retirement embodied the contradiction of retirement as a post-work phase. This has allowed Japanese senior citizens to counter negative stereotypes of the old as being passive and dependent on the one hand and provided them with a neoliberal pathway for the regeneration of responsible selves in their second lives on the other. By shifting from being the recipient of support to being the provider of support, the seniors become "ageless."

Ageless Seniors with Bad Boy Charms

The activities that silver backpackers undertook in the Japan Cultural Center—from choir to dancing—bore striking resemblances to activities promoted by the Ageless Life and Community Participation awards from the Cabinet Office. Some activities in the Japan Cultural Center also promoted intergenerational ties, such as the children's book-reading club where seniors read books to children of Japanese expatriates. Many silver backpackers narrated their motivation to engage in these activities as *boke boushi*, that is, means of delaying the onset of senility. Additionally, there was a class aimed at exercising their brains at the Japan Cultural Center where members were instructed to sing Japanese folk songs while playing the drums, maracas, and castanets. Participants told me that they were trying to maintain their health so that they could maintain their independence and not become a burden for their children (Thang et al. 2011; Jenike 2003; Kavedzija 2015; Shea 2014).

In addition to becoming upper class in terms of their attitude to life, the postcolonial landscape of Malaysia allowed some retirees to transcend the burden of financial class based on their familial financial backgrounds to achieve the dream that was denied to them in their younger age. One of my male interlocutors who volunteered to teach Japanese at a local Malaysian Chinese high school described himself as "a diplomat." In his youth, he had wanted to become a diplomat but only the graduates of top universities could enter such prestigious public service jobs (see Chapter 1). When he didn't get accepted into a top public university, the man gave up his dream and instead became a high school English teacher. He thought to himself, "If I learned

English, I would one day be able to travel overseas." He took early retirement at the age of fifty-eight so that he could teach Japanese to Japanese war orphans left behind in China (*Chuugoku zanryuu koji*). After relocating to Malaysia in his early sixties, he had wanted to continue teaching Japanese to Chinese children. He told me that it was through teaching Japanese to local children that he finally achieved his dream of becoming a "Japanese diplomat."

The transcendence of economic class was also enabled by the favourable exchange rate of yen to ringgit (see Chapter 2 for more discussion on postcolonial relations). Regardless of their financial backgrounds in Japan, in Malaysia, the retirees consumed like middle- to upper-middle-class Malaysian people. The average cost of living in Malaysia for a retired Japanese couple, including their expenditures on hobby activities, ranged between MYR 7,000 to MYR 10,000 (around USD 1,700 to USD 2,500) a month. In 2014, Japanese retirees' average expenditure was significantly higher than the average expenditure of Malaysian citizens (MYR 5,559, around USD 1,360) (Department of Statistics Malaysia 2015b).[7] For Japanese residents who were leading the expatriate lifestyles, however, their expenditures in Malaysia were not too different from the average spending of a household of a retired couple in Japan, an amount of JPY 247,815 (around USD 2,200) (Ministry of Internal Affairs and Communications of Japan 2016).[8] With the same expenditure, in Malaysia as in Japan, the Japanese retirees could live in a gated community in the city center close to all amenities. While they frequently ate at expensive European and Japanese restaurants or even at international fivestar hotels, they also regularly ate at local hawker stalls which sold simple meals for less than RM 8 (USD 1.5). The same pattern went for the consumption of clothes, where the Japanese expats oscillated between cheaper working-class malls and more expensive high-end malls selling designer clothes. The lower cost of living gave the retirees the option to choose their lifestyle—a choice that they did not really have in Japan. The lower cost of living in Malaysia also made it possible for Japanese seniors to enjoy active lifestyles.

By crossing transnational borders, silver backpackers were also able to overcome a rural-urban geographical divide in terms of access to public and private infrastructures. Eddie, for instance, enjoyed attending concerts by the Malaysian Philharmonic Orchestra (MPO) every week. In Japan, similar concerts were not only unaffordable but also inaccessible to people who lived in rural areas. From the city of Nagoya where he had lived, Eddie would have had to travel on an expensive bullet train for two hours to reach a concert hall in Tokyo. In Malaysia, it took him only fifteen minutes by taxi to go from the apartment he rented in the heart of the city to the performance hall. The ability to frequent such venues also allowed Eddie to obtain social distinction (Bourdieu 1984). After a concert one evening, Eddie and I entered a lavishly decorated concert lobby full of expatriates and rich locals mingling around with glasses of wine. Eddie moved around the lobby greeting other Japanese concertgoers. I recognized a few familiar faces, including a former businessman whose daughter became a professional pianist in Japan. He and Eddie acknowledged each other and exchanged pleasantries. Eddie told me that he enjoyed being among the "distinguished crowd." In Japan, he had lived close to *Shogai Gakushuu Daigaku* (lifelong learning universities), but there, he had felt as though he was mingling with *roujin* (old people). In Malaysia, in contrast, Eddie felt that he could mingle with like-minded people—the social upper class.

Living in Malaysia also gave transnational retirees opportunities to travel around the world. Mr. and Mrs. Korematsu, for instance, took advantage of cheap fares offered by AirAsia. As soon as AirAsia released its promotional fares, they snapped up tickets to different destinations around the world. With these cheaper fares, they could also go back to Japan frequently. Return airfare from Kuala Lumpur to Tokyo or Osaka at a special discounted rate cost as little as 30,000 yen in 2014 (USD 200). The low cost of flights made transnational boundaries almost obsolete. In contrast to the feeling of immobility that the couple had felt in Japan, their lives in Malaysia were characterized by hypermobility (Shakuto 2017, 169).

In these myriad ways, in Malaysia, the male silver backpackers could alter their existing state of feeling as "old men" by transforming themselves into "upper-class" seniors who were "willing to try new things" (Bardsley 2011, 118). Through setting new goals and aspirations to guide them through their retirement years, transnational Japanese retirees could become the normative ageless seniors of the twenty-first century.

It is important to note, however, that very few Japanese men I met in Malaysia saw themselves as exemplary seniors in the eyes of the Japanese state. Rather, it was more common to hear of them speaking of themselves as *furyō rōnen*, that is, the delinquent elderly. The word furyō (wicked, delinquent) is often used to refer to youth (*furyō shōnen*) who have become derailed from a normative lifecourse. Some of these older self-identified deliquients were explicitly critical of the work-oriented lifestyles and temporality in Japan. Mich exemplifies these critical attitudes.[9]

At the beginning of my fieldwork in early 2014, I met Mich, a seventy-two-year-old retiree who was staying in a hostel in downtown Kuala Lumpur. Although his real name was Mr. Miyake, he liked others to call him Mich. He divided his time equally between his home in Japan, and his favourite hostel in Kuala Lumpur. Mich was almost 1.8 meters tall, had pale skin, and his lean body moved about gently. He was dressed in a yellow Hawaiian shirt with a light grey floral print when I met him for the first time. Even to my unacculturated eyes, it was obvious that his shirt was made of expensive silk. Mich reminded me of a classic painting of an aristocrat from the Heian Period.

"I like it here. Time passes slowly here." Mich said softly as he stretched deeper into a yellow sofa in the Kuala Lumpur hostel. He continued:

> Whenever I return to Japan after spending some time in Malaysia, I feel strange the moment I get off the plane at Kansai airport. In Japan, I am constantly reminded of time. People follow timetables too strictly. Once, my train was delayed for three minutes. At every station after that, the train master announced his apology. Just for a three-minute delay! At the expense of following timetables, we sacrifice our emotional experiences. There is no need for fixed rules on time. I have stopped wearing watches here. But when I go back to Japan, they say I am weird.

I looked at him curiously. Mich's indifference to time seemed to dismiss the very idea of productivity that the postwar Japanese state cultivated in its citizens. But he had not always been "weird," he said, noticing my curious look. In his youth, Mich was on what he called "an elite path." Being the second son of a wealthy family in one of the most exclusive neighborhoods in western Japan, Mich went to an all-boys private school. After graduating from a prestigious university in Osaka, he began working for a large trading company in Osaka. He was ambitious; for three consecutive years, he woke up at dawn, jogged for an hour, and went to work until midnight. He reduced his sleep to produce more than his coworkers. Mich was promoted rapidly. "I was like a horse on a racecourse, blinkered so that I could see just one path laid out in front of me," he said. Mich was indeed set on a capitalist lifecourse, numbing his senses, and racing rapidly into the future.

But the race ended abruptly for Mich. At the age of thirty-five, he fell seriously ill. The machine that didn't rest finally broke. He stayed in and out of the hospital for three years. "I was, at first, restless. I was thinking about work from the hospital bed." But he eventually came to a cruel realization. "The company would run normally without me." He was quickly replaced by a younger worker. His marriage also broke down. He had no children. Mich felt lonely. Without a sense of progress, he felt as if time had stopped.

Mich likened his period of sickness to a period of retirement. In the same ward with him were retirees. He saw them die one by one. "There was no difference between them and me. I effectively experienced an early retirement."

After Mich recovered, he went back to work in the same firm, but he no longer worked like before. Instead, he started to travel the world with a view to relocating to one or more of the places he visited when he retired. He no longer believed that he had to retire at an age set by the company. He began investing in stocks with the aim of accumulating enough funds to retire early.

On the day Mich accumulated one hundred million yen (approximately 700,000 USD), he quit his job. He was fifty-seven. His colleagues thought he had gone mad. If he had waited for three more years, he would have qualified for a full pension. "But life is too short to waste it on mindless work," he said to me.

He took off on his adventure. When I met him in 2014, Mich was about to fly to Nepal. "The doctor said I may live up to sixty-five. But now I feel better than ever at the age of seventy-two!"

He then recited a haiku from his memory.

Hito no iku uramichi ni michi ari hana no yama
Behind the road are there paths and flowers

The dislocation experienced by Mich was significant because it suggested a stark difference between the life of a company elite and the life of a non-working man. Of course, multiplicities of self are inherent in human life (Humphrey 2008, 359). It has never been the case that work was the only defining feature of self. But, under the capitalist lifecourse to which sarari-iman successfully belonged, the idea of productivity brought singularities to the multiple strands of personhood (Humphrey 2008). Yet Mich's narrative of loneliness highlighted the fragility of this association between work and personhood. Although the capitalist lifecourse provided people like him with a clear manual for upward mobility, their lives were "being made and unmade according to the dictates and whims of the market" (Berlant 2011, 192).

Mich's sickness made him deviate from the normative path and made apparent to him what the dreamworld of progress simultaneously meant: it is attainable for only so long as one continued to work. He derailed from the lifecourse, abandoned his watch, and left Japan. He was fully embracing the life of a weirdo in Malaysia.

Similarly, many male retirees in Malaysia liked to think of themselves as slightly deviant. I observed that there is a desire among transnational retirees to attain the social upper-class status while at the same time being deviant. Some of these men called themselves *choiwaru jii-san* (an old man with a bit of bad-boy charm) borrowing from the term, *choiwaru oyaji* (a middle-aged man with a bit of bad-boy charm) (Bardsley 2011, 117). The latter term was popularized by the middle-aged men's fashion magazine *Leon* in 2001 (Bardsley 2011, 117). As exemplified by the drinking game whose prize is a brain exercise game, the male transnational retirees created an identity: ageless seniors with bad-boy charm (Shakuto 2017).

Rupture: Liberation from Gendered Personhood

In many ways, coming to Malaysia allowed retired sarariiman who may have felt emasculated in Japan to repossess their gendered and racial privilege. But how do women, who had generally experienced a lesser degree of rupture in their old age, experience their lives in Malaysia? In what follows, I will show how some women described their move to Malaysia as a form of "a rupture" in their gendered personhood, albeit an incomplete one. I will highlight the narratives of those who felt that the transnational retirement gave them an opportunity to peel away their gendered personhood in later life.

When I was initially struggling to find the narratives of women (see Introduction), a female interlocutor introduced me to Ms. Saito, who lived alone in Kuala Lumpur. Ms. Saito agreed to be interviewed, and two days later, I was sitting in a café at the heart of the city with her. Words poured out of her mouth as if they had been waiting to be heard for a long time. Ms. Saito's story reveals the hardship of being a divorcee and how coming to Malaysia liberated her from some of the gendered constraints that she had experienced throughout her life.

Ms. Saito got divorced in the 1970s when her three children were still very small. She had been working in a kindergarten as a nanny. She really liked children and enjoyed working there. After her divorce, however, the income from being a nanny was not enough to support her three children. Ms. Saito studied and obtained a license to become an accountant assistant. She got her first job as an accountant assistant at a small family firm.

The firm was run by a few men from the same family. All the women except her were part-time workers providing minor assistance. Despite her qualifications, Ms. Saito also was asked to provide menial labor. She recalled countless times she had to run and buy cigarettes for men or cook lunch for them. She was outraged by the contradiction in the workplace. "During my high school years, we learned about gender equality. When I worked at a kindergarten, every other worker was a woman. After I got divorced and started working in the corporate world, I realized there was so much discrimination against women. I was shocked." She then promised herself, "I will make these men recognize me!" Ms. Saito studied more and passed a national license exam to become an accountant. She worked in the firm for ten years and was promoted to a senior staff member. She took on more responsibilities and started administering advanced accounting. As she was enjoying the challenges of her new role, the CEO warned her. "If you take on more responsibilities, your male colleagues will be intimidated." She ignored the advice and continued performing at her best. Then, just as she was about to be promoted to a role as a section chief, her male manager began to harass her. He would refuse to sign documents and pass hostile comments to those who were friendly to her at work. The work environment became toxic. She had no choice but to resign. It took her many years to find another stable job. During those years, she developed a chronic hearing problem that made her lose her sense of balance. She felt that her life was spinning out of control.

Ms. Saito finally found a stable job and stayed until her retirement. That company's bookkeeping was initially in an appalling state. Two months after she started at the second company, the National Tax Agency came for an inspection and took away millions of yen from the company. The employees gossiped that she must have been the whistle-blower. Despite the hostility, Ms. Saito persevered. She patiently executed her job and eventually rose up to the number two person in the company which had been steadily growing in size. By the time she resigned, it had more than a hundred employees. She eventually left the company due to a disagreement with the CEO about management strategy; Ms. Saito suggested that he adopt a new strategy to manage the increasing number of employees, but the CEO insisted on sticking with the old ways. Her last job was to make the CEO's will. After finishing it, she retired at the age of sixty-one.

After surviving various forms of gender discrimination and hostility at different workplaces, Ms. Saito told me, looking back, that she was nonetheless happy to have worked for these companies. All of them were small family-run companies, and at least she was not a cog in a wheel like many elite sarariiman. She was proud that she had experienced many types of work while raising her three children on her own.

After retirement, Ms. Saito felt that she could still contribute to people's lives. She started volunteering at a daycare center and earned a side income as a babysitter. This brought her back to the first job she had loved, kindergarten. When she was younger, she had held a negative perception of volunteerism. She had thought that it was for rich housewives, not for working mothers who were struggling to make ends meet. Her resentment echoed the conflict that 1980s feminism saw between housewives and working mothers. While the former expanded their participation in various women's activities including volunteerism, the latter did not regard such housewives as feminists and even somewhat resented them because of their financial dependence on their husbands' income. Ms. Saito's retirement liberated her from that resentment. "When I was working, I did everything because I had to. After retirement, nothing I did was compulsory. I was choosing to volunteer. And I kept volunteering because it was so much fun." She felt it was natural for her to do what she could for the community.

Yet after retirement, Ms. Saito experienced a new type of constraint. Being an old and single woman evoked a perception of vulnerability and dependency in the eyes of her own three children. They were concerned about her living alone. Her daughter's family lived in the same apartment complex, and after Ms. Saito's retirement, they invited her to have dinner with them every weekend. They offered to drive her everywhere and for every small task, they rushed to do it for her. Although Ms. Siato enjoyed spending time with the children and appreciated their intentions, she hated the feeling of being a burden and wished for a more independent lifestyle. She didn't want to resign herself to being a vulnerable older woman.

After her mother passed away, Ms. Saito had even more time to spare. She decided to enroll in an English school in the neighborhood. There, she met a flamboyant lady called Tsubaki-san. She reflected on her encounter.

> Tsubaki-san was opposite me. She was rich. She used to manage her own real estate properties. She was sociable. She loved drinking. I was none of these, but I liked her. Even her husband was different

from any men I knew. He could do all the household things. He didn't say the old-fashioned nonsense like "I don't do this because I am a man." He could live by himself. Before meeting her, I didn't like to try new things. But she encouraged me to come with them to Malaysia to enroll in an English language school for one month. I thought I'd give it a try and rented a unit in the same condominium complex as them.

The English language school in Kuala Lumpur hosted mainly Japanese university students and retirees. There Ms. Saito met many different types of Japanese people that she had never met before. It was a liberating experience.

> Japanese people I met in Kuala Lumpur were non-conventional. Here, I didn't feel judged. In Japan, I was entangled in so many social obligations. My children were always concerned about me, and I couldn't be alone there. Here, for the first time in my life, I could live freely without social ties [*shigarami no nai jiyuu na ikikata ga dekiru*].
> In Malaysia, I set myself a rule: "one challenge a day." For instance, yesterday, I tried buying my meal from a new vendor. Today, my challenge was to order a takeaway fresh juice and drink it from a plastic bag! When I first arrived, I rode a taxi everywhere and ate at Japanese restaurants. Now, I take trains everywhere and eat at Hawker centers. Oh, I also set myself a challenge to speak English at least once a day. Small little challenges like these. They make me feel nervous but also excited [*doki doki suru*].

Ms. Saito initially had bought a ticket for a one-month stay, but she decided to extend it for an additional two months. For the past two months, after Tsubaki-san had gone back, Ms. Saito was living alone without any ties to anybody. She felt, for the first time in a long time, that she was living life for herself. Not for her husband, her employers, her colleagues, or her children. Just for herself.

The narrative of Ms. Saito highlighted the effects of gender constraints on single women both during working times and in their retirement. For Ms. Saito, her retirement and subsequent relocation to Malaysia liberated her from the social sanctions of being a divorcee and a single woman in Japan. Once retired, she could act just as other housewives, enrolling in English school

and spending her time volunteering. But she soon felt that she was being perceived as being vulnerable because she was a single older woman. Going to
Malaysia gave her a sense of control and independence. Ms. Saito could be
someone with her own dreams and aspirations, far from the assumed image
of vulnerability so often placed upon older single women in Japan. In Malaysia, just like men, and as equal to men, Ms. Saito could embark on her own
"retirement project."

Ms. Saito's story also highlights her liberation from the gendered expectations in Malaysia. Karen Kelsky (2001), an anthropologist of Japan, studied a group of young Japanese women in the 1990s, women who had sought
the idea of the West and Western men as progressive alternatives to resist gendered expectations of the female lifecourse in Japan. Unlike the Japanese
women whom Kelsky had studied in the 1990s, the older female interlocutors in Malaysia in the 2010s did not idealize foreign locations or foreign men
as enablers of their more progressive future. For them, it was not so much
that Malaysia was associated with liberal virtue. Rather, the better future was
enabled by the older women's own investment in themselves, as well as by
their solidarity with other women, regardless of the status of marriage or
wealth. Toyota and Thang's comprehensive studies of Japanese retirees in
Southeast Asia also show that Japanese women tend to lead very active and
independent lives there. Female transnational retirees "enhance[d] their
independence by redefining and enlarging their space of engagement" (Toyota
and Thang 2017b, 570). Transnational retirement to Malaysia physically expanded Japanese women's spaces of engagement.

This narrative of living a later life for oneself was also evidenced among
some Japanese women who came alone to Malaysia even though they were
still married to their husbands who had remained in Japan. Mrs. Yoshida was
an example of such a case.

Mrs. Yoshida called me at seven-thirty in the morning a day before I left
the field. "Did I wake you up?" she asked. I said no, but my voice betrayed
me. "I heard that you were leaving tomorrow. I wanted to tell you my story
before you left." I jumped out of bed, while holding the mobile phone, and
sat on a desk with a pen.

> I worked for thirty-two years before retiring at the age of sixty. Then
> I went on a cruise for three months by myself. It was a memorable
> experience, but I felt disappointed with myself for not being able to
> communicate with others in English. I am an ambitious person, and

I couldn't let this realization slip. So, I sent a fax to my husband
from the cruise ship: "I have decided. When I get off this ship, I will
devote the rest of my life to myself. I would only take care of my
own mother and you would have to take care of your own mother."
I knew that if I waited until I left the ship, I would not have had the
courage to say this to him. I went back to Japan, and then three
months later, my mother was diagnosed with terminal cancer.
I looked after my mother intensively for six months. Then she
passed away. Upon her death, I came to Kuala Lumpur by myself
and my dog.

In this early morning phone call, I was surprised to hear that Mrs. Yoshida had not only left her husband in Japan to come to Malaysia but also
that she had freed herself from the much-expected social obligation of looking after her husband's mother. It appeared that with the physical distance
away from Japan, and in the bubble of a cruise ship, she had the courage to
jump out of her gendered expectations. After coming to Malaysia, she enrolled in an English class.

As soon as I reached Kuala Lumpur, I started to look for an English
class. I've always dreamed of studying at the British Council. When
I went for their trial lesson, I realized that there were no Japanese
people in their class. This was ideal. I was so anxious that I wouldn't
make a cut to enroll in the class. But I did! I cried with joy when I
passed my entrance exam to the school. For the next year and a half,
I advanced from one level to another. Everyone was so pleasantly
surprised that an old woman like me could acquire a new language!

Unlike Ms. Saito, who slowly rid herself of ties to Japanese people in Malaysia, Mrs. Yoshida jumped into an environment without any Japanese to
achieve her goal of speaking English. Coming to Malaysia on her own,
Mrs. Yoshida challenged the stereotype that older women and independence
were an oxymoron.

This sense of liberation was also felt by women who had largely followed
the normative female lifecourses of marriage and childbirth and then came
to Malaysia with their husbands. Mrs. Ishida, who used to feel watched by
her neighbors in Japan (see Chapter 1), enjoyed the liberation from her shigarami (social ties) in Malaysia. She said, "No one passes judgment even if

I am playing all day because that's precisely the social norm here [among fellow Japanese retirees]. I have so much time for myself." Mrs. Ishida started to keep an online blog in Malaysia. She named her blog after a tea house which was built to commemorate Michizane Sugawara, an aristocrat from the Heian period (794–1192) who was sent to Mrs. Ishida's hometown as *shimanagashi* (banishment). Despite the punishment, he found the place beautiful. Perhaps, like Michizane Sugawara, Mrs. Ishida found Malaysia to be a hidden gem in what initially looked to be shimanagashi. For her, going to Malaysia was less about starting a new retirement project than it was about liberation from existing social obligations.

Other women disposed of their possessions—both physically and symbolically—before coming to Malaysia. When Mr. and Mrs. Hara decided to come to Malaysia, their daughter objected to their international move. The daughter complained that it was unnatural for parents to leave their children. But Mrs. Hara told me: "I used to live one hundred percent for my family. I looked after my parents and parents-in-law, daughters, and grandchildren. It's time to live one hundred percent for myself now." This discontent about having to care for others in later life may be specific to Mrs. Hara, but it could also reflect the general trend in which grandmothers around the world are called to provide unpaid care as state institutions are cutting welfare. Cross-culturally, the idea that "the early sacrifices of motherhood are later rewarded with meaningful care [by others] in elderhood" (Livingston 2007, 166) is becoming increasingly uncertain in the post-Fordist restructuring of capital. In an edited volume entitled, *Generations and Globalization* (Cole and Durham 2007), anthropologists explore the changing intergenerational relations in various countries within a new economic context that witnessed the growth of flexible labor and sharp class divisions. For instance, Julie Livingston (2007) observes how the shifts in global capital in relation to the practice of disability increased the demands on grandmothers to be basic care providers in Southeastern Botswana. Instead of being cared for themselves, the elderly grandmothers had to become primary caregivers in their old age (C. Goodman and Silverstein 2002; Rodriquez-Galan 2013). In Japan, grandparents, especially grandmothers, tend to look after the newborn grandchildren with their daughters or daughters-in-law given the lack of, or very short amount of, paternal leave given to male spouses. In 2021, while 95 percent of women took more than six months of maternity leave, the majority of men took less than two weeks (Ministry of Health, Labor, and Welfare of Japan 2021). Even in cases where there is a good paternal leave policy, very few men take it. In

2021, only 14 percent of men took parental leave in contrast to 85 percent of women (Ministry of Health, Labor, and Welfare of Japan 2021). The majority of women, therefore, return to their maternal homes to give birth and stay there for the first few months (Ministry of Health, Labor, and Welfare of Japan 2018). Even after daughters go back to their marital residences, many grandparents continue to help look after the grandchildren given that the average man only spent less than one hour on childcare a day in 2016 (Ministry of Health, Labor, and Welfare of Japan 2021).

Having provided care for their children and grandchildren, Mr. and Mrs. Hara were ready to live their lives for themselves. They sold their house in Gunma Prefecture and got rid of all their winter clothes. Mrs. Hara donated all her valuable kimonos to a resale shop. They arrived in Kuala Lumpur six months later with two suitcases. Mrs. Hara said that she felt lighter. I interpret Mrs. Hara's sense of being light as indicating liberation from the larger reproductive roles. The "destruction of matter matters profoundly" in the erasure of familial obligations (Tusinski 2016, 15) because the removal of objects, especially kimonos which are usually passed down through generations, symbolized their departure from the reproductive roles. By getting rid of material accumulations, women may have unbound themselves from various values and practices that had made them reproductive laborers in Japan.

Some women also embarked on trips by themselves. Three female members of the Language Club at the Japan Cultural Center went to Europe on their own without their male partners. One of them was Ms. Isobe, who was a gently spoken woman who followed her husband to Malaysia when he was hired by a Japanese aid organization as a senior volunteer after his retirement. On the third day of the women's eight-day Europe tour, Mrs. Isobe's bag was stolen. A man splashed ink on her dress. He offered to wipe it off for her, and she momentarily took her eyes off her handbag. When she looked again, the bag was gone, and so was the man. The three women cancelled the rest of the trip and returned to Kuala Lumpur. When I met Mrs. Isobe after her trip, she was undiscouraged by the experience, in ways uncharacteristic of what I remembered as a gentle and quiet woman. "They took everything that was in my handbag. I had no idea what to do, whom to call, or where to report. I realized then that I had been completely dependent on my husband. But now I learned an important lesson. I must become more independent."

Undeterred by her experience in Europe, Mrs. Isobe soon signed up for another trip to Kota Kinabalu with the members of the Language Club. Her husband did not come with her. With the lesson learned in Europe, all the material things in her handbag—her passport, wallet, credit cards—were renewed, just as she was herself.

Conclusion

The political-economic conditions of the aging state produced the discourse of "second life," which focused on the values of independence and mutual-support. As contradictory as it may sound, the movement to Malaysia, and the activities in the Japan Cultural Center in particular, allowed many former productive sarariiman to adhere to the new aging ideals of the Japanese state. Their adherence was aided by the postcolonial conditions in which the strength of the Japanese currency allowed for the retirees' pensions to stretch further and even to lead a much more active lifestyle in comparison to life in Japan. At the same time, many men saw themselves, quite confidently, as normatively deviant, as they departed from the social pressure to keep working and instead found a lifestyle in which they could pursue a social upper-class status with a bad boy charm.

Some women could depart from the social constraints and gendered expectations placed upon them in their old age by coming to Malaysia. The move gave them an opportunity to find a new life away from their families' or neighbors' watchful eyes and, further, gave the women an opportunity to dispose of some material possessions which had symbolized their reproductive roles within the family.[10] It was not so much that Malaysia was associated with progressive gender values. Rather, by going overseas, women could invest in themselves in solidarity with other women, which for many of them was done for the first time.

Japanese women and men, in different ways, both adhered to and at the same time deviated from the aging ideologies of the Japanese state. While this chapter focused on the creation and negotiation of aging personhood among transnational retirees, the next two chapters will focus on their social relations in Malaysia, especially their spousal and family relations.

Interlude

I n Malaysia, it was quite common to witness Japanese men publicly avowing their affection for their female spouses, especially during dinners involving fellow members of the Japan Cultural Center. One of the most common types of rhetoric appeared in the stories of how the men had met their wives— even though most of them did so through *omiai* (arranged marriages). Mr. Shimizu, for instance, told the story of his omiai in the following way.

> When I reached the marriageable age, I had a few omiai. The first woman was too beautiful. She worked at Shiseido [a Japanese cosmetics company] as a model. She was way beyond my league. I couldn't be myself in front of her. I politely declined. The second woman didn't even put her makeup on. She had cheeks so red that they looked like a pair of apples. The gap between the first woman and the second woman was too great. I felt I was flung from one side to another. Again, I politely declined. The third woman was introduced to me by a Japanese flower arrangement teacher. She gave me a photo that had three women in it. The girl on the left was so-so-looking. The girl in the middle was a teacher. The girl on the right was very pretty. For the next two weeks leading up to the omiai date, I was unable to sleep, consumed by thoughts about which girl it would be. On the day of the omiai, the teacher and I arrived at the meeting point early, and we waited and waited. The clock had hit the appointed time, but she was nowhere to be seen. I felt so anxious. Then, after seven long minutes, she finally arrived.

Mr. Shimizu turned and asked me. "What would you have said if you were the girl?" Without a thought, I replied, "I am very sorry to be late." "Exactly!" he said with glee. "But you know what she said? She said, 'I got hungry, so I stopped to have ramen on the way.' I was so amused by her boldness! I immediately liked her. And you know what, she was the pretty one! I was planning to propose to her after a year of courtship, but I couldn't wait. So, I proposed to her after three months."[1]

He told the story so effortlessly that I suspected that it was a tale Mr. Shimizu had told many times before. I was surprised to witness these public displays of affection in the Japan Cultural Center. As we saw in Chapter 1, love was considered antithetical to marriage, which had long been considered an economic and national matter in Japan (Ryang 2006). The relationship between spouses used to be downplayed in favor of relationships within the household as a whole (Kondo 1990, 133–34), and the sentiments associated with the partners in a marriage were patience for women and responsibility for men (Tokuhiro 2010, 19). In contrast, Mr. Shimizu portrayed his wife as a bold woman who would not perform submissive femininity before a prospective husband. His narrative suggested that the couple was bound together by choice and "love at first sight" rather than obligations (Giddens 1992).

As exemplified by this story, there tended to be greater intimacy between couples, and even burgeoning romance, in Malaysia. Many Japanese couples jointly participated in social activities at the Japan Cultural Center and, like Mr. Shimizu, many Japanese men in Malaysia employed romantic rhetoric to narrate spousal unity. The couples' attention seemed to have shifted to highlight their own relationships after their move to Malaysia.

In cases where Japanese men were alone in Malaysia, however, talking about their absent wives was considered taboo at the Japan Cultural Center. In fact, Japanese silver backpackers routinely teased these wifeless men as being somewhat shady. They were constantly suspected of looking for local girlfriends even though in reality, it was rare to witness Japanese men with Malaysian partners. During my fifteen months of fieldwork, I encountered only two such couples, and in both cases, the Japanese men felt the need to explicitly tell others that their Malaysian partners had more savings and drove better cars than they did. In other words, the men were trying to say that they were not exploiting poorer local women, or vice versa. Nevertheless, rumors circulated of men who, having been "abandoned" by their Japanese wives, employed domestic workers with the aim of eventually marrying them. Single men's sexuality and moral standards were constantly cast in doubt.

CHAPTER 4

Romantic Partnership

ingle Japanese men in Malaysia are not the only ones attracting suspicion or a tinge of moral disapproval from fellow travelers. The popular imaginings of men from developed nations coming to Southeast Asia to form relations with local women are so pervasive that I now automatically add an explanation to anyone who asks about my research. My interlocutors often came as couples, although there were cases where single women came alone, or women returned to Japan before their husbands who had decided to stay in Malaysia by themselves.[2]

At the same time, these popular imaginings were the very things that informed my interlocutors' framing of Malaysia as a morally exceptional place—as a couple's place. Malaysia was where people like Mr. Shimizu could publicly avow his attraction to his wife and reframe his arranged marriage into a romantic one. The moral landscape of the host country, Malaysia, went hand in hand with the moral anxiety of older Japanese men in the domestic spousal context to create a particular ideal of spousal companionship that could be realized in Malaysia.

"Companionship" has been defined by anthropologists as a "marital ideal in which emotional closeness is understood to be both one of the primary measures of success in marriage and a central practice through which the relationship is constituted and reinforced." (Hirsch and Wardlow 2006, 4). Companionate marriage emerged as early as the sixteenth century in Europe which witnessed the decline of parentally arranged marriage (Simmons 2015, 137; Stone 1977). Such marriage reflected a vision of marriage as the union of two individuals bonded through choice and pleasure rather than via institutions of kin and property (Hirsch and Wardlow 2006, 4). In its more recent forms, companionate marriage is broadly defined as a form of marriage characterized by friendship and romantic love; this form emerged in the United States and Western Europe in the 1920s to adapt marriage to accommodate the growing social and political role of women and civil equality (Simmons 2009, 105, 136–37; Giddens 1992; Hirsch 2003, 9). Since the 1980s, the Japanese feminist movement has called for more equality between the roles of husbands and wives, and along with that equality there emerged what Ueno (1994, 35) calls the *do-kokai kappuru* (interest group couples). These couples are united by their common interests and characterized by their openness to allowing others to join the couple's hobby activities. This idea of companionate marriage in which spouses are closely linked through emotional connections captured the imaginations of middle-class Japanese men in contemporary Japan (Alexy 2020, 17). As the occurrence of later-life divorce spread in Japan, Japanese men's magazines started to propagate a new model of masculinity along the lines of companionate marital ideals.

When separate gendered socialization had been the norm for women and men, how did spousal companionship become the norm among the community of silver backpackers in the Japan Cultural Center in Malaysia? And why did this expatriate community demoralize wifeless men? By questioning how some spousal relations came to be defined as "ideal" or even "normal" and others "taboo" (Povinelli 2006), I began to comprehend the nature of the spousal intimacy that was sought after men's retirement. This chapter provides multiple answers to the above questions by first laying out the racial and sexualized ways in which Malaysia became the imagined utopia for Japanese silver backpackers to enact romantic partnerships. It will then look at the nature of the romantic partnerships that have been enacted by the Japanese couples, and how they can be both empowering and constraining for women. More often than not, in pursuing an independent retirement as a couple's joint project, women were made more dependent on their husbands than they had been when they were in Japan.

In this chapter, I want to focus on the ways gendered lifecourses trouble the nature and pursuit of romantic partnerships. Although the romantic partnership is envisioned as having a sense of oneness and equality between the spouses, various power imbalances, particularly those related to transnational retirement, complicated these ideals and practices. I explore how gendered value production processes led to tensions within a couple's pursuit of a "joint project." Through this examination, I will show how patriarchal value production processes were privileged in the pursuit of romantic partnerships.

The chapter launches a critique of the patriarchy which persists in retirement and the pursuit of "romantic partnership."

Companionship Ideals in Malaysia

I mentioned in Chapter 2 that two of the main reasons why many transnational retirees chose Malaysia were financial and racial. The readers may still be wondering whether other Southeast Asian countries would have been equally appealing. The gendered relations within the Japanese couples became the key element in distinguishing Malaysia from the rest of Southeast Asia and in making it the utopic landscape for middle-class Japanese men.

Southeast Asia is one of the most popular destinations for international backpackers (Sørensen 2003, 847; Spreitzhofer 1998; Westerhausen 2002). The past three decades have seen the rapid growth of backpacker tourism and related infrastructure in the region, and in turn, the increase in Asian backpackers going there (Bui et al. 2014; F. K. G. Lim 2008). Southeast Asia is a popular destination for young Japanese backpackers too. Backpackers from Japan tend to avoid tourist places and consume local food in inexpensive stalls rather than frequenting restaurants serving foreign food (Muzaini 2006, 148–49). Some backpackers even try to pick up the behavioral patterns of the local community by speaking the local language (Muzaini 2006, 150–51).

Despite the name silver backpackers, few of the interlocutors I met in Malaysia exhibited these characteristics or intermingled with the local communities (see Introduction and Chapter 2). Some, in fact, positively avoided being seen to be too close to the local communities. My male interlocutors often used the term "the sunken class" (*chinbotsu gumi*) to refer to older Japanese people who were longer-term residents or backpackers in other parts of Southeast Asia, such as the Philippines, Cambodia, and Laos. Such retirees were sunken because they were believed to have lived among the locals to save costs, unlike the Japanese retirees in Malaysia, who lived in expatriate enclaves. The cost of living in the rest of Southeast Asia was significantly lower than in Malaysia, and the motivation for overseas retirement in the other countries was considered primarily economic (Mizutani 2015). Those sunken Japanese were stereotypically depicted as working-class single men, whose financial positions didn't allow them to find partners in Japan. Instead, they were suspected of having gone to Southeast Asia to meet young local partners—a practice that the more affluent Japanese men in Malaysia regarded as morally questionable. The companionship of Japanese wives put these retired elite sarariiman in a morally superior position in relation to retirees in other parts of Southeast Asia. The presence of Japanese wives prevented the former from "sinking" into a liaison with local women.

Ann Stoler, a historical anthropologist, argues that companionate marriage ideals in the colonial setting often arose in conversation with domestic socioeconomic arrangements. In Victorian England, for example, formations of race and class were in conversation with domestic labor arrangements in the colonies that naturalized the idea of a companionate couple whose bond relied on emotional ties and mutual respect (Stoler 2002, 70–75). European women were valorized as European men's moral partners who safeguarded the latter's sexual and cultural purity, preventing the contamination of contact with the colonized (Stoler 2002, 71). The control of European women's sexuality was, therefore, essential to the structure of colonial racism and making of the empire respectable (Stoler 1989, 634).

Similarly, the formation of an idealized intimacy in Malaysia was in conversation with both Japanese domestic arrangements as well as the practices of Japanese men in the rest of Southeast Asia. The companionate couplehood of husband and wife in Malaysia allowed male retirees to distinguish themselves from their domestic counterparts, who were feeling dislocated from familial and spousal ties as discussed in Chapter 1. The socially upper-class men in their old age were the ones who were still desired by their wives as demonstrated by their wives' coming to Malaysia to pursue a second life with them. The socially lower-class men were the ones who had lost their spaces of belonging at home. Even worse were the sunken class men who were the ones who had to move to Southeast Asia alone and find a new partner there.

In this racialized, gendered, and sexualized landscape, the enactment of middle-class respectability in Malaysia was contingent upon the maintenance of the image of Malaysia as a moral place. Any other image was quickly dismissed or concealed by both women and men. I was once on a crowded train in Kuala Lumpur with one of my female interlocutors. There was only one seat available. She sat on it while I stood in front of her. The train mechanically moved from one station to another and we both fell silent. She was aimlessly looking at passengers until her eyes fixed on a local teenage girl sitting opposite her. The girl was dressed in a pair of short trousers and a mini tank top exposing her skin. "The taste for clothes among the local girls is shocking," my female interlocutor whispered to me in Japanese as she scanned the girl's revealed skin from top to bottom. Before I could respond, she changed the subject to an upcoming visit by her daughter's family. My interlocutor planned to bring them to a cultural dance show held at the Malaysia Tourism Center. The locals must be "innocent" and conservatively dressed for retirees to enact their respectable selves. At the Malaysia Tourism Center, in contrast to the girl on the train, local girls will be dressed "appropriately" in their traditional costumes.

In summary, the postcolonial setting of transnational retirement provided a key background to the making of normative couplehood among the silver backpackers. They viewed retirement in Malaysia as the more respectable choice when compared to other destinations in Southeast Asia due to Malaysia's restrictions on sex industries, the retirees' own residential arrangements in expatriate exclaves, and importantly, their positions as couples enjoying second lives together. Couplehood safeguarded both the moral and class positions of these formerly elite corporate workers in relation to their domestic and overseas counterparts. Coming to Malaysia with their wives allowed older Japanese men to acquire and maintain middle-class respectability. The next section will look at the nature of the romantic partnership enacted by couples in Malaysia.

From the Division of Labor to Romantic Partnership

Some men referred to the greater sense of spousal togetherness as *ittaikan*, which refers to a sense of unity in which a couple's feelings are so united that they seem to share a single body. In its original meaning, this idiom idealizes intimate relationships as best when they are understated; a relationship is considered mature when the partners do not need to verbally communicate (Alexy and Cook 2019, 92–98). The idiom is especially relevant in a Japanese context where silent communication, or *ishin denshin* (heart-to-heart communication) is the preferred medium over words (Lebra 1976, 115). An intuitive grasp of each other's feelings and the reading of subtle signs and signals are considered more affectionate than explicit communication (Lebra 1976, 115). Furthermore, silent communication made sense in postwar Japan where the dominant model of intimacy was "disconnected dependence" (Alexy 2020, 36), an emotionally distant union of housewives and salarymen who were nevertheless inseparable because of the divisions of labor (Ikeuchi 2021, 478). In this context, the European or North American notion of love that is defined by "shared interests, friendship, communication, and endur-ing romantic passion" (Borovoy 2005, 89) has been understood to be less common.

However, in recent years the Euro-American model of men and their pre-sumed romantic tendencies has been marketed as the pinnacle of masculin-ity in Japanese magazines targeting a retired audience (Bardsley 2011, 115). This may also reflect a wider social trend in which youths' ideals of a desir-able man have shifted from one who can provide financially to one who is cooperative and communicative (Roberts 2014, 31; Cook 2014).[3] According to Allison Alexy, an anthropologist of Japan, the "disconnected dependence" model of intimacy has come under increasing criticism, and has given way to a model of "connected independence" (Alexy 2020, 62) which encourages a marriage based on a companionate romance between spouses who are best friends, and bound by love and support for each other (see also Ikeuchi 2021, 478). Japanese magazines are deploying discourses about romance and love as means to claim modern gender relations or progressive person-hood (Masquelier 2013, 226; Cole and Thomas 2009, 5; Alexy 2020, 8).

In this transformative moment, the term ittaikan has been given an ad-ditional meaning by Japanese men in Malaysia, arguably in alignment with the perceived romantic practices of the West. My interlocutors explicitly used ittaikan when discussing husbands and wives performing activities together. Mr. Kawai, who joined the Karaoke Club at the Japan Cultural Center with his wife, captured this sentiment. He told me that after being married to his wife for such a long time, he thought that there was very little that he didn't know about her. Then her singing at karaoke made him realize that his wife had a beautiful voice. He said, "The moment I put my shoulder next to my *waifu*'s shoulder and listen to the sound of her music, I achieve *mentaru haa-moni* [mental harmony] with her." Echoing Euro-American discourses of romantic love in which the self and the other seek to fuse together (Lipset 2004, 2–5), Mr. Kawai explained that when their voices harmonized, the sounds transcended the individual body and united their two bodies into one (Shakuto 2019a, 306).

I also noticed some men calling their wives "waifu," which is a term de-rived from the English word "wife." This way of referring to one's spouse is uncommon in Japan, where the more usual terms are *oka-san* (mother) or *kanai* (wife, but literally, "inside the house") (Lebra 1976). Japanese feminists have discouraged the use of these terms because their Chinese characters and origins imply that women are inferior within the household (Carroll 2006, 115).

A counterpart to these terms is *shujin*, which is commonly used to refer to male partners. The feminist movement in the 1970s discouraged the use of shujin because it literally means "master." Feminism of the 1970s diverged from that of the 1950s which had encouraged women to be in charge of household savings (see Chapter 2). 1970s feminism raised concerns about absent fathers and called for greater involvement of men in household tasks (Nakatani 2006, 96).[4] The later feminism was also closely linked to the feminist movement in the West. Following the declaration of the United Nations' International Decade for Women in 1975, public money in Japan was poured into conferences and centers for women (Mackie 2003, 179). Some municipal governments even sponsored women's study trips to visit overseas women's organizations. One of my female informants in Kuala Lumpur had been on one such trip organized by the Fukuoka City Council. She spent two weeks visiting different feminist organizations in the UK and France. In the Japan Cultural Center, she often called out other Japanese women who used the term shujin. Instead, she urged others to use the term *hanryo*, which was a more gender-neutral term for a partner. She repeatedly told me that the term we used demonstrated our level of idealism.

Unlike the term, kanai, the foreign term waifu was supposedly free of prescribed gender roles (Carroll 2006, 115). While it was taken from English, the term's meaning and significance were different from the original English context. In the Japanese context, its use signified that the speaker was aware of the 1970s Japanese feminist discourse described above. Furthermore, by choosing to use the English term waifu as opposed to the Japanese version of the gender-neutral term hanryo the speaker demonstrated himself to be "Western." The speaker thus portrayed himself as a liberal and progressive man who saw his wife as an equal. Mr. Otani, who scorned Mr. Yamamoto for making his wife prepare tea for the guests in the Prologue, typified such an attitude. Mr. Nishiguchi also epitomized such a modern gentleman. He repeatedly emphasized his affection for his wife, saying that his waifu's happiness was the source of his vitality (*waifu no shiawase ga watashi no genki no minamoto desu*). Men's affectionate narratives in Malaysia seemed to have redefined their spousal relationships from unions based on a division of labor to bonds formed out of a romantic partnership.

Indeed, the public display of couplehood was encouraged in the Japan Cultural Center. For instance, the Karaoke Club encouraged the participants to join its weekly activities as a couple and demanded husbands and wives have equal voices. Whenever a new couple joined, they were encouraged to

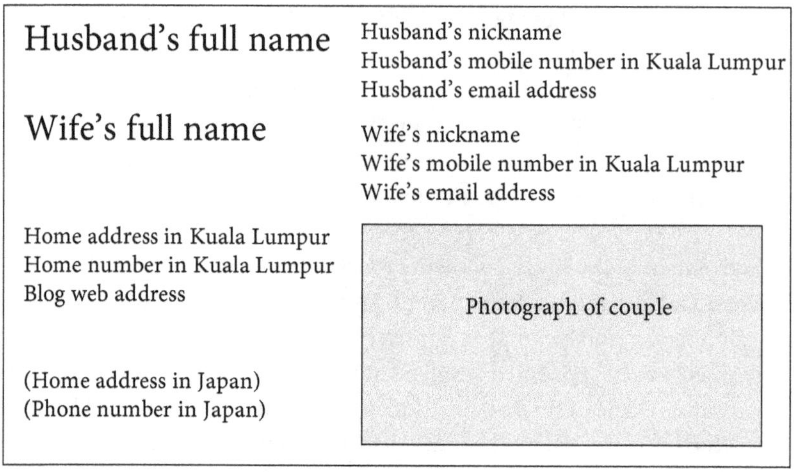

Husband's full name	Husband's nickname Husband's mobile number in Kuala Lumpur Husband's email address
Wife's full name	Wife's nickname Wife's mobile number in Kuala Lumpur Wife's email address
Home address in Kuala Lumpur Home number in Kuala Lumpur Blog web address (Home address in Japan) (Phone number in Japan)	Photograph of couple

Figure 3. Schematic reproduction of a typical Japanese couple's name card used in Kuala Lumpur, Malaysia.

introduce themselves. Often a man would talk on behalf of the couple, while his wife stood quietly next to him. Somebody from the crowd would shout, "please, we want to hear from your wife too!" (*okusan no koe mo kikasete kudasai*). After being "corrected," the woman would either smile and shake her head to indicate that she did not want to speak, or utter in a soft voice, "If you could please let us be part of this community, we would be very grateful" (*nakama ni irete itadakereba saiwai desu. Douzo yoroshiku onegai itashimasu*). A couple would then jointly choose a song to sing together.

The practice of exchanging name cards materialized the romantic partnership and its emphasis on spousal equality. In joining activities and classes for the first time at the Japan Cultural Center, couples exchanged name cards (*meishi*). Such an exchange is an essential business practice in Japan. The card usually has one's name, the name of the company, and one's position in the company. After retirement in Malaysia, the sliver backpackers exchanged joint name cards (Figure 3). These cards typically bore both spouses' full names, their respective nicknames to be used in Malaysia, their phone numbers in Japan and Malaysia, a Malaysian address, sometimes a link to their blogs, and most importantly, their joint photograph. These photographs were often playful pictures of the couple singing in a choir, dancing, or posing in their vacation clothes together. The exchange of these joint name cards materialized the couple's position as a unit in the public domain of the Japan Cultural Center (Shakuto 2019a).

Exchanging joint name cards, reinventing the narrative of their omiai (arranged marriage), harmonizing their voices in the choir, and men calling their female partners, waifu—these practices and expressions showed that spousal intimacy after one's working life ended revolved around a particular understanding of spousal equality, one that emphasized a sense of oneness. In their retirement, gender norms previously based on a strict division of labor shifted to emphasize instead a sense of oneness between husbands and wives.

Negotiating Gender Roles

Some women took advantage of the rhetoric of equal partnership to accumulate public recognition in ways that had not been possible for them when they were younger. The story of Martha Hasegawa is an illuminating case.

Martha Hasegawa came to Malaysia with her husband after he retired from public service. Her real name was Mariko, but she preferred people to call her Martha. A slender woman in her early sixties, Martha regularly invited me to have breakfast with her at local food stalls in Kuala Lumpur. She enjoyed the local food much more than many of the other female or male interlocutors I met. Like Mrs. Otani who enjoyed her life in Malaysia (see Prologue), Martha too embraced the local designs and often wore tailored summer dresses made of batik fabric.

Over breakfast, Martha often called herself, *hutsuu no shufu*, that is, "an ordinary housewife." But she was no ordinary housewife. After graduating from a music college, she taught piano briefly to neighborhood children. Although it was not common for women from the baby boomer generation to work after marriage (see Chapter 1), some women gained employment in what were considered women's professions such as teachers of artistic pursuits, including piano, calligraphy, and flower arrangement (Ueno 1994, 58; Saso 1990, 9). Martha enjoyed teaching music, but she felt pressured to resign when she saw younger music graduates struggling to find jobs. Women were taught to give up their positions when they got married or if they saw others needing jobs. They had to constantly justify why they should keep their jobs. After her career was cut short because of the social expectations for her to become, in her words, "an ordinary housewife," Martha volunteered at an after school childcare center in a neighborhood school to continue participating in public life.

When she arrived in Malaysia with her husband, Martha noticed a call for a conductor at the children's music class at the Japan Cultural Center. She immediately applied and got the position. She conducted at least twice a week. She also eventually took over the conductor position at the adult's choir club.

"I just wrote to my mother thanking her for teaching me music so that I can contribute to a community here in Malaysia." Martha told me during a Chinese New Year party that she and her husband had organized at her condominium, located less than a five-minute walk from the Japan Cultural Center. "It's important that I live in this condominium complex. It's more expensive than other condominiums, but it's close to the Japan Cultural Center. I can walk there whenever I need to. I have so many responsibilities there," she said, looking out the balcony. "When I was in Japan, I was known to people as my husband's oku-san [wife] or my children's okaa-san [mother]. When I met my husband's colleagues, I would bow and tell them how grateful I was for their looking after the interests of my husband in public service [otto ga osewa ni natte orimasu]. Like this." She turned and bowed to me. We laughed. "But here in Kuala Lumpur," she continued, "I am known as Hasegawa-san. Here, we [Mr. and Mrs. Hasegawa] make friends with others as a couple, as equals."

Martha's narrative reminded me of Morisaki Kazuko, the forerunner of the women's liberation movement. When she launched a new women's journal called *Mumei Tsushin* (Correspondence with No Name) in 1959, she declared, "We return the names given to women. We want to return to having no names. Because we are called by so many names. Mother. Wife. Housewife. Lady. Daughter. Virgin" (Quoted in Ueno and Tabusa 2020, 57). This was a striking statement in the late 1950s when the model of feminism focused on creating better housewives and better mothers (Ueno and Tabusa 2020, 57). Morisaki's activism laid the groundwork for the women's liberation movement in the 1970s. Hasegawa-san would have only been six years old in 1959, but half a century later, she had managed to get rid of the labels given to her.

Indeed, she acquired a new label: she was referred to by many as Hasegawa-sensei, or Martha-sensei. The term *sensei* is used for a teacher, and it denotes respect. The title sensei muted Martha's gender as opposed to the previous terms used to refer to her, that is, oku-san (wife) or okaa-san (mother). She never had business cards in Japan, but she did in Malaysia—a couple's joint name card. In terms of public recognition, Martha accumulated equal, if not more, respect than her husband who assisted her in the cultural center.

We stood on her balcony looking out at the magnificent night view of Kuala Lumpur. "My mother is happy in Japan because she knows that I am doing well here. The education that she gave me forty years ago is finally being used for a good cause!" Suddenly, Martha's face was lit by the reflection of fireworks celebrating the arrival of the Chinese New Year. They coloured her eyes from pink to yellow to green. Her face glowed with confidence.

Transnational retirement in Malaysia, and the transgression of gender boundaries it allowed for, provided an opportunity for women like Martha to enjoy the public recognition that was denied to them in previous years as housewives. It empowered Martha to redefine expressions of gender.

As part of the new gender practice, Martha stopped managing the household accounts. Although the majority of Japanese women managed the household accounts as part of their domestic duties (see Chapter 2), Martha told her husband that it would be his role after his retirement. "We have limited pension, and he must see that for himself to control the number of social outings." He had reduced the number of drinking sessions since taking charge of household accounts.

What was striking here was that even when women like Martha seemed to enjoy participating in public activities with their husbands, they seldom used the word ittaikan to describe their spousal togetherness. Martha told me that she was known in Malaysia as "Hasegawa-san" or "Hasegawa-sensei." She emphasized her individuality and her independence from her husband, not a sense of unity with him. She enjoyed making friends with others as couples, "as equals," but her sense of equality was the partnership of two independent people, as opposed to the coming together of two people into one. In the next section, I will explore these differences and the extent to which women like Martha could become equal to men as individuals.

Partnership Contested

When the fireworks were over, Martha and I went back into the living room to join her husband, Kenny, and his Japanese friend, Richard. Initially, Richard had come to Malaysia with his wife, but she decided to return to Japan a few years later while Richard stayed in Malaysia. When Martha and Kenny arrived in Malaysia, Richard showed them around Kuala Lumpur and helped them settle in. Martha and Kenny regularly invited Richard to their home for meals as they were worried that Richard might be feeling lonely.

That evening, Richard was showing a newsletter to Kenny. It was an alumni newsletter from one of the most prestigious private universities in Japan. Richard and Kenny were alumni, and they had met through an alumni event in Malaysia. Richard asked Kenny if he knew other graduates in Malaysia. Martha interjected halfway in a dismissive manner. "Who cares which school you went to? Now we are all retirees in Malaysia. We are all the same!" Martha seemed frustrated by the circulation of material signifiers of which few women could be part.

This interaction between Martha and Kenny raised questions about the hierarchy of practices and values that couples would pursue in Malaysia. After all, although husbands and wives were "equal," the signifiers of what men saw as distinction, such as one's alumni status in prestigious universities and pub-lic acclaim, continued to circulate among men in Malaysia. Few women had access to the same signifiers. Technology also prevented many women from taking up leadership roles in the clubs and activities of the Japan Cultural Center because most communications were done over email. Some men, how-ever, did try to provide such signifiers to their wives in Malaysia to equalize their status. Mr. and Mrs. Uchida are a case in point, as Mr. Uchida took it upon himself to "elevate" his wife's "mere hobby" to public recognition in Malaysia.

One afternoon, Mr. Uchida asked me to help him make posters for his wife's patchwork exhibition. Patchwork is a needlework popular among older women in Japan. Similar in style and method to quilting, women sew together pieces of discarded fabric to give them a new life as bags, blankets, and wall hangings. Mr. Uchida had booked a room in the Japan Cultural Center to showcase his wife's patchwork. "My wife's patchwork is very spe-cial. It should be shown to the world!" He proclaimed with excitement and conviction. I happily assisted his poster-making and soon after, I saw Mr. Uchida walking around the Japan Cultural Center putting up posters for his wife's exhibition.

A few days earlier, I had met Mrs. Uchida for the first time during a lunch outing with the members of the Language Club. In contrast to her energetic husband, Mrs. Uchida was a petite, softly spoken woman in her early sixties. Her hair curled, she was dressed in a black summer dress with a matching flower pendant. She gently touched her face with a white handkerchief to wipe off sweat. She then carefully folded her cardigan and hat and placed them into her handbag before slipping into a seat next to Mr. Uchida. She didn't join the weekly activities of the Language Club, but her husband had urged her to join the lunch after a class one day. If he didn't ask her out, Mr. Uchida told the classmates, his wife would be making patchwork all day at home. Mr. Uchida had been lamenting that his wife had not been adapting too well in Malaysia. She had been a housewife since they got married, and he thought that moving to Malaysia would liberate her from domestic duties as they could eat out more frequently. But according to him, his wife didn't seem to enjoy leaving the house, nor did she have a taste for Malaysian food or the environment. When she complained of insects in the room, he bought mosquito nets and put them up against all the windows himself. But Mrs. Uchida still seemed unhappy. That day, Mr. Uchida chose an Italian restaurant for the group outing because Italian was her favourite meal.

The exhibition that Mr. Uchida organized for his wife attracted a large audience both within and outside of the Japanese community in Kuala Lumpur. Mrs. Uchida was soon asked to give a demonstration of her work to students of creative art at Malaysia's top university. Mr. Uchida was very proud of her achievement. He told me afterwards, "My wife's sewing work is exhibited at the nation's top art school! If she were in Japan, she would have never had a chance to showcase her skills to students. Her sewing would have been a mere hobby in Japan but here in Malaysia, it is recognized as an artwork. I am really proud of her." He was not only happy that his wife's long-standing hobby was generating public recognition in Malaysia but also that he could assist her in gaining this recognition. There was a sense that this was their joint project and a joint achievement.

A few weeks after the exhibition, Mr. Uchida organized a tempura party at their home for classmates of the Language Club. Although Mr. Uchida prepared the tempura, it was his wife who cleaned the house, prepared the side dishes, and washed the dishes after the party. Contrary to the liberating rhetoric of "freeing your wife from the household task" as it was advertized in the promotional material, most women ended up doing most domestic tasks in Malaysia. This was in contrast to middle-class locals in Malaysia and the British senior migrants in Malaysia among whom it was common to hire paid help, often Filipina or Indonesian migrants (O'Reilly and Benson 2015, 424). No Japanese women I met in Malaysia had live-in domestic help, and only a few employed a cleaner for a few hours a month. Many Japanese women considered their home to be a private space and they were exceedingly uncomfortable with the idea of having a home helper (Lock 1993, 122). One female interlocutor who had a cleaner said to me one day, "Shiori-san, I need to rush back to clean the house because the cleaner is coming!"

I arrived at Mr. and Mrs. Uchida's home a few hours before the party to help Mrs. Uchida prepare for the gathering in the kitchen. Her kitchen was full of edible Japanese herbs that she had brought from Japan. I congratulated her for the recent exhibition and asked if I could see some of her work. While replying that it was no big deal, Mrs. Uchida showed me a few wall hangings and cushion covers she had made in Malaysia. They were, even to my inexperienced eyes, sewing work of the highest quality. As I admired her patchwork, she told me how she started making them back in Japan and then again in Malaysia. She took lessons in patchwork at a local community center when her grandchildren were born. She originally had wanted to make them for her grandchildren, but after giving away a blanket and a bag, she decided to make other things for herself. Over the years Mrs. Uchida had made fifty works with different types of fabrics that she had collected. When they decided to move to Malaysia, however, she threw away all the fabrics she had collected in Japan. There would be no time to use them, she thought, because her husband promised that they would be travelling around the world from Kuala Lumpur.

But Mrs. Uchida's husband committed himself to so many leadership positions at the Japan Cultural Center that there was hardly any time to travel. Sitting at home all day with nothing to do, she decided to resume her patchwork-making. Mrs. Uchida had to rebuild a collection of fabrics from scratch. From that day, the landscape of Malaysia changed for her. Her eyes searched for things she could use for her sewing. She would go to a market to find fabrics with interesting patterns. She would even keep some packaging just in case she might be able to use it for her work. Patchwork embedded her in this new place.

Mrs. Uchida paused and stroked the wall hanging of Alice in Wonderland she had made. Then she revealed her side of the story about the exhibition. She would happily spend four hours a day sewing at home in Malaysia. Time flew so quickly when she was sewing and thinking about patterns. But her husband became concerned that she was not getting out of the house, so he organized a public exhibition for her. She was not at all keen to showcase her work, but she didn't want to disappoint her husband. Mrs. Uchida reflected on the exhibition with some discomfort. "Before my demonstration in the class, two teachers from the university came to our apartment to see my patchwork. They looked at my work, whispered something to each other and laughed. I didn't understand Malay or English, so I didn't know what they were saying. I just felt very uncomfortable." In the unfortunate miscommunication between cultural gestures, the laughter which may well have been an expression of admiration, was interpreted by Mrs. Uchida to be the sound of disapproval.

In contrast to her husband's excitement about the exhibition, Mrs. Uchida's ambivalent narrative about the same event was striking. From Mr. Uchida's perspective, his wife's exhibition brought her out of home and allowed her to accumulate public recognition for what was otherwise "a mere hobby" in Japan. But this was a logic within the largely male domain of value production which discursively linked one's value with public performance. Mrs. Uchida made these patchworks initially for her grandchildren and later, for herself. When her patchwork was brought to the public for viewing, she felt judged and uncomfortable.

The inconsistency between Mr. and Mrs. Uchida's perceptions of the patchwork exhibition typified an instance of spousal anxiety in Malaysia. In many cases, the way that women embedded themselves in the new environment was not recognized by their husbands. Mr. Uchida was dismissive of his wife staying at home to work on patchwork and encouraged her to go out. In Mr. Uchida's eyes, bringing her hobby out from the domain of home to the domain of public space was an instance of a "romantic partnership" where he played a supportive role in their joint project. Yet when Mrs. Uchida did not enjoy going out or showcasing her work to the public, he felt dismayed and became concerned that she did not like Malaysia. From her perspective, in contrast, the Malaysian landscape became animated from the moment she started to look for fabrics to use for her patchwork. She was very observant of colours that were used in people's clothing in Malaysia, and she recycled many local materials in her work. She was hardly disengaged from the local environment.

Mr. Uchida's dismissal of his wife's staying at home may have been derived from a larger devaluation of home in the discourses of second life and successful aging, which encourage the seniors to pursue active lives in the community (see Chapter 3 for a discussion of new aging ideals). Yet at the same time, in both Martha and Mrs. Uchida's cases, when men organized home parties for their friends, it was women who did the cooking with all the domestic products that they had brought from Japan. Although the rhetoric of romantic partnership seemed to liberate women from their gendered roles, it was still women who created the affective community to which men could in turn belong. Yet at the same time, women's gendered labor at home was disguised and devalued under the same rhetoric.

Furthermore, in many cases, some women who would otherwise have liked to lead an active life outside of the home in Japan were nonetheless confined to domestic spaces in Malaysia due to the immobility they experienced. Most women did not speak the local language or drive in Kuala Lumpur. Although the city had a developed public transportation system, the expatriate population tended to travel by car (Butler and Hannam 2014). Most of my interlocutors preferred to travel by car because of the frequent robbery attempts on pedestrians near the Japan Cultural Center. Consequently, many women had to rely on their husbands to drive them around and to translate for them during their daily activities. Many women I spoke with missed their mobile and active lives in Japan, which had increased after their children left home and their parents-in-law passed away (see Chapter 1). The women used to drive or walk to participate in different activities and many of them were keen to continue this into older age. In Malaysia, however, women found it difficult to reinvent, let alone regenerate, their social lives outside the confines of their condominiums or the Japan Cultural Center. Mrs. Uchida told me as we prepared some dishes for the gathering in the kitchen. "My husband and I didn't use to fight so often in Japan, but I just can't do anything on my own here. And he's frustrated that I am not adjusting." She lowered her voice. "But I know I can't change my husband's mind about bringing forward the return date. He is so stubborn." Mr. Uchida was on his computer in the dining room. He could have heard us but Mrs. Uchida didn't seem to mind either way. In Japan, she used to go everywhere on her own, including the community center where she had learned patchwork. In Kuala Lumpur, she didn't drive, and she didn't speak the local language. She had to rely on her husband to drive and translate everywhere she went. Before men's retirement, women were dependent on their husbands for financial resources; after transnational retirement, they were dependent on their husbands for language and mobility.

Women's frustration was exacerbated by the fact that their social lives were restricted to largely the same group of people, either in their condominium complexes or in the Japan Cultural Center. Within this restricted sociality, *shigarami* (ties of obligation) were quickly produced. Mrs. Ishida, who initially thought that she escaped the neighborly shigarami in her small town in Japan by coming to Malaysia (see Chapter 3), nevertheless told me that she had joined the female choir and ballroom dancing classes in the Japan Cultural Center out of an obligation to her Japanese neighbors who were teaching them. If they stopped attending classes at the Japan Cultural Center, there were few alternative places women could go. Confined within the walls of the Japan Cultural Center and their condominiums, the sense of immobility that characterized men's retirement life in Japan was experienced by many women in Malaysia.

The temporal experience of women's free time was also affected by their immobility. For instance, Mrs. Fujisawa was a regular attendee at Mrs. Aoi's sewing sessions (see Chapter 2), but she always had to leave before the end of the session because her husband came and picked her up before the traffic began. She lived in a suburb at least forty-five minutes' drive from Kuala Lumpur to be close to her husband's golf club.

One cannot ignore that romantic partnership as the Japanese retirees practised it in Malaysia was ultimately founded on the assumption that women could participate in men's activities (Shakuto 2019, 309). Women were typically incorporated into the men's activities by taking up the men's hobbies, particularly golf which was popular among former sarariiman because it had been part of their corporate entertainment activity (Ben-Ari 1998) (see Chapter 1). As more experienced players, men taught their wives in retirement. Women, by playing along, participated in their husbands' activities, but as their juniors. While they shared men's hobbies, women's household tasks were seldom shared. The model of oneness incorporated women into the men's activities, not the other way around. Here it might be illuminating to use the phrase which was used to describe the companionate marriage in the Victorian era: "the husband and wife are one, and the husband is that one" (Stone 1977, 331; Davidoff and Hall 2013, 327).

In this context, the male rhetoric of romantic partnership in Malaysia proved somewhat fraught. There was contradiction between the ideological rhetoric of ittaikan and the practical difficulties preventing women from leading an independent life—the former scripted a new spousal model in the eyes of men, while the latter presented a lack of choice for women to act otherwise.

From Mother to Waifu

The difference in a couple's perceptions of spousal relations was enshrined in kinship terminology. Although some men called their wives waifu, women continued to refer to their husbands as *oto-san* (father), as was customary in Japan (Shakuto 2019, 209). One night, I was walking with Mr. Nishiguchi to a Chinese restaurant after Karaoke Club. I suddenly heard his wife calling him from behind. "Papa! Papa!" Mr. Nishiguchi blushed in embarrassment. He turned back and grumpily replied, "Why can't you call me *daarin* [a Japanese adaptation of the English word darling] or at least *anata* [an affectionate way of saying you]?" Mrs. Nishiguchi ignored her husband's words, passed him a car key, and joined other women in front of us. Mr. Nishiguchi shook his head and recounted a story. "Once, we were staying at a five-star hotel in Tokyo. I was waiting for my waifu in the lobby. Everybody was well-dressed and sipping cocktails while listening to the gentle jazz music playing in the background. Then suddenly there came my waifu shouting from across the lobby. 'Papa! Papa!' Everyone turned to my waifu and found a sixty-year-old woman calling me papa!"

Mrs. Nishiguchi's calling her husband by the familial role—papa (otosan)—may have reflected how she continued to see their relationship in terms of the family unit. By going to Malaysia, some women were liberated from their reproductive roles as mothers only to be incorporated into another discursive role as their husband's waifu. In women's eyes, the relationship was not transformed.

Despite the contested experience of transnational retirement, the rhetoric of love and ittaikan naturalized couples' decisions to come to Malaysia together. For instance, Mr. Kosaka told me that the decision to come to Malaysia was mutually made with his wife and that his wife was equally excited to be in Malaysia. "It didn't take any convincing [of my wife]. When I told her that I wanted us to move to Malaysia, she seemed keen, as if we were always destined to be here!"

His wife later told me that it was her husband who wanted to come to Malaysia. She hesitated at first because of her unmarried daughter back in Japan. After moving to Malaysia, their daughter was diagnosed with a mental health condition. Mrs. Kosaka returned to Japan immediately. She decided to base herself in Japan and continued to visit her husband in Malaysia every two months. Every time she was in Malaysia, she was non-committal as to how long she would stay, or when she would visit again. Over time, she spent less and less time in Malaysia. Sometimes Mrs. Kosaka came to Kuala Lumpur with her female friends from Japan. She would be busy bringing them around Kuala Lumpur and barely had time to spend with her husband.

Other men emphasized how they appreciated having their wives in Malaysia, although they seldom seemed to consider if the women would have said the same about them. Mr. Nakai, for instance, told me that he couldn't have survived the initial few years of setting up a new life in Kuala Lumpur without his wife. He had wanted to go back to Japan so many times. But because his wife was there with him, he could stay strong and persevere. Mr. Nakai's narrative suggested that the relocation to Malaysia was made possible through the coming together of husband and wife as partners in the second life. I could also sense a deep affection and gratitude in his voice. But when I asked him if his wife was happy in Malaysia, he looked surprized, as if he had never thought about the question. He became quiet for a while. Finally, he said, "I don't know. I never asked."

In a cultural context in which silent communication was preferred, the discourse of ittaikan made men assume that women wanted the same thing as them. But as we have already seen, women and men marked their retirement differently, especially if the women had been housewives. Retired men who otherwise faced a reduced status at home could reinstate their spousal privilege vis-à-vis their wives in Malaysia. As men said, often it was thanks to their wives that they could pursue the new retirement project transnationally. But it was a mistake to assume that it was also a women's project. Transnational retirement for many women was not their new retirement project because they continued to provide the same affective care to men as before. Instead, transnational retirement reproduced the same pre-retirement gender roles for women, roles in which they cared for, entertained, and otherwise offered affective closeness to husbands from their homes.

Rikon and Sotsukon

If they were not on board with the idea of a "joint retirement project," why did some women still come with their husbands to Malaysia? The following story of Mrs. Okada may partially answer this question. In Chapter 1, I told the life story of Mrs. Okada, who gave up her career upon marrying her husband. He had asked her to quit work, but it was also the most viable option within the cultural and economic framework that demarcated women's roles at home. Neither could she let her daughter pursue a life abroad because, again, her husband objected. When the members of the Language Club decided to go on a trip to Kota Kinabalu, I sat next to Mrs. Okada in an airport shuttle.

Her husband sat behind us with another male member of the group. I asked her if she minded not sitting with her husband. "Not at all! After forty years of being together, I get sick of him sometimes," she quickly smiled and said she was kidding. But a moment later, she lowered her voice and told me in a serious tone. "Once in a while, though, I do contemplate a divorce [*rikon*]. I never pursued it because if I got a divorce at this age, it would render my past life *mottainai* [a waste]. If I left him now, I would ask myself, 'what was the point of my life with him?' [*kono hito to issho ni sugoshite kita watashi no jinsei no imi ha nani?*] So, I must not get a divorce. It's for myself."

For Mrs. Okada, the pursuit of a retirement life with her husband was not a demonstration of a commitment to a joint partnership. Rather, it was a commitment to her decision to stay married. This commitment may have also been motivated by financial reasons. Across the world, the divisions of labor and lower paid female employment result in older women having lower savings and pension benefits than similarly aged men (Arber et al. 2007; Gunnarsson 2002; Carmel 2019). In Japan, if a couple gets divorced in later life, a woman who had been a housewife will not get half of the couple's total pension. This makes the decision to get a divorce very difficult for women.

Ironically, I saw more traces of "romantic" relations between couples who lived apart. Here I refer to single Japanese men in Malaysia who were seen as somewhat suspicious by couples in the Japan Cultural Center. At the very least, the public discourse of a wifeless man as a morally and sexually dubious figure did not necessarily correspond with the subjective experience of these men. Some such men used the term *sotsukon* (graduation from marriage) to describe their spousal relationships. Men who had graduated from their marriages typically came to Malaysia without their wives. Mr. Okamoto, whom I met at the ballroom dancing club, was one of them. He was still married to his wife, but they lived apart and led separate lives. He described his sotsukon relationship in the following way:

> I came to Kuala Lumpur by myself. My wife lives in Japan. After I retired, we agreed to live separately and pursue our own lives. She graduated from a music college with a degree in singing but never had a chance to put that to use. Now she is employed in a hostess bar. She sings there four times a week. She is really enjoying it. As for me in Malaysia, I rented an apartment near a local university so that I could easily make friends with university students. I go to the

gym every day and play squash with them regularly. It's been four and a half years since we started living apart.

It's not that hard living apart from my wife. Before my retirement, I worked as a pilot and so I was only home for ten days a month anyway. In fact, I think it's better this way [to live apart]. Living by myself now, I appreciate how hard it was to do household tasks. The fact that I finally appreciated her work seemed to have mattered to her. We still Skype each other once a week for about thirty to forty minutes. That's just enough. No more, no less. The distance keeps our relationship. I felt closer to her after living apart.

Mr. and Mrs. Okamoto both had independent second lives—one in Malaysia and another in Japan. Mr. Okamoto did not depend on his wife to achieve his retirement project. What drew them together was not the incorporation of his wife into his activities, as many men in the Japan Cultural Center tried to do. Rather, it was the valuing of household tasks done at home. It was also Mr. Okamoto's valuing of Mrs. Okamoto's activity. By graduating from marriage, they may have also graduated from regulatory forms that naturalized women's enabling of men's projects. Mr. Okamoto recognized that his wife was an individual with her own dreams and aspirations. This was what many women wished, including Mrs. Watase, who had exclaimed in frustration at her husband that women could have their own dreams and goals (see Interlude to Chapter 2).

Conclusion

This chapter explored tensions between husbands and wives' articulations and expectations of the "joint retirement project." It considered various linguistic, material, spatial, and social practices used by men to reorganize their spousal relations from being based on a strict division of labor to being based on a romantic partnership. By discussing how the practices of this new marital intimacy had hidden costs for wives, the chapter showed how such gestures were at once touching and fraught. In Japan, the husband's wages made the wife dependent on him; he in turn relied on his wife for maintaining the household. Men's retirement and their inability to provide wages had in many ways liberated their wives from this social contract. In pursuing romantic partnerships in Malaysia, however, language and mobility replaced wages in making wives dependent on their husbands.

Here, in addition to the transnational lens, I used the feminist notion of partnership as an entry point for articulating how senior citizens' imaginings of companionship connected with or diverged from their interpretations of partnership. I deconstructed the narrative of companionship that the male silver backpackers used to understand how women experienced the idea of companionship differently and how gendered power relations complicated the actual practice of this ideal. In the case of Japanese transnational retirees, companionate relationships did not simply erase the previously meaningful hierarchy or gender roles. The forms and expressions of gendered hierarchy merely shifted as dependency and power were recreated in nonfinancial forms. The seemingly liberatory rhetoric of love and equality obscured the nature of power and the underlying gender hegemony that were reproduced. Thus the overt performance of togetherness between husband and wife reflected both the anxiety and the fragility of spousal relations in later life. People who pursued a life independent of their spouses would have been an anxious reminder of the fragility of spousal ties.

Interlude

Mrs. Khadi had been teaching language classes at the Japan Cultural Center for over thirty years. Wrapping herself in a colorful Malay baju and glancing at the classroom from the top of her pink-tinted glasses, she conducted her classes with charismatic charm. Mrs. Khadi's class covered all sorts of topics, from what we ate for breakfast to where we went on holiday—rarely sticking to textbooks. None of the students seemed to mind.

Five minutes before the end of each class, she would disappear. Nobody ever found out where she went, but she'd always come back with a bag full of Malaysian *kuih* (traditional sweets). Some days, it was pandan coconut cake, other days, she brought peanut cookies. We each took a piece, but there were always more. She'd pass the excess kuih to Mr. Uchida, the class leader, to distribute during the after-class coffee sessions. But there were few takers; quite a few students suffered from diabetes. Others didn't quite get used to the taste of coconut.

Nevertheless, Mr. Uchida didn't tell Mrs. Khadi to stop bringing the sweets, for he was afraid of hurting her feelings. Instead, every week, he passed the sweets to a waiter at a café in the cultural center. There was a weekly circulation of kuih from the local vendor to Mrs. Khadi, to the Japanese seniors, and to the café waiter. It was a circulation of kuih as well as everyone's goodwill.

This interlude is dedicated to Mrs. Khadi, who passed away after I left my field in 2016.

CHAPTER 5

Negotiating Families from a Distance

I often heard silver backpackers say, "Japanese people nearby are more valuable than relatives far away" (*touku no shinseki yorimo chikaku no nihonjin*). Sharing drinks and meals had become one of the defining features of sociality among Japanese people in Malaysia. Mr. Takahashi, one of the regulars at the Language Club, told me that the after-class coffee session with Mrs. Khadi's kuih was the reason why he stayed in the club, even though his proficiency had not improved after two years. Over coffee, people shared information about interesting places to visit in and out of Kuala Lumpur. They often ended up going to these places together. One time, a group of women went to Little India in search of beautiful local fabrics. Another time, a group of men went to a rural rice field in search of "fat" rice resembling Japanese rice.

The club members regularly invited one another to their homes for meals, even though inviting non-family members to one's home is rare in Japan. Mr. Yoshimoto, for instance, regularly invited the members of the Language Club to his home for sushi parties. He used to work for a sushi restaurant when he was a university student and he enjoyed making sushi for his friends. Once I followed him to a wholesale fish market at two o'clock in the morning to shop for a party the following day. The bright fluorescent lights of the industrial fish market loomed over the pitch-black residential neighborhood. The temporal and visual contrast served as a dramatic reminder of the inequalities that separated middle-class Malaysians and working-class migrant fishermen and their dealers. Mr. Yoshimoto was an oddity at the market, but he didn't seem to mind. In less than half an hour, he was holding plastic bags full of tuna and squid. "My wife had asked me not to host parties anymore, because as you can see, it is a lot of effort! It is so much work, but for my *nakama*, it is worth it!"

This chapter focuses on family relations that were made and unmade by Japanese transnational retirees in Malaysia.[1] Here, the ties of "family" as they were experienced were not necessarily biological. Many silver backpackers saw relationships formed in Malaysia as akin to family. They called each other *nakama*—a term that conventionally refers to a close community of people. These retirees said that nakama were "like-family" or fictive kin (Lynch 2013, 195). I use the term "fictive family" cautiously here because it has come under constructive critique by scholars such as David Schneider (1980), who argues that all kinship, including biological kinship, is in some sense fictional (see also Weston 1991, 105). Nevertheless, I use the term fictive here in order to encompass the interlocutors' narrative word choices, *kazoku-mitai* (like a family).

To understand the nature of the Japanese retirees' fictive families in Malaysia, it is useful to first talk about men's relationships with their biological families. The chapter will begin by illustrating the transformation in the parent-child relationship in contemporary Japan, and how men in particular have tried to care for their children and vice-versa from a distance. Transnational retirement enabled retired sarariiman to transform the meaning of "absent fathers" into caring for children from a distance. The rest of the chapter will focus on the making of fictive kin both inside and outside the Japan Cultural Center. Women's relationships with biological kin will be addressed in more detail in Chapter 6. This chapter will instead highlight how women consolidated men's fictive ties through their affective labor in different times and spaces.

Shifting Parent-Children Relationships in Contemporary Japan

Most couples from the baby boomer generation had lived with the man's parents and looked after them into their old age (see Chapter 1). In 1980, nearly 70 percent of the baby boomer generation lived with aging parents. Yet by the time the baby boomer generation itself got older, the norm of co-residence was quickly disappearing. When my interlocutors retired in the early 2010s, the rate of inter-generational co-residence had dropped to 40.6 percent (Cabinet Office 2015, 10).

Several factors caused the drop in the rate of inter-generational co-residence.[2] Firstly, as more Japanese people worked in urban areas, it became increasingly difficult to accommodate multiple generations in the limited living spaces available (Ferries 1996). By looking at the correlation between the rate of co-residence and the income of the children's generation, Ferries (1996) found that middle income families had the highest rate of extended family co-residence while lower-income groups tended to adopt the nuclear family structure. He speculated that lower income families were constrained by the lack of living space and high rents. In such a family, typically husband and wife both had to work and could not afford to support a chronically sick parent in the same household.

Second, the longevity of the aging population made caregiving a long and strenuous activity for daughters-in-law (Jenike 2003). In 1972, the life expectancy was 70.50 years for men and 75.94 years for women (Ministry of Heath, Labor, and Welfare of Japan 2010). By 2014, the life expectancy had risen to 80.50 years for men and 86.83 years for women (Ministry of Heath, Labor, and Welfare of Japan 2015). As life expectancy had increased by almost ten years, the period of caregiving also increased. Men from the baby boomer generation who retired at the age of sixty in 2014 were expected to live on average for another 23.36 years, and women another 28.68 years (Ministry of Heath, Labor, and Welfare of Japan 2015). Having provided the caregiving to their parents-in-law, many of my female interlocutors told me that they did not want their children to go through a similar burden.

Third, and most significantly, starting in the 1980s, more women had been entering the workforce to supplement their family income (Peng 2002). In 1985, after the Japanese government signed the Convention on the Elimination of All Forms of Discrimination Against Women, it passed the Equal Employment Opportunity Act which prohibited gender discrimination in recruitment, hiring, promotion, training, and retirement (Mackie 2003, 184). Coupled with this legislative change, Ueno and Tabusa (2020, 11) observe that women from the baby boomer generation had taught their daughters to earn qualifications that would allow them to undertake jobs that offered flexibility for mothers, such was the improved female lifecourse that they envisioned. By 1988, the employment rate for female university graduates climbed to 75.2 percent, approaching the figure for males, 78.8 percent, in the same year (Upham 1993, 336–337). Of course, the statistics must be qualified. Most women continued to work part-time while raising children and in much less prestigious positions than men (Kimoto 2005; Izuhara 2006, 166). Despite this, the mid-1980s witnessed an upsurge in media reporting about the "new career women" (*kyaria uuman*) (Upham 1993, 337). By 1990, only 13.8 percent of young women saw marriage as "a woman's happiness" (*josei no kofuku*) (Tokuhiro 2010, 20), as compared to 39.7 percent in 1972 (Dales 2009, 21). The shift in gender norms was reflected in the survey done by the Japanese Cabinet Office in 2014. The survey asked, "what do you think of the idea 'men should work outside, and women should protect the family at home'?" Overall, 49.4 percent of those who answered the survey disagreed, in contrast to 34 percent in 1992 (Cabinet Office 2014, 1). Among the respondents between the ages of between twenty and twenty-nine years, however, 56.1 percent disagreed with the statement (Cabinet Office 2014, 1). With a rise in the number of women working outside of the home, fewer and fewer women were willing to take care of their in-laws (Traphagan 2003).

As it was no longer able to rely solely on women's invisible labor to provide welfare support for the seniors, the Japanese government had to introduce a series of welfare reforms called *Kea no Shakaika* (the Socialization of Care) in the 1990s. It introduced the Gold Plan, a ten-year strategy aimed at redistributing the responsibilities of personal aged care between the state, market, family, and community. A further New Gold Plan and Gold Plan-21 were introduced in 1994 and 2000, respectively, to respond to the growing demand for professional care services including home help, daycare, and nursing home care (R. Goodman 2002, 14; Toyota 2006). This was in striking contrast to the earlier Japanese-style welfare system, which had relied heavily on the family to take care of seniors. By 1996, the public message had become one that privileged the merits of professional institutionalized care over informal home care.

To finance this, a new long-term care insurance system was introduced in 2000 to require individuals above the age of forty to contribute to personal professional care services. This allowed the costs of long-term care to be shared between the citizens and the state (Izuhara 2006, 168).

Despite the individual financial contribution, the government expenditure on social welfare increased from JPY 4.799 billion (around USD 43 million) to JPY 8.323 billion (around USD 74 million) between 1990 and 1998. This was not an insignificant amount for a country that had been hit by an economic bubble burst in 1991 (Peng 2002; Allison 2013; Morioka and Nakabayashi 1994). Between 1989 and 1992, the Nikkei Stock Index dropped by more than 40 percent (Hamada 2005, 138). The attributes of the Japanese-style productivity discussed in Chapter 1, which once had made it the archetype of the nation's economic superiority—lifelong employment, seniority principle, and high savings (Duke 1986, xvii)—were criticized as the nation's greatest liabilities. Rural local governments especially suffered because they had larger populations of senior citizens (Peng 2002). Conditions further worsened after the humanitarian, economic, and political fallout from the 2011 tsunami, subsequent nuclear disaster, and the retirement of the baby boomer generation in 2012.

Japan's situation became more urgent because of the demographic crisis; there was not enough younger population to support the rising welfare costs of the older generation. The Japanese population growth had been falling below a replacement level for decades. On New Year's Day in 2015, BBC News kick-started the year with a grim headline: "Concern as Japan's 2014 birth rate falls to record low." The birth rate had declined to a rate of 1.43 children per woman. The prediction by the National Institute of Population and Social Science Research showed that Japan's population would decrease from 126 million in 2000 to 92 million by 2050, and 50 million by 2100 (Douglass and Roberts 2000, 19). In 2017, the population over sixty-five years of age became more than a quarter of the national population (World Bank 2017). By 2049, the proportion of the elderly is predicted to increase to one in three (Douglass and Roberts 2000, 19). The media warned that a dwindling band of workers would have to support rising social security payments as the number of retired people continued to grow. The support ratio of workers to pensioners was five to one in 1995 (Toyota 2006), but it is projected to drop to 1.2 to one by 2050 (Cabinet Office 2012a, 2). The declining number of young people, coupled with the increasing life expectancies of older people, made the provision of health services extremely difficult.

It was in these economic conditions that older people, more than other vulnerable groups in society, became the problem: "the aging society problem" (*koreika shakai mondai*) (Garon 1997, 222). In 2013, the government announced a proposed increase in consumption tax from 5 to 10 percent to cover the increasing cost of welfare for seniors. Following the announcement, Aso Taro, who then served as the finance minister, publicly shamed those on life-prolonging medical treatment. "Heaven forbid if you are forced to live on when you want to die. I would wake up feeling increasingly bad knowing that [treatment] was all being paid for by the government." He continued, saying that seniors should be allowed to "hurry up and die" to relieve the costs of state welfare (McCurry 2013). Once upon a time, the state cheered the baby boomers as the nation's "heroes" behind the miraculous growth that the country had experienced in the postwar years. By the early 2010s, however, the state was labeling the retiring members of the baby boomer generation as a "burden" on the nation's weakening economy (Shakuto 2018b, 187–88).

Despite being called a burden, men and women from the older generation and who thus had lived through the high-growth period were in general more financially well-to-do than the precarious Japanese youth who were living through the long recessionary era. Life for the younger generation had not been so easy (J. Hirayama and Kashiwagi 2004). Anthropologists of Japan, including Anne Allison (2013), have noted shifting working conditions where lifetime, permanent employment is no longer available for many youth. Even for those with fulltime jobs, the lifetime employment and financial security that large corporations used to afford the baby boomer generation are quickly becoming a thing of the past (Allison 2013). According to a survey conducted by the Cabinet Office (2015, 11), about 71 percent of people above age sixty—mostly retired—answered that they were financially secure. Each person in the household received about 1,928,000 yen (approx. USD 17,602) on average, per year, which was almost as much as the national average of 2,053,000 yen (approx. USD 18,750) (Cabinet Office 2015, 11). When it came to savings, seniors also had more money. On average, a household headed by a person over sixty-five had savings of about 24,990,000 yen (approx. USD 228,163), which was about 1.4 times higher than the national average (Cabinet Office 2015, 12).

In such socioeconomic conditions, rather than emphasizing filial piety as the ultimate virtue, a new trend was emerging where seniors were expected to be "useful" to their children instead of the other way around. The next section will explore ways in which transnational retirement allowed retirees from the baby boomer generation, particularly men, to be useful to their children.

Caring for Family from a Distance

Transnational retirement transformed the meaning of "absent fathers" for some men, since, as contradictory as it may sound, the physical distance allowed these men to rematerialize their ties to their biological family. For instance, many silver backpackers who moved to Malaysia had vacated their homes in Japan and let their children stay there (Shakuto 2018, 190). This gesture was much appreciated by their children. Buying a house had been part of a middle-class lifecourse for baby boomers but it was no longer the case for their children (Y. Hirayama 2011). The stagnating economy had also led to reduced numbers of marriages among youth (Rebick and Takenaka 2006,

9). This economic factor, combined with a cultural context in which one is not considered independent until marriage (Kato 2009; Suzuki 2002), had raised the rate of co-residence of unmarried children with elderly parents from 16.7 percent in 1985 to almost 20 percent in 2000 (Borovoy 2010; Ogawa, et al. 2006; Kato 2009). By vacating their homes for the precarious youth of Japan, silver backpackers in Malaysia were able to provide housing which, in an earlier era of high growth and full-time employment, Japanese youth would have been more likely to be able to pay for themselves.

The youth of Japan were also living precariously in that they faced the threat of another earthquake and the ongoing nuclear pollution after the Fukushima nuclear disaster in 2011. The number of Japanese MM2H visa holders rose sharply after 2011, from 195 in 2010 to 423 in 2011, 816 in 2012, and 739 in 2013 (Ministry of Tourism and Culture Malaysia 2015). The statistics do not provide a reason for this increase, but given the timing, it is likely related to the tsunami and Fukushima disasters of 2011.[3] Some silver backpackers who arrived after 2011 told me that they were creating a safe haven for their children in Malaysia just in case another disaster hit Japan. One such couple was Mr. and Mrs. Kutani. They had been living in Ibaraki Prefecture just outside of Tokyo when the radiation accident occurred in 2011. Initially, they fled to Nagano Prefecture, but a journalist friend warned them that the government's report on radiation levels was false. Mr. Kutani's cousin, who lived in Australia as an anti-nuclear activist, confirmed their suspicions. Having lost confidence in the Japanese government, Mr. and Mrs. Kutani moved to Malaysia. Although their children were still in Japan, the older couple were ready to receive them in Malaysia if another crisis hit Japan, whether that be a natural disaster like the 2011 tsunami or a financial disaster like the bursting of the bubble economy in the early 1990s. By vacating their homes or by providing a safe haven, silver backpackers' retirement period in Malaysia became a "useful time" (*yakuni tatsu jikan*) as opposed to the "wasted time" of retirement (*mottainai jikan*) in Japan.

Care through absence was also performed by the silver backpackers' children. Many retirees watched Japanese TV programs in Malaysia by installing a device on their children's televisions in Japan. Mr. Uchida, for instance, installed a device on his son's TV in Tokyo. Whenever Mr. Uchida switched on his TV in Kuala Lumpur, the device in his son's home would flash red lights. Every morning, his son could see the flashing red lights and know that his father and mother were alive and well in Malaysia. On days when Mr. Uchida was too busy to watch TV, the son would call to ask if they were okay. Other seniors used their blog posts as a similar communication tool with their relatives back home. One male interlocutor liked to paint the landscape of Kuala Lumpur and posted his paintings on his blog so that his family in Japan could see that he was well. Both the TVs and the blog posts allowed families geographically split between Malaysia and Japan to maintain familial bonds of care without verbal communication.

Indeed, many male silver backpackers found it difficult to connect with their children through more traditional forms of communication which depended largely on talking. Mr. Kosaka lamented once how he found it difficult to communicate with his daughter over Skype. "When my wife is with me in Kuala Lumpur, we regularly talk to our daughter using Skype, but I have nothing to say to my daughter whereas my wife can talk to her for hours and hours. Once, my daughter called when my wife was still in the shower. I had to talk to my daughter on my own. [Big sigh.] The awkward silence! It was so hard to find anything to say to my daughter."[4] One female retiree insightfully articulated to me what constituted the best relationship between men and their children: "one in which both parties are healthy and distant." Susan Long (2014, 194), an anthropologist of Japan, also noted cases of good relationships when two generations did not live nearby: "Perhaps when they saw less of each other there was less to complain about." For some men, it seemed easier to spend time with their children or grandchildren through the mediation of technologies from abroad. Mr. Yoshimoto, for example, regularly played an online game with his seven-year-old granddaughter. Each played the game independently on his or her own time, and they competed by comparing each other's scores. I regularly saw him playing the game briefly during coffee breaks after language class. "Ah! My granddaughter just beat me. Let me play it again." After a few minutes, he would show me the score. "See! I beat her again! I am sure she will play it now to beat me." He gazed gleefully at the screen.

The communication was not just limited to the moment, as sometimes the transnational retirees transcended generational temporality to bridge intergenerational temporality through their online blog entries. In 2016, there were more than 440 Japanese-language blogs about Malaysia. A significant portion of them was written by retirees and around six of them were consistently ranked one of the ten most visited blog sites. Mr. Uchida diligently blogged about his life in Malaysia online. He had begun daily blog entries the day he decided to go to Malaysia. He detailed the processes of applying for the MM2H visa, finding accommodation, setting up an Internet account, using public transportation, and travelling to nearby Southeast Asian countries. His activities were so well documented that one could follow and replicate the exact same experiences. Indeed, many prospective residents in Japan read his blog posts online. As his blog grew in popularity, Mr. Uchida began receiving emails from sarariiman in their late fifties who were planning to relocate to Malaysia after their retirement. When I asked him why he blogged, Mr. Uchida answered without hesitation: "It is for my grandchildren. It is a testimony of how their grandfather lived in this world" (*kawaii magotachi ni okuru, jiiji ga konoyo ni ikita akashi*). "My grandchildren are now aged seven and five. They are too small to know what I am doing in Malaysia. I will probably die before they fully understand it. But my blog posts will remain after my death. When my grandchildren grow up, they can read them and understand how I lived my life in Malaysia. It will serve as a testimony to how their grandfather lived his life."

Mr. Uchida's blog, which kept the records of his life in Malaysia, acted as an archive of "lost letters" (Garcia 2016, 89) sent to distant family members—some not even born—in a distant future.[5] After his death, Mr. Uchida's letters, in the form of blog posts, would become a primary source of his family's history or legacy (Garcia 2016). The gifting of these letters to his grandchildren allowed him to transcend a generational form of kinship to form an intergenerational kinship.

During their working lives as absent fathers, wages had materialized men's ties to their families. After their moves to Malaysia, the materiality of absence—such as an empty house, the red lights on the TV, and the words of blog entries—reconsolidated men's ties to their children and grandchildren, both present and future. Male silver backpackers managed to transform the meaning of absent fathers into something positive by moving to Malaysia.

Reimagining Family in Malaysia

While men rematerialized their ties to their biological families through absence, at the same time, they made new fictive families in Malaysia. Although the Japanese retirees I met were from different geographical and professional backgrounds, many of them met almost every day in and outside of the Japan Cultural Center. The following section will focus on the making of fictive kin through a few prominent practices at the center.

These men first and foremost became family-like through dining and doing things together (Weston 1991). In *Families We Choose*, Kath Weston

(1991) explored the growing sense of relatedness within queer friendships as meals were shared regularly in a domestic setting. This form of mutual assistance went beyond just cooking and cleaning to include tasks such as collecting mail while one was on vacation, feeding the cats, and other similar activities. The emotional support that Weston's interlocutors provided to each other created a sense of family. In Japan, the practice of eating together had been regarded as the central backbone of homeliness (Goldfarb 2017, 250). The ideal home would have family members all "eat the same food at the same time at the same table" (Goldfarb 2017, 250). Allison (2013, 97–98), however, notes the more recent decline of homeliness or family dining (*shokutaku*) in contemporary Japan. As mentioned in Chapter 1, many sarariiman who worked long hours could only return home after their children had gone to bed. Instead of eating meals with their family, sarariiman often ate their meals with colleagues. No doubt, this contributed to men's dislocation from family life in their retirement. In Malaysia, instead of eating meals with their families or colleagues, silver backpackers ate meals with their friends. One of the most iconic social clubs in the Japan Cultural Center was the Karaoke Club. Between twenty and fifty retirees met every Saturday evening to sing Japanese and American pop songs from the 1960s through the 1980s. Each person or a couple could choose one song from the list and then sing it together. After ninety minutes of singing, most participants went for dinner at a nearby Chinese restaurant. They told me that Chinese cuisine was well-suited for socializing because they could share a meal from one big bowl. Over dinner, they talked about where to find delicious Japanese food, where to pay parking tickets, and to where to visit for the next holiday. For some members, socializing during dinner was more important than the singing itself. "I look forward to this dinner every week," one male retiree who had come to Malaysia by himself told me. "The food doesn't taste good when eating alone."

Members of the Language Club also went on vacations together. I had the opportunity to join one of these trips. During the vacations, the couples did not share the same bedrooms. Instead, the men slept in one room, and the women in another. This arrangement fostered a sense of an emotional culture in which the members of the Language Club, as a whole, felt like a family rather than a collective of a few couples. We would reminisce later about the trip at weekly coffee sessions, and it gave us a sense of a shared past. When a female member of the club decided to return to Japan, she invited all the others to her home and gave her clothes to the other women—a practice that would only happen among the closest family members in Japan.

In addition to these family-making practices, discursive customs were also at play in creating and maintaining a sense of equality within the Japan Cultural Center. For instance, the use of nicknames was an important practice. Most silver backpackers adopted English nicknames, such as Kenny, Martha, Eddie, Paul, and, to my amusement, Thatcher (Shakuto 2019a). Given that most retirees in Malaysia were retired elite sarariiman, it was quite possible that they met their former colleagues or in some cases, former bosses at the Japan Cultural Center. Nicknames enabled them to engage with each other as equals, no matter what occupations they had performed in their working lives. Similarly, any explicit mention of one's previous occupation was considered taboo. Instead of relating to each other through their former positions in a company, the men tried to relate to each other as nakama.

Interestingly, there was a sense of nakama even among those who had never met before. The consciousness of nakama was created through the shared project of transnational retirement. To recall from Chapter 2, Mr. Kosaka picked up Mr. and Mrs. Uchida from the airport on their trial visit after he was contacted by the couple. Mr. Uchida read an online post by Mr. Kosaka where the latter provided useful information about transnational retirement. Just like Mr. Uchida, many prospective migrants read Mr. Kosaka's posts and sent him emails with questions and, sometimes, requested to meet with him personally when they visited Kuala Lumpur on their trial visits. Mr. Kosaka happily obliged and extended his assistance as he would have to his biological kin, even though he had never met most of the retirees before. This sharing of information before and during the international relocation made the idea of transnational retirement conceivable for the group of Japanese retirees, many of whom had not visited the country previously. Through this, they had a network of fictive kin which gave them a sense of familiarity and homeliness.

Creating and Consolidating Family Outside
of the Japan Cultural Center

Individuals formed intimate relationships outside of the Japan Cultural Center, too. In fact, it was often outside the formal spaces of the Japan Cultural Center that these fictive relationships were consolidated and extended by women. The following story of the women's yogurt network illustrates this point.

One day, Mr. and Mrs. Kosaka came to pick me up from my condominium to go to the Karaoke Club at the center. As soon as I slid into their car, Mrs. Kosaka passed me something in a plastic bag. I looked inside and, to my delight, I found a box of homemade yogurt. "You can use this as a starter and make your own next time," she smiled at me. She taught me to scoop two spoons of yogurt and drop them into a container of milk. This was all that was needed. A day later, it produced another container of yogurt!

The giving of yogurt started with Mrs. Kosaka bringing back a packet of yogurt starters from her home in Tottori Prefecture. She thought that she could share this magic food with other Japanese women who lived in the same condominium complex. Many Japanese retirees lived in the same complex because the location was recommended by one of few real estate agents who spoke Japanese in Kuala Lumpur (see Chapter 2). Over the years, the real estate agent became a safety net for new and existing retirees as they often contacted her for advice beyond real estate matters, such as when they faced bureaucratic challenges in Malaysia. In addition to the recommendation by the real estate agent, Mrs. Kosaka's husband also wrote about their condominium in the online forum. Every time there was a prospective resident, they came and had a look at Mr. and Mrs. Kosaka's apartment.[6] Like her husband who was volunteering to assist the new residents, Mrs. Kosaka told me that she used to volunteer at a local primary school for children with physical and mental disabilities. She tried volunteering in Kuala Lumpur too but found it difficult because of the language issue. She thought that sharing yogurt with her neighbors was a small contribution that she could make to the community. After she gave the yogurt to some Japanese neighbors, her yogurt became an instant hit among the Japanese women. The most recent recipient was Mrs. Watanabe. She was from Tottori too. She liked the yogurt so much that when her daughter came and visited her from Tottori, she gave her daughter a packet of yogurt to take home with her. The yogurt that travelled with Mrs. Kosaka from Tottori went around the condominium complex in Kuala Lumpur and then returned to Tottori!

In addition to connecting women of different generations in Japan and Malaysia, Mrs. Kosaka's yogurt connected women who were outside the networks of the Japan Cultural Center in Malaysia, specifically single women. Few single women participated in the Japan Cultural Center since couples dominated its activities. One female interlocutor told me that she felt uncomfortable in the Karaoke Club. She was a divorcee without children, and she did not feel welcomed in the center which emphasized couplehood so much (see Chapter 4). She instead attended a local choir. Neither Ms. Saito nor Ms. Yoshida, both single women in Malaysia, attended the Japan Cultural Center (see Chapter 3). Instead, they took English lessons in local schools. Mich, a single man in his seventies, stayed in a hostel despite his wealth (see Chapter 3). Although there were a few single people in the Japan Cultural Center, single people, in general, seemed to have stayed outside of it.

One such woman in the yogurt network was Ms. Machida. She was one of the few single women I met in Kuala Lumpur, and she had been living alone for the past two years. As a single mother, Ms. Machida used to live in council housing in a Tokyo suburb. After retiring as a social worker, she did not know what she wanted to do. She had one daughter, who had recently gotten married. "I could have continued working until sixty-five, but I wanted to retire while I was still healthy so that I could do what I wanted to do. But I didn't know what I wanted to do." Most of her female friends were looking after their grandchildren, but her daughter did not have a child. "If I had grandchildren, I might have felt that I had a role in the family. I could help my child look after her children. But there were no signs of any grandchildren coming anytime soon. So, I thought, 'what should I do? Where do I belong?'"

Then one day, Ms. Machida saw an advertisement for Malaysian retirement visas on TV. "Surely it was advertised before, but I never paid attention to it. But this time, I felt as if Malaysia was calling me from the TV screen. I was sucked in by an image of a paradise on the TV." She said that she instinctively knew that she was coming to Malaysia. "I knew it was God's reward [*Kami-sama no gohoubi*] for my hard work." For Ms. Machida, an opportunity for a second life came unexpectedly when, as she said, Kami-sama came and took her to Malaysia.

Ms. Machida's time in Malaysia started with a search for suitable accommodation. After a few inspections, she stumbled across a one-bedroom apartment in the same condominium complex as the Kosakas. She posted a note to the online Japanese network of transnational retirees, asking who else lived there. Mr. Kosaka responded swiftly to her post. When she arrived, Mr. Kosaka assisted Ms. Machida with everything from paying bills and setting up an Internet account to grocery shopping. She eventually decided to sign a long-term lease for the same condominium as she had become good friends with Mrs. Kosaka.

When we met in her one-bedroom apartment during the Christmas season, Ms. Machida served me the yogurt that she had just made from Mrs. Kosaka's starter. The TV was on, and it was showing an NHK program (the Japanese equivalent of CNN) featuring Asada Mao, a figure skating national icon. "Even if I am not watching it, the sound of a Japanese TV program makes me feel at ease," she explained. On the dining table, I noticed a few origamis. "I just made an origami Santa Claus," Ms. Machida showed me a few Santa Claus figures that she had made with red and white origami papers. "I hid one of them by the Christmas tree in the condominium reception area." She told me with a charming smile. We sat on her balcony overlooking the enormous Duke highway. The noise of the traffic was the only reminder of where we were—the heart of the Southeast Asian megacity. "Life is strange, don't you think?" She asked me. "Watching the TV program about Malaysia, finding this apartment, and meeting Kosaka-san; if one of them did not happen, I wouldn't have been sitting here chatting with you. I don't believe in a particular deity. I believe that both Christ and Allah existed. Indeed, I believe in all Kami-sama. They all brought us here."

It might well have been Kami-sama that brought us there. But it was also the yogurt that brought us together in the women's network in this condominium complex. I was amazed at how the lives of women from different geographical locations, classes, and marital statuses became connected in Malaysia, importantly, outside of the Japan Cultural Center. Ms. Machida told me that she did not participate in the activities at the Japan Cultural Center. She didn't drive and it was too difficult to get there. Instead, Ms. Machida immersed herself in the activities of the complex. She didn't speak English, but she was an active resident. During the festive seasons, she voluntarily decorated the condominium lobby with origami. This aroused curiosity among the staff of the management office, and despite the language barrier, they became good friends. She was invited to the wedding of one of the employees. This was extraordinary for a transnational retiree since few made friends outside of the Japanese community.

Ms. Machida was also exceptional in that she had developed a close relationship with younger Japanese expatriate wives who took origami lessons from her in the same complex. This contrasts with retirees in the Japan Cultural Center who seldom mixed with the younger expatriate population. In fact, when the Japan Cultural Center increased the annual fee from MYR 40 to MYR 70 in 2015, a few retirees at the center thought that the club's younger expatriate population had demanded a fee hike to get rid of older members. Such fear of ageism was frequently uttered by male retir-ees, who also in the same breath asked me, "What's the value in studying the old who are just playing around in Malaysia?" The same older group of people would ask me to study something "more important," like youn-ger Japanese expatriate communities. Their internalized ageism also re-flected a value system which regarded the non-waged activities of retirees as unimportant.

In contrast, some Japanese women reached out to expatriate groups be-yond the Japanese community. Mrs. Aoi, who regularly hosted a sewing ses-sion for Japanese female retirees in her condominium (see Chapter 2), was one such example. One day, she saw a social tennis club advertisement on the condominium complex's elevator notice board. A few days later, she saw a British woman with a tennis racket on the same elevator. For the next few days, Mrs. Aoi dreamed of playing tennis with a group of female friends from around the world. When Mrs. Aoi saw the same British woman again in the elevator, she asked if the woman was part of the tennis group. The woman smiled and invited her to join. Since that day, her life in Malaysia has revolved around tennis with British women and sewing with Japanese women. When her daughter visited them in Malaysia, Mrs. Aoi hosted a big party in her unit and invited both the British and Japanese female friends and their partners.

The giving of food and handcrafts among women seems to have opened wider doors to connect differently positioned people, from single female re-tirees to couples, to expatriate wives, and to local staff members in Malaysia. The women tended to form close relationships with a defined circle of people regardless of their different positionalities. Many were neighbors, like Mrs. Kosaka and Ms. Machida. Some gave the yogurt to their children, like Mrs. Watanabe. This women's yogurt network reproduced a network akin to the neighborhood community in Malaysia. This contrasted with men who readily formed fictive relationships with those whom they had never met based on the joint project of transnational retirement.

Although the ways in which women and men formed friendships and fic-tive ties were distinct, women's creation of fictive ties was essential for con-solidating men's fictive ties. Mr. Kosaka might pick up someone like Ms. Machida from the airport and spend a few days with them, but he might never see them again. In contrast, people in the women's yogurt networks were more immediate and, significantly, more permanent. Mrs. Kosaka's yogurt distribution to Ms. Machida consolidated the space of relationality within the intimate community of neighbors to which Mr. Kosaka could in turn belong. Yogurt, in this context, signified reproduction. Because it was physically reproductive, it assisted the women to reproduce some of their sources of belonging and homeliness. Furthermore, whenever a man organized a home party for his nakama, it was often women who did the preparation and clean up. In both cases of home parties discussed in Chapter 4, it was Mrs. Uchida who prepared the side dishes for her husband's classmates, and it was Martha who prepared the Chinese New Year party dishes for Ricky whom she was worried would be eating alone. In other words, the eating of meals together was the central part of nakama creation in the Japan Cultural Center, and it could not have been done without the assistance of women at home.

Cross-culturally, too, women have been found to be "kin and friend keepers" (Arber 2004; Calasanti 2004; Coe 2022). For instance, in Sri Lanka, female migrants would consider the needs of their children, partner, and their parents in deciding their own migration journey. Once the women migrated, they would develop social networks for themselves and their partners, and they also maintained connections with their family members back home through food giving and frequent phone calls (Wilding et al. 2022). Back home, migrants' mother, mother-in-law, and other female relatives would take on domestic duties such as childcare for the migrants (Gamburd 2020).

Despite this, women's domestic activities were often taken for granted by men, because what the women exchanged to create this network tended to be "seemingly ephemeral and valueless" (Weiner 1992, x).[7] Women's conversations in the kitchen were also often dismissed as trivial. The story of Mr. and Mrs. Otani with which I started this book is telling. Mr. Otani, who left Malaysia earlier than planned because he lacked a sense of purpose there, dismissed women's *idobata kaigi* (housewife's gossip) at the poolside as a non-worthwhile pursuit. This was problematic not just because this was what his wife enjoyed most about living in Malaysia; it was also because it was through his wife's engagement in idobata kaigi with her neighbors that she had gotten to know Mrs. Yamamoto, who in turn invited the couple to their home.

Taking the seemingly mundane scoops of yogurt as seriously as men's activities in the public domain of the Japan Cultural Center reveals that men's fictive kin in Malaysia and in retirement more generally were derived from women's assistance and networks behind the scenes. From circulating yogurt to preparing meals with domestic products from Japan, it was women's hidden affective labor and networks that men relied upon to create a family in Malaysia.

Death in a Family

In addition to consolidating men's fictive ties in Malaysia, women also bridged and connected fictive and biological kin. The final section of this chapter will turn to moments of death which illuminate women's extraordinary capacity.

Because of the commanding presence of my DSLR camera, I often became a default photographer at events organized by silver backpackers. Once, at the Karaoke Club, I took a picture of Mrs. Nishiguchi which I thought was rather well done. She was pleased to see the picture and asked, "Can you email the photo to me? I may use that picture as my funeral portrait." I was taken aback by her morbid comment, which predicted her own mortality and by extension that of others, but people around us did not seem particularly disturbed by it. They laughed it off.

Most of my interlocutors still had long years to live after their returns to Japan, yet the prospect of death was constantly on their minds. The vitality with which they had lived their lives in Malaysia made me often forget their ages and any potential health issues that they might have had. I was reminded of them, however, through numerous events. For instance, one day in the lobby of the center, they set up a machine to test blood sugar levels. A few people that I knew from the Igo Club took the test. A normal blood sugar level was eight but their readings were eleven and fourteen. I was shocked, but they were not. "That's ok; I am already diagnosed with diabetes." "Me too." They said to each other. Later I offered to buy them drinks from the vending machine. One of them asked for coffee. "Make sure it's reduced sugar," he winked.

Just as how they approached their health issues, most interlocutors handled the topic of death with surprising pragmatism. One of the staff members at a migration agency in Penang advised a Japanese client that he should not get a joint bank account with his spouse just in case one of them died. The post-death transition would be much smoother if they had separate accounts. The staffer further told the client that not many Japanese in Malaysia opened term-deposit accounts because they might die before the accounts mature. One Japanese couple told me that they never got on the same flight just in case it crashed. They said in a matter-of-fact way that, if both died at the same time, it would be very inconvenient for their children. Many couples told me that they had already drafted their wills. It seemed that even death had become a project to carefully plan for so as not to burden the loved ones.

A few months into my fieldwork, someone passed away. Mr. Ichiro Shigeta, who was affectionately known to others as Ikuo-san, died unexpectedly. He was traveling on a train when he had a heart attack and fell near the Kuala Lumpur Central station. He was immediately taken to the nearby clinic but was pronounced dead soon after. His body was flown to Japan a few days later so that his funeral could be conducted there.[8]

The news of Ikuo-san's passing spread rapidly among fellow silver backpackers. He was an active member of the Japan Cultural Center. He and his younger wife still had teenage children, so he participated in the activities mostly alone while his wife looked after the children. He also helped many people settle into Kuala Lumpur. I had maintained an email correspondence with him when I started my fieldwork. He was extremely generous with his information, and many interlocutors spoke highly of him. Although I did not get to meet Ikuo-san in person, I could tell that he was a much-loved member of the silver backpackers' community. People posted numerous obituaries on online social networks.

Before Ikuo-san's body was flown back to Japan, Mrs. Komura, one of the active members at the Japan Cultural Center, volunteered to represent his friends at the center and, as such, went to see him for the one last time at the hospital. She later wrote on the public mailing list about her encounter with Ikuo-san's family members who had come from Japan to receive his body.

> I just came back from the hospital. I saw Ikuo-san with his family. No tears came out of my eyes because I am still in disbelief. It is as if we lost him in the wrong time and space. He would wake up later, and we would have a good laugh about it. What a bad dream.
>
> I met and talked to his family members—his wife and his two older brothers. I knew immediately that they were his brothers because they looked so much alike. "Why did you go before us?" the brothers lamented before Ikuo-san.
>
> I thanked the brothers for Ikuo-san's contribution to the activities of the Japan Cultural Center. They laughed and said, "he did nothing at *uchi* [literally, "inside," but here it could mean family and home], but it's good to hear that he was useful at *soto* [literally, 'outside,' but here it could mean non-family members and outside the home]."

I have printed out everyone's obituaries and passed them to his wife. They added to eleven pages. By reading these obituaries, his brothers will understand how much people loved and relied on Ikuo-san [here in Malaysia].

I just bought a new notebook. If you would like to send a message, please write them in this notebook. His wife said that the family didn't have many pictures of him. If you have photos of Ikuo-san, please stick them in this notebook too so that I can pass the notebook to her.

Tomorrow, let's host a wake for Ikuo-san at our weekly dinner event after the Karaoke Club.

Mrs. Komura's letter started with the mourning of his sudden passing. It then introduced Ikuo-san's family members who came from Japan to collect his body. Ikuo-san's brothers referred to Japan and Malaysia by the terms uchi and soto. Kinship terms frequently used for one's family are *ie* and *uchi*. Ie refers to family and to its dwelling, and it can be translated as family, house, household, stem family, and genealogy (Hendry 1981b, 15). Joy Hendry (1981, 15) writes, "perhaps the closest English idea is that of 'House' as in 'House of Windsor'." An ie is organized on the basis of a stem family structure rather than a nuclear family structure, and it encompasses both the living and the (deceased) ancestral members of the household (Kondo 1990; Traphagan 2003). Ie transcends the lives of individuals and therefore, after death, all will join the ranks of their ancestors (*senzo*). Hence the living members of a family usually honor their ancestors and ensure that their descendants would follow them (Hendry 1981, 15). Uchi, on the other hand, denotes both inside and home. It contrasts with soto, which means outside and outsiders (Ohnuki-Tierney 1993; White 1988). In the high-growth period, women's work was largely associated with uchi (inside, with family members) and men's with soto (outside, with outsiders).

The practices of silver backpackers in Malaysia blurred the boundaries between uchi and soto. Men in the public domain of the Japan Cultural Center used the term nakama to incorporate each other into fictive kinships. Thus, when Mrs. Komura organized Ikuo-san's "wake," which was usually done by family members, it nonetheless felt natural among the community of his fictive kin. But Ikuo-san's biological family in Japan did not recognize this form of family. By contrasting the terms uchi and soto, Ikuo-san's brothers jokingly pointed out how Ikuo-san was useless (*yakuni tatanai*) within the family but he was useful (*yakuni tatsu*) outside of it.

Recognition of one's presence within the household has implications in the spiritual domain. Jieun Kim (2016, 845) observes that those who spend the last years of their lives disconnected from familial ties may become *muen-botoke* (disconnected spirits). The term muenbotoke refers to the spirits of the deceased whose deaths were not grieved by loved ones. Susan Long (2005, 61) writes that in Japan, "dying without the presence of others is considered a terrible fate." These spirits cannot enter the collective ancestral world because the descendants do not perform the necessary posthumous rites or look after the gravestone (Kim 2016, 850). Instead of becoming venerable ancestors, muenbotoke are "doomed to wander around this world restlessly in a state of hunger, misery, and resentment" (Kim 2016, 845).

In this socio-religious context, Mrs. Komura's letter took on a project-like narrative, refocusing her attention on ensuring that the legacy of Ikuo-san's contribution to the Japanese community in Kuala Lumpur (soto) was recognized by his family members back in Japan (uchi). Mrs. Komura swiftly collected people's obituary letters to Ikuo-san and bound them together into a notebook to be given to his wife. Mrs. Komura's notebook of letters was an attempt to get Ikuo-san's contribution to his fictive family in Malaysia (soto) recognized by his family in Japan (uchi). Ikuo-san's wife also played an important role in this transition; she received the notebook and transformed his activities into a form recognizable within the family (uchi): legacy.

The incident of Ikuo-san's passing highlights women's roles in consolidating men's ties to both their fictive and biological kin. Both women—Mrs. Komura and Ikuo-san's wife—took charge of ensuring men's recognition by the family members. As the producers of the affective environment of home, Japanese women were placed at the heart of the men's rematerializing of their ties to both fictive families in Malaysia and to biological families in Japan.

Conclusion

For the precarious youth of Japan, their formerly absent fathers transformed the meaning of absent fathers into something positive by going to Malaysia and leaving the family home to the younger generation. The families cared for each other from a distance, through the mediation of the materiality of absence. In Malaysia, transnational retirees formed a close fictive kinship with others to feel a sense of homeliness. They did so through dining and doing activities together around the Japan Cultural Center, and by adopting nicknames to emphasize the flat relationships between them. Women materialized these ties through the exchange of ordinary objects such as yogurt and origami papers with neighbors outside the formal spaces of the Japan Cultural Center. In doing so, women transcended the discursive boundaries between the Japanese and the locals, and between retirees and expatriates. Upon one's death in Malaysia, women were also the ones who consolidated the ties between fictive families in Malaysia and biological families in Japan.

What this chapter shows was that family, both biological and fictive, has become a key aspect of aging successfully in one's second life. In the aftermath of social welfare and life-long employment, the neoliberal state demanded self-responsibility and individualism on the part of its citizens. The ways in which people dealt with such a socio-economic shift centered on relying heavily on family—both fictive and biological—to fill in the affective gap. The excess of independent retirement projects was the enfolding of friends into fictive kin, and women's exchanges assisted men in maintaining those ties (Alexy 2020, 11). It was women who were depended upon to enable the family to become a wholesale alternative to the welfare state. I will show in the next chapter how women's flexibility and their ability to bridge reproductive and productive domains allowed some women to negotiate a return.

Interlude

As I arrived at the lobby of the Japan Cultural Center to meet Mr. Nishiguchi for the first time, I noticed a man standing still in his crisp business suit. He appeared to be in his late sixties or early seventies. With gray hair and sharp features, he reminded me of Mahathir Mohamad, the former Malaysian prime minister who returned from retirement to assume prime ministership again at the age of ninety-three.[1] One of my interlocutors introduced Mr. Nishiguchi to me as a very knowledgeable man and said, "You will learn a lot from him." When I approached him nervously, Mr. Nishiguchi looked surprised. Later, he revealed that he thought he was meeting a client for his business. In his "retirement" in Malaysia, he started a freelance consultancy to advise potential investors on business opportunities in Malaysia. We formed a close friendship over the course of my fieldwork. Mr. Nishiguchi was an avid reader widely acquainted with topics from Malaysian and Japanese politics to fine distinctions between anthropology and sociology. He often recommended books for my research.

One day over a coffee, Mr. Nishiguchi emphasized the importance of being useful to others (*yakunitatsu*) in old age. "One needs to keep giving" (*atae tsudukeru koto ga daiji*), he said. "A person is aging successfully if he or she continues to gather information and disseminate that information to others." I imagined a group of senior citizens exchanging information. I nodded in agreement, "that's a great way to survive in a foreign country. You give out what you know, and you take what others know."

Immediately, Mr. Nishiguchi protested. "No! I hate the concept of 'give and take' [*gibu ando teiku*]. Why can't one keep giving?" Noticing my puzzled expression, he elaborated. "You see, 'give and take' is two-dimensional." He lifted his right finger in the air and drew a horizontal line from right to left. "You give." He then drew back the line using the same finger from left to right. "Then you take," he said. "You repeat that movement—give and take. You would forever stay at the same height."

While keeping the right finger in the air, Mr. Nishiguchi asked me, "But what if we call it 'give and give' [*gibu ando gibu*] instead?" He drew the same horizontal line from right to left. "You give. Now, instead of taking from another person, that person will also give to you." He then lifted his left finger and drew a horizontal line from left to right above the first line. Now we had an additional line on top of the first line. "See, 'give and give' is three-dimensional," he smiled. "Every time you give, you uplift yourself." He repeatedly drew new horizontal lines above the previous lines with two fingers. When he couldn't draw any higher, he looked at me. "Shiori-san, to live is to add different layers of color to your life. Each person you meet will give you a different layer of color, and this is how you get your own color."

CHAPTER 6

Regeneration, Repair, and Return

Anthropologists have long been fascinated by the topic of gifts and exchange. What compels people to give and receive gifts? In the classic text *The Gift*, Marcel Mauss (2011 [1925]) argued that the norms of reciprocity enabled the creation and the maintenance of social relations; other economic anthropologists followed (Lévi-Strauss 1969; Sahlins 1972). In the Japanese context, gifting practices were formed during the Kamakura and Muromachi periods (twelfth–sixteenth centuries), which saw the emergence of the *samurai* (warrior) class (Sakurai 2011). Samurai, along with aristocrats and priests, frequently gave gifts of visits and swords to the *shogun* (the military commander in chief). In return, the shogun maintained political stability and secured their territorial land (Sakurai 2011, 179–80). Gifting practices between superiors and subordinates remained an important part of Japanese corporate culture of which many silver backpackers were part (Rupp 2003). In the 1970s, it was common for employees to send gifts to their employers or superiors as part of a yearly cycle of gifting, similar to a feudal practice. In exchange, the employers or superiors would provide the employees with "guidance, protection, and benevolence," which helped secure the employees' positions within the company (Lebra 1975, 557; Nakane 1970).[2]

Yet Mr. Nishiguchi's give-give relationship, and the ways silver backpackers readily helped people, did not seem to reflect the value of reciprocity as understood in the classic anthropological theory of gift exchange. In Malaysia, the givers and the receivers of "gifts"—in the form of service—were, in most cases, not the same persons due to the temporariness of their stay. Most silver backpackers returned to Japan after one to three years in Malaysia. An experienced resident like Mr. Kosaka might give assistance to the newcomers like Mr. Uchida, but by the time the newcomers had settled in Kuala Lumpur, chances were that Mr. Kosaka would have returned to Japan. The silver backpackers seemed to give and to only give, just as Mr. Nishiguchi had encouraged everyone to do.

I turned to feminist economic anthropologists who have analyzed unreturned gift practices, not in the framework of gift and relationships, but rather in the framework of gift and personhood (Weiner 1980; Munn 1986; Chu 2010; Schuster 2015). Calling it "generalized reciprocity," these scholars situate the classic norms of reciprocity beyond the limitations of the present, instead placing them within the broader dynamics of value production (Weiner 1980; Munn 1986; Chu 2010; Schuster 2015; Weiner 1977, 22). For instance, Annette Weiner (1977, 220) observed that in Trobriand Island, men gave away their valuable possessions, but they kept respect and prestige. Mr. Nishiguchi's articulation of the give-give relationship alludes to generalized reciprocity; by providing services, the gift givers acquired and kept the color.

What is the color exactly then? This chapter analyzes the practices of generalized reciprocity that took place within and outside of the Japan Cultural Center. While I focused on the remaking of geopolitical relations, self, spousal relations, and family relations in previous chapters, this chapter treats the act of giving as the very grounds on which my interlocutors experienced transnational retirement. I suggest that silver backpackers transformed the practices of giving into the creation of *ibasho*, "a space where one feels comfortable and at home" (Allison 2013, 174). This analysis recasts the feudal and corporate practices of giving in affective terms and treats the retirees' desire to be useful (*yakunitatsu*) as a medium through which they dealt with the maintenance and contradictions of gendered personhood in later life.

The chapter will first describe silver backpackers' desire to be useful and juxtapose their sentiments with the wider feeling of dislocation felt by different generations in Japan and beyond. The subsequent section will show how women and men both acted on this desire through their understandings of roles and ibasho, albeit in different ways. The concepts of roles and ibasho were fluid and their meanings and practices were open for reinterpretation in the aftermath of work. This chapter illustrates the fragility of these terms and how the work of repair led some couples to return to Japan.

The Desire to Be Useful

Most men talked about service to others as a reflection of their desire to be useful (*yakunitatsu*). Mr. Kosaka regularly helped prospective migrants experience living in Kuala Lumpur. Sometimes it took Mr. Kosaka half a day to reply to enquiries sent to the online forum or to bring an interested couple around the city (see Chapter 5). Most of these activities were not remunerated. It was time-consuming and physically exhausting, yet he did not see this as exploitation. Just as how sarariiman did not tend to see long working hours as exploitation (see Chapter 1), people like Mr. Kosaka felt rewarded by their experiences with potential migrants. Mrs. Kosaka said to me, "being useful to others gives me *ikigai*, the meaning of life" (*hito no yakuni tatsu koto ga watashi no ikigai desu*). As discussed previously, other silver backpackers became useful to their biological children by vacating homes in Japan or by providing safe havens in Malaysia (see Chapter 5). By doing so, their retirement period in Malaysia became a "useful time" (*yakuni tatsu jikan*) as opposed to the "wasted time" of retirement (*mottainai jikan*) in Japan. Many retirees in Malaysia seemed to share a similar desire to be useful to others in later life.

This desire to be useful in old age is shared across different cultures and societies. For instance, Schulz (1980, 251) notes that among older American men, performing a useful function in a community was one way for them to feel needed and desired. These discourses seemed to transform the act of giving into one's moral obligation to others. Yet such desire does not simply signal people's absorption of the state's aging discourses into a "moral neoliberal" subjecthood that fills in the welfare gap created by the state's failure to provide one (Muehlebach 2012). To recall Chapter 3, while silver backpackers became "ageless" in Malaysia by adopting the normative aging ideals of the Japanese state, they also actively deviated from those same ideals, either by becoming a *choiwaru oyaji* (senior with a bad boy charm) or freeing themselves from gendered expectations.

Instead, I argue that the desire to be useful was closely linked to the generation of roles, which in turn provided ibasho. One could make ibasho with anyone, including family, colleagues, or friendship groups. But when an anthropologist Anne Allison (2013, 47) did her fieldwork among youth in Japan in 2008–2010, many lived without a place or space where they could feel comfortable. An extreme example of socially dislocated youth is *hikikomori*, which refers to the socially withdrawn youth of Japan, mostly young men who are socially withdrawn into their rooms, and who rarely, if ever, leave for school or jobs. Having not found a permanent job, such youth live day by day on temporary work or become what is popularly termed, *parasaito singuru* (parasite singles), who live "parasitically" off their parents for years (Allison 2013, 30). Other troubled youth include NEETs (not in education, employment, or training) and *furiitaa* (freeters), youth with casual work or who are between such jobs (Hidaka 2010, 122). Hikikomori and other troubled youth in Japan are often viewed as a symptom of wider sociological trends such as the breakdown of communication and collapse of human relations more generally (Allison 2013, 74; Horiguchi 2011). Allison (2013, 119) concludes that one of the most pressing problems facing troubled youth today is an inability to find a role within society (*yakuwariga mitsukerarenai*).

As discussed in Chapter 1, this sense of dislocation was also felt by retired male corporate workers. In their retirement, these men felt dislocated from their formal identities as workers at the same time that they were struggling to find their places within their families and the larger community. Male silver backpackers frequently mentioned that it would have been *mottainai* (a waste) to spend their healthy years in Japan, where their only options were to keep working for a company that didn't value them anymore or to spend their days doing nothing "useful" at home.

Over the course of my fieldwork in Malaysia, I observed that the provision of service to others earned retirees "roles" (*yakuwari*) in the Japan Cultural Center. For instance, members of the Malaysia My Second Home (MM2H) club gave their services to others without expecting a material return, but through that service, the former acquired an official role. The person who volunteered the most to help prospective migrants was given an official title within the group. The membership in the group was hierarchically organized, from chairperson (*kaicho*) to captain (*kyaputen*), officers (*yakuin*), supporters (*sapota*), and ultimately ordinary members (*ippan kaiin*). These titles came directly from corporate practices.

Some of these roles were endowed with the gravitas of waged labor, as shown by the adoption of corporate terms (Muehlebach 2011, 74). The names of the committee members were published on the center's official website along with its constitution. Officers attended monthly committee meetings in the boardroom of the Japan Cultural Center. Some officers even turned up to these meetings in business suits and exchanged their name cards (see Chapter 4).

These roles, in turn, generated ibasho in the Japan Cultural Center. The following story of Mr. Uchida and Mr. Higashi in the Language Club shows how a role could lead to the security of ibasho within the Japan Cultural Center. Mr. Uchida and Mr. Higashi had been the club's class leader and treasurer, respectively, for two consecutive years. One of the leader's tasks was to assign a role to each classmate. One day, Mr. Uchida was about to assign a role of a note-taker to a new female member, but she hesitated to accept the position because it would require a strong language ability. Instead, she suggested that she take over Mr. Higashi's treasurer role; Mr. Higashi was absent that day. Her suggestion seemed reasonable given that Mr. Higashi had had this role for over two years. But Mr. Uchida immediately dismissed the suggestion. "You can't take that role from him. Although Mr. Higashi is one of the oldest members of the Language Club, he made little progress with the language. Aside from account keeping, he can't really take any other roles. If you took that role from him, he would lose his ibasho in the club and he would quit!"

Mr. Uchida's social maneuvering suggested that there was a complex melding of service, roles, and belonging within the Japan Cultural Center. Male silver backpackers incorporated themselves into the gifting framework of waged labor, thus their giving of themselves to the community gave rise to a role and ibasho in that organization.

At the same time, the silver backpackers were extending corporate practices to the distinctive relationships formed in retirement. The relationships formed in their retirement, and in Malaysia in particular, were very different from those they had formed in their respective corporations. Silver backpackers themselves insisted that the nakama made in Malaysia was of equals, regardless of gender or previous occupations (see Chapters 4 and 5). This was distinct from the corporate, waged relationships which were formed between hierarchical members. This gap in practice, as the retirees negotiated the work and retirement practices to define their ibasho, caused some contestations. I will now turn to the anxious negotiations of work and post-work practices which gave rise to an unexpected conflict for some, indicating the fragility of the post-work sociality that is based on work practice.

Negotiating the Terms of Ibasho

One day, I was running late for a session of the Art Club at the Japan Cultural Center. As I was trying to hastily remove my shoes before entering the classroom, I noticed Paul smoking outside the classroom with Mr. Z. Mr. Z and Paul were good friends; they always wore colorful shorts and they dressed almost identically, except for Paul's red glasses. That day, Mr. Z was wearing a T-shirt that Paul had designed for the Art Club a year before. But seeing them together outside the classroom was a little unusual. They seemed to be discussing something serious.

As the pair finished talking and came into the classroom, Mr. Mori, the leader of the Art Club, stood in front of the classroom to announce the election of a new leader: "The leader should be a man, the deputy leader should be a woman, and the accountant should be a new member. So, I have asked Mrs. Kitano, who just joined the club, to be the accountant, and Mrs. Taniguchi to be the deputy leader. I then asked Paul to be the leader, but he declined. So, what shall we do now? Some people say that I should continue to stay as a leader."

Mr. Miwa, one of the oldest members of the club, spoke up. "Well, let's have a look at what the club's constitution says. It says, 'A leader shall change every year, although the continuation of the leader shall not be prevented.' It is clearly stated that the leader should change every year." Mr. Mori responded:"But last year, we amended the constitution to add a phrase, 'although the continuation of the leader shall not be prevented.'"

Azuki-chan, one of the founding female members of the Art Club, raised her hand to ask a question."Why can't we just follow the seniority principle? The oldest member in terms of the year that they joined the club becomes a leader." Mr. Miwa responded swiftly. "This discussion should be held at the annual general meeting, which, according to the constitution, shall be held at the end of March."

Mr. Mori looked away. Mr. Miwa caught him and said: "Wait, don't tell me you are not planning to hold an AGM? You have to, according to the constitution, you know that, right?" Mr. Mori responded, "Alright I know. I will hold an AGM in March, but we need to have this discussion before the AGM." Mr. Miwa looked puzzled, but before he could continue, someone else spoke up: "It's really difficult to select a group of leaders when we are a group of nomads! Mr. Mori himself is temporarily leaving for Japan at the end of March [Later, Mr. Mori sent an email notifying the club that he would not be able to attend the AGM because he was going to Japan for a medical check-up]. How to hold an AGM without a leader? Half a year we are travelling. I suggest that the three executives share the loads." Mr. Z responded in an eloquent manner, supporting the anonymous speaker and the earlier suggestion by Azuki-chan.

I have been in this club for more than eight years now. Initially, we rotated the leadership according to the order in which one joined the club, no matter how good or bad he or she was in their painting ability or their leadership skills. But since about three years ago, we have shifted to demand a more charismatic style of leadership. That's why no one wants to take over the leadership now. They don't want to shoulder responsibilities and be compared with previous leaders. I suggest abolishing the hierarchy among the three executives altogether. Three of them are co-leaders. That way there will be less pressure on each of them. It'd be easier for people to take up the roles. The most important thing is to emphasize that it is by seniority! Then, one would feel that there is no choice but to take the role. People will support whoever is the leader.

Mr. Miwa protested: "Wait, wait. That's completely against the constitution. Do you mean to say that we should change the constitution?"

Paul ignored Mr. Miwa and supported Mr. Z.: "Indeed, in the past when the leadership was chosen by ability, and not by seniority, there were lots of disputes." I realized that this was what Paul and Mr. Z had been discussing outside the classroom. Their dialogue was premeditated. Mr. Z wore the T-shirt that Paul had designed to show solidarity with him. I then noticed that a few other members of the Art Club were also wearing Paul's T-shirts. Paul might have had similar private discussions with many more members prior to that meeting.

Mrs. Taniguchi, who had been appointed by Mr. Mori to be the deputy leader, raised her hand to ask a question. "But if we go by seniority, there will be years with only women in the executive position." Mr. Mori nodded in agreement, suggesting that was a problem. But Mr. Z responded quickly. "So? What's wrong with that? I am sure women can handle it." Mrs. Taniguchi protested, "Oh, but women are not very good with computers!" Someone shouted from the crowd. "Ask your husbands!" The crowd burst into laughter. The consensus was reached.

"Fine, we will follow a seniority order," Mr. Mori said decisively, although he sounded a little disappointed. People applauded. But Mr. Miwa objected again. "What is the point of the constitution if we don't follow it? Last year, we had a similar leadership dispute, and we amended the constitution. If you continue to ignore the constitution, next year we will face the same problem again. I can already tell. I used to work in an executive position before retirement. I can tell you that what you are doing [ignoring the constitution] is wrong."

Someone from the crowd teased him. "You are saying that because you don't want to be the leader!" People giggled. Another shouted, "What's the big deal? We can just change the constitution again to explicitly state, 'seniority'."

In the meantime, Mr. Mori scribbled down the names of members in the order of seniority. He separated men from women. "Alright, I have a list now. Since the leader must be a man, it would mean that the next leader is . . ."

Paul and Mr. Z intervened simultaneously. Paul said, "Forget the gender! The constitution doesn't say it has to be gender balanced!" just as Mr. Z. said, "What's wrong with all three women? Let them do it! Women are stronger anyway!"

The crowd laughed again. Mr. Mori had no choice but to appoint three women. "Fine, so the oldest members were Mrs. Taniguchi, Mrs. Sekine and Mrs. Kawashita. They can divide the roles among themselves." The discussion was over. Mr. Miwa spoke up for one last time as people started to pack their bags. "I am saying this for the last time. This is not a deliberation process according to the constitution. The discussion should have been held only at the AGM. What we are doing now is *nemawashi* [an informal process of deciding before the actual meeting]. It is not a procedure according to the constitution."

When I finished packing my bags, Mr. Miwa was already gone. He never returned to the Art Club. I later heard that he had resigned shortly after the dispute.

After Mr. Miwa's departure from the Art Club, women—who had largely been silent during the meeting—continued to gossip about what happened at the meeting for several weeks. Among them, Azuki-chan, the woman who had raised her hand to ask why they couldn't just go with the seniority principle, said that Mr. Miwa was being too inflexible. The women did not blame him, however. Instead, with almost a sense of pity, they blamed his previous occupation—that of a high-level civil servant. As a civil servant, women gossiped, Mr. Miwa had been moulded into following the law with no exceptions. He could not get rid of the old habit even in his retirement.

In a way that evoked Bourdieu's (1984) habitus, both women and men said that these embodied dispositions from previous lives were ingrained in people no matter how hard they tried to get rid of them. Although asking about another person's previous occupation was considered taboo (see Chapter 5), people always looked for material and social signs of those previous occupations. Paul, for instance, liked teasing his friends who were former public servants. He would comment on their taste in clothes. "You can spot former public servants from miles away. They wear a pair of trousers the same color as the floor so that they can blend in. Whereas people who were self-employed or used to work for foreign corporations [like myself] wear bright colors." Finding material signifiers of socioeconomic status is not unique to Japanese people. Oliver and O'Reilly (2010) who conducted their research among British senior residents in Spain also found that the migrants' aspirations for "a new life" were ruptured by non-economic signifiers of their positions in society. For the most part, I found that people socialized with others of the same gender and of similar occupational and class backgrounds.

In a lifeworld in which previous occupations loomed large in the imaginations of the silver backpackers, the deliberate adoption of casual nicknames (see Chapter 5) demonstrated the coexistence of the continuities and discontinuities that had defined their former lives. Within the complex web of social relations from which one could not unbind entirely (Robbins 2010, 648), the distinction between work and retirement practices was finely drawn. After all, the rest of the Art Class agreed on applying the seniority principle, which was a practice widely used in large corporations in their former working lives. But the justification for using the seniority principle in the Art Club was different from the corporate justification. In corporations, seniority was to ensure loyalty to the company. At the Art Club, in contrast, seniority was to ensure that those who became leaders would not feel the pressure to prove themselves worthy of the position.

I interpret the conflict within the Art Club as an instance of fracture as people negotiated post-work sociality with fellow retirees. Ibasho was created within the Japan Cultural Center through a person's commitment to a role as well as their relationships to one another as nakama, but, because the former draws from the practices of "work" while the latter tries to depart from it, retirees had to oscillate between proximity to and distance from capitalist waged work practices to define their social belonging in retirement.

In this context of fluid and indeterminate sociality, the attribute suggested by women—flexibility (*juunannsei*)—became the valued attribute. Chie Nakane (1970, 122), who studied the social structure of Japanese *mura* (villages), notes that in return for emotional security within the mura-like social organizations, a person must "adjust himself to group demands and accept the group consensus, even though it might seem unreasonable both in content and the method of presentation." In the case of the dispute at the Art Club, Mr. Miwa's insistence on following the constitution seemed reasonable, but his insistence on opposing the group consensus cost him his membership. Mr. Miwa's resignation resulted from his own inflexibility in adjusting to the post-work indeterminate sociality that had blurred the boundaries between work and non-work practices.

Women's Roles and Ibasho in Japan and Malaysia

It is important to note that many older female transnational retirees who had children in Japan also felt a sense of dislocation from their ibasho. As the women's ibasho in the lifecourse were largely shaped by their reproductive roles (see Chapter 1), the presence or absence of grandchildren seemed to have mattered in terms of ibasho-making both in Japan and Malaysia. For instance, Ms. Machida, a single mother (see Chapter 5), reflected on her retirement in Japan and mentioned that she might not have come to Malaysia if she had had grandchildren. After she retired as a social worker, Mrs. Machida felt she did not have an alternative role in society. An older single woman without a role was seen as being liminal. Such women were out of place in a country which for so long has placed women in the domain of the family and the household. In their old age, the women felt that they needed to justify their positions in society, for instance through a role as a grandmother. Going to Malaysia liberated them from these constraints and expectations, at least momentarily. The older women invested in themselves through English lessons and created selective social relations. Yet, when I met Mrs. Machida a year after our first encounter, she was getting ready to return to Japan. She told me excitedly, "My daughter just gave birth to a grandchild! I can finally go home now. [*yatto kaereru wa*]." The language used here—that she can finally go home now—showed a sense of relief. Although Mrs. Machida had enjoyed the freedom from gendered constraints afforded to her in Malaysia, her new role as a grandmother gave her an ibasho in the family to which she could return.

Similarly, many women who did have grandchildren and thus had a role as a grandmother seemed to prefer to go back to Japan. Claire Tachibana, a woman in her early sixties, often touched my cheeks and said that I reminded her of her children. One evening, she invited me to her home in Mont Kiara along with some others. She and her husband used to own a house in Karuizawa, an exclusive hill station in Japan where the rich and famous competed to buy their second and third properties. After his retirement, Mr. and Mrs. Tachibana went back and forth between Malaysia and Karuizawa. But after a third summer, she suggested selling the house in Japan as she was tired of maintaining two houses. They sold their Karuizawa house and instead bought and renovated a unit in an exclusive condominium complex in Mont Kiara. Mrs. Tachibana used to work as a wedding planner. She painted the walls of the new apartment white and chose furniture made of marble to resemble the interior of the lavish church weddings that she used to organize. But when I visited her beautiful apartment in Mont Kiara, she told me that she had been homesick. It had been eight years since she and her husband had moved to Kuala Lumpur. She regretted selling her house in Japan. "I have grandchildren. And I want to be close to them." She was looking forward to hugging her grandchildren during her visit to Japan the following month. Then she quickly looked at her husband, who was enjoying drinks with his friends at the dining table. "But Tachibana says he wants to die here." She called him by his surname, a practice considered cold and distant between spouses. "After all, it was my idea to sell the house in Japan." She looked down and sighed.

Many women continued to feel an obligation to their distant neighbors in Japan. For example, Mrs. Miyakawa from Penang related to me how she was troubling her neighbors by being abroad for a long time. "We are not there [in Japan]. But the grass in our garden will grow. Leaves will fall. Mails will arrive. So, my neighbors cut the grass, sweep the leaves, and take in the mail. Otherwise, it's obvious that our house is empty. Thieves will come to our neighborhood. I am troubling them by being absent [*inai kara meiwaku wo kaketeiru*]."[3] She looked worried and somewhat sad throughout our conversation. When Mrs. Miyakawa smiled, her eyelids slanted downwards, and she seemed to forcibly pull up the corners of her mouth. While men sought to reduce the burden (*meiwaku*) on their children by being away (see Chapter 5), some women felt that they were creating a burden upon their Japanese neighbors by being away.

Just as how some men had found their value being wasted in post-retirement in Japan, some women who followed their husbands to Malaysia found their value being wasted in Malaysia. Mrs. Hara, who had disposed of all her winter clothes before coming to Malaysia as a means of liberating herself from shigarami (social ties, see Chapter 3), nevertheless described her life in Malaysia as mottainai, a waste. "It is very free in Malaysia. I can wake up and eat anytime I want. I can devote as many hours to my hobby as I want.

But it is mottainai. What a waste." The anxious sentiment around wasting time (c.f., Musharbash 2007; Jeffrey 2010; Masquelier 2013), even when the period of retirement was supposedly characterized by the abundance of free time, was further captured by Mrs. Miyakawa, a retired woman I met in Penang. "Here in Penang, time doesn't chase me, but I wish it did [*jikan ga otte-kurenai*]." By phrasing her sentiment as "I wish time chased me" as opposed to a more descriptive term, *owanai* (time doesn't chase me), Mrs. Miyakawa suggested an unrealized wish for a sense of fulfilment.

In these myriad ways, some women in Malaysia lamented their lack of roles in Japan and expressed feeling liminal there, while other women felt liminal in Malaysia precisely because they did not have the roles which they otherwise had in Japan. The different ways that husbands and wives imagined their ties to family in Japan translated into the different ways that they viewed their moves to Malaysia. While female partners often called their stays in Malaysia a "prolonged holiday" (*chouki ryokou*), their husbands tended to call it a "migration" (*ijuu*). This different understanding had a significant effect on their perception of the home. While women tended to consider their home to be in Japan, husbands tended to call Malaysia their new home (*atarashii uchi*). In addition, women made more frequent trips back to Japan than their male counterparts.

Here, it is helpful to compare the gendered temporality of capitalism. The linear progression of a capitalist lifecourse was regulated by a generational temporality which started with birth, ended with retirement, restarted again in the second life of retirement, and ended again with death. Many former sarariiman felt that there was no sense of future after retirement in Japan but could resume their sense of progress by taking up the new "projects" of transnational retirement in Malaysia. The men achieved agelessness through their cyclical engagement in social roles related to the work practices that had dominated their younger lives. In contrast, women's lifecourses continued well past the men's retirement because women's reproductive roles went beyond the corporate timeline. The husband's retirement often coincided with the birth of grandchildren, and women were usually called in to help with their children's household tasks. Many women also continued to care for unmarried children as the stagnating economy had led to reduced numbers of marriages among youth (Rebick and Takenaka 2006, 9). Housework and care labor did not follow the same linear progression as capitalist temporality. Mr. Kosaka half-jokingly captured this difference. "In their old age, women are still useful to their children. Men just take up space." The sources of women's value were found through generations. In other words, while men's temporality tended to be generational, women's temporality tended to be intergenerational.

Gendered conceptions of time are not unique to Japan. Anthony Giddens (1992, 59), a sociologist of British society, famously said that "men have assumed that their activities constituted 'history', whereas women existed almost out of time, doing the same as they had always done." Annette Weiner, a feminist anthropologist of the Trobriand Island societies, evaluated this situation differently. "The importance of women's wealth exceeds the importance of the historical time controlled by men" (1977, 210, 231). Weiner argues that "the final control by women of the cosmic cycle leaves men destined to borrow some of the symbols of women's power and to create through women, artificial extensions of their own historically bounded time" (Weiner 1977, 23).

Indeed, as we saw throughout the previous chapters, both schemes of corporate capitalism and second life relied primarily on women's labor for their enactment. In Malaysia, Japanese men were in need of women to give substance to their joint retirement projects as well as to create fictive ties. But the men's nakama was a transient one. The photographs on the couple's joint name cards showed not just the spousal intimacy but also how brief their encounters were going to be, for they needed pictures for identification. After their return from Malaysia to different parts of Japan, it was difficult for former silver backpackers to keep in touch with each other. Although their acts of giving in Malaysia, from sharing information to helping each other, created roles and ibasho, it did not erase the sense of anxiety retired men felt about their ibasho, both in Japan and Malaysia.

It was here, toward the end of the Malaysian chapter of their second lives, that women played a crucial role in creating an ibasho for men in Japan. The concluding section of this chapter focuses on women's affective labor of care in creating ibasho for men in the family life in Japan, which in turn allowed some women to negotiate their own return.

Repair and Return

Although the MM2H visa allowed them to stay in Malaysia for ten years, most silver backpackers I met returned within three years. Some returned when their bodies declined. Some returned to look after their elderly parents. But many couples returned because the women insisted on returning.

Mrs. Hara, who told me that her value had not been realized (mottainai) in Malaysia, excitedly approached me one day in 2014. "The other day, my daughter called and asked us to help our grandson with his schoolwork. Our grandson will be entering junior high school next spring. I think it's a good idea for us to go back and help our grandson."

Mrs. Hara's excitement at going back to Japan typified the experience of many Japanese women. She said that she was planning to leave for Japan in two years' time. But when I returned to my field site a year later, Mr. and Mrs. Hara were already gone. Mr. Kosaka, their neighbor, told me that they had gone back to look after the grandson.

In persuading their husbands to return, women evoked the possibility for men to have "a role" and "be useful" within the biological family. The value that was generated by their service was their ibasho within the family. By suggesting her husband teach their grandson, Mrs. Hara tactically invited her husband to establish intergenerational ties.

In addition to teaching their grandson, Mr. Kosaka told me that Mr. Hara had developed a hearing problem. For many men, their wives were the few people whom they could rely on in old age. Women of the baby boomer generation tended to have a better relationship with their family members than their male counterparts in retirement. According to the statistics collected from people who lived by themselves in old age, 58.2 percent of women answered that they would want their children to look after them when they were ill. But only 41 percent of men responded the same, and 21.5 percent of men who had children answered that they did not have anyone who could care for them (Cabinet Office 2016, 33).

Mr. Kosaka himself had become partially deaf in the one year I didn't see him. Mr. and Mrs. Kosaka were leaving Kuala Lumpur when I met them for the last time at the end of my fieldwork in 2016. As the three of us met over a meal, Mrs. Kosaka caringly repeated our conversation to her husband in a louder and slower voice so that he could follow. Borovoy (2010), who worked with Japanese wives, notes the persistence of a nurturing ideology among women even if they had developed a distance from their husbands. While Borovoy's female interlocutors acknowledged the exploitative dimensions of caregiving, the women ultimately wanted to continue to be the caregivers and be appropriately appreciated for it (Borovoy 2005, 101). In these affective conditions, women's abilities to care for men and to incorporate them into family ties provided women with the power to negotiate a return.

Some women also seemed to have been able to renegotiate the terms of their joint partnership, shifting it from one in which women join men's projects into one in which men value women's lives and their value production processes. Mrs. Okada, who felt that her life had always been constrained by men—first by her father and then by her husband—eventually returned from Kuala Lumpur to her natal village in Miyazaki Prefecture to look after her mother. Her husband quit the Language Club in the Japan Cultural Center and returned with her. In Miyazaki, he took up a job as a delivery truck driver. Mr. Uchida later told me that Mrs. Okada had made her husband promise her after two years in Malaysia that when her mother needed care in Japan, they would go back to *her* natal home to look after *her* mother, because she had come to Malaysia to realize *his* dream. It was Mr. Okada's turn to follow her decision, even though it meant that Mr. Okada would take up a job unrelated to his previous occupation. Over the period they spent in Malaysia, there seems to have been a partial shifting of spousal relations between Mr. and Mrs. Okada.

As for Mr. Uchida, he too slowly negotiated the terms of his retirement "project" with his wife. He was initially planning to stay in Malaysia for ten years, but I received an unexpected New Year's greeting from him during his sixth year in Malaysia.

2 January 2019

New Year's Greetings, everyone.

We are very sorry for all the trouble we caused last year and for leaving Kuala Lumpur without properly saying goodbye. We are now settled into our new home and new life in Japan.

On New Year's Day yesterday, we were surrounded by our children and grandchildren. It had been a long time since we celebrated New Year's Day with our family. We held the party at our new home with eight of us, just the family members. Of course, I made tempura at the party. My children and grandchildren were amazed to witness my skills and I felt very good.

Because of that, I had a little too much to drink, and I failed to send this new year greeting on New Year's Day. My sincere apologies.

We decided to return to Japan earlier than planned due to our failing health. The pain in my waist and lower limbs has gotten worse since our return. Sometimes I can't even walk. I'm surviving on painkillers from the local clinic, but I should see a specialist doctor soon. My wife, on the other hand, seems to be doing much better since our return, and in fact, she no longer seems to have any problems. Perhaps the Japanese climate and the food agree with her better.

Unlike Malaysia, I find Japanese winter cold and harsh. Despite that, with children and grandchildren who live nearby, I believe that the rest of our lives will be filled with warmth.

I would like to share with you my aspiration for the next few years. I will improve my health, get used to the new life and the new place, rekindle old friendships in and out of Japan, and continue to challenge myself by becoming a language volunteer at the Tokyo Olympics 2020.[4]

Mr. Uchida concluded with the customary greetings and wished for the health and wealth of everyone and their family members. He signed off his email with both his and his wife's names. The address that followed was a suburb of Tokyo near where his children lived.

Mr. Uchida's return to Japan came a few years before his planned date, and what had provoked their eventual return was the failing health of both Mr. and Mrs. Uchida. Yet his email was characteristic of his project-driven nature. Mr. Uchida had already set multiple new goals to achieve in Japan, from improving his health to becoming a language volunteer at the Tokyo Olympics. I was surprised, however, that he did not mention that he would make new friends or nakama in Japan. Instead, Mr. Uchida spoke of rekindling ties with his old friends, and he foresaw his future in Japan to be with his children and grandchildren. He bought a new family home near where their children lived. Instead of dining and doing activities with his nakama, he made tempura for his children and grandchildren. "With children and grandchildren who live nearby, I believe that the rest of our lives will be filled with warmth." It seems that he had a new ibasho within the family.

After his return, Mr. Uchida updated his blog: "Now, every article I wrote previously about Malaysia, my hobbies, and my personal thoughts have become my *zaisan* [legacy]." His life in Malaysia had become his legacy. When they returned to Japan, men borrowed some of the symbols of women's power and created through women extensions of their generational time into intergenerational temporality (c.f., Weiner 1977, 23). In the same blog post, Mr. Uchida referred to his wife as "My Better Half" in English. When I knew him in Malaysia, he had never called his wife in this way. His email also acknowledged that the Japanese climate and food agreed with his wife, who was feeling much better in Japan, even though his own conditions had gotten worse. Although the regulatory work of gender may not have been reordered completely, there may have been a partial shift in the norms of Mr. and Mrs. Uchida's relationships over the course of their transnational retirement and their return.

Conclusion

This chapter described how the roles, or the sense of being useful to others, became the principal idiom through which the silver backpackers talked about their claims to ibasho in the Japan Cultural Center. I argue that what fed the flow of giving was the desire to be useful on the personal level, which was symbolic of ibasho on the discourse level. In other words, the desire to be useful through one's role in the Japanese community was a performative cultural production of belonging. Male retirees appear to have subjected themselves to seemingly endless and exhausting tasks of service because it was ibasho that they were laboring to reproduce. Their practice of service fed these ambitions, and these became prominent features of male retirees' activities in Malaysia.

In defining their roles, men borrowed some of the practices from their previous working lives, yet this borrowing also gave rise to anxieties because conflicts frequently erupted as men negotiated the terms of a new sociality. The question of where and how to draw the boundaries between work and non-work practices caused some disagreements among retirees, and some of these conflicts resulted in one losing membership to their new ibasho.

For many women, in contrast, what rendered their lives mottainai in Malaysia was not the dislocation from the gendered lifecourse—most women thought it was liberating. Rather, it was the disregard for the feminized lifecourse that they had led. For women, their pasts and the communities that they had built, no matter how resentful of them they might have been in their younger years, provided them with a source of value, roles, and ibasho. Given the fragility of men's ibasho in Malaysia, women's ability to create belonging for their male partners both in Malaysia and Japan generated the possibility for women to negotiate a return, in many cases, much earlier than the husbands originally planned.

Conclusion

Beyond Work-Life Balance

I n this book, I have moved outward from my interlocutors' experience of the transnational retirement project to examine emergent forms of personhood and relationality in retirement. I showed what this retirement abroad both promised and thwarted. From men setting up clubs to help new retirees, to women sharing Japanese yogurt among neighbors, and to husbands declaring love to their spouses, who nevertheless continued to call the men oto-san, the everyday dramas that played out in the Japanese retirement community in Kuala Lumpur provided openings into the ambiguous nature of post-work lives. The experiences of silver backpackers highlighted specific ways that transnational mobilities in later life enabled, and sometimes hindered, the creation and maintenance of affective communities.

To what extent did transnational retirement rearrange the gender roles and gendered values that had been previously associated with capitalism and their working lives? For many men, transnational retirement may have been about shaping an uncertain future. This form of retirement emerged around moments in the political and economic history of the Japanese state when the terms of productivity and belonging were particularly uncertain and fluid. Baby boomers were situated on a tectonic shift as the Japanese economy plummeted from postwar growth to enter its fourth decade of depression. Just as Japan struggled to find its footing, many male silver backpackers also struggled to live through the structural consequences of having led a life as a sarariiman. The idea of an independent and mutually supportive retirement, and a neoliberal economic system that promotes successful aging more broadly, had set up anxieties around the temporality of productivity and intimacy in their later lives. The sense of "being stuck," that is, of not filling their time with useful activities, framed the moral debates over the politics of retirement's temporality as former sarariiman differentiated the productive, meaningful time of transnational retirement from the perceived wasted time of many male retirees in Japan (compare Chu 2010, 258).

In such context, senior citizens' access to transnational mobility, expatriate enclaves, and lifestyles in Malaysia may have enabled a version of aging that was unattainable in Japan. The movement to Malaysia allowed some retirees to re-create the middle-class respectability that they had enjoyed in Japan in Malaysia, an act made possible by global inequality. The practice of transnational retirement is important for understanding how Japanese seniors created an emotional, social, and physical space in which they could begin their second lives afresh. As many men transitioned from being sarariiman to ageless seniors in their second lives in Malaysia, intimate concepts which were once considered antithetical in the former system, namely, equality and love, were nevertheless used to enable the latter. As the men cared for their children by being away, friends in Kuala Lumpur became fictive kin. From the giving of one's service, to inviting each other to their homes for meals, and to calling each other by nicknames, nakama became one of the idioms which men used to stake a belonging that they felt had been missing upon retirement. Women were a very important part of this process as their romantic partners. Men who were once called the nation's heroes became wet fallen leaves in retirement, but some tried to regain their social upper-class masculinity by performing the liberal self. These male retirees demonstrated their affection for their wives and encouraged the women to pursue joint activities in public as a unit. The desires to be useful to one's friends and be intimate with one's spouse were fundamentally shaped by and, in turn, influenced by the cultural meaning of the transition from work to retirement. Specific historical and gendered socializations of the postwar, high-growth period, as well as the shifting welfare policies, made these sentiments persuasive, especially among the male baby boomers. In pursuing independent retirement abroad, friends and spouses, as well as Malaysia itself were enfolded to become a wholesale alternative to the welfare state or to the biological kin which would otherwise have offered affective security and closeness.

Yet that was "such a male perspective," as Mrs. Yamamoto might have said. Some Japanese women differentiated themselves from men by calling out men's search for purpose in retirement as evidence of their inability to handle freedom. The tension between some spouses was sparked when gendered and racialized expectations about retirement and inter-Asian mobilities came to a head. The assertions that people, regardless of gender or previous position, were equal in Malaysia and that the liberal model of companionate marriage was encouraged in the Japan Cultural Center, reflected men's value production processes which attributed values to public roles. Many women instead developed their own social networks based on activities including the material circulation of domestic products and everyday interactions in the neighborhood. For those (mostly women) whose identities and belonging had been shaped by the heavy participation in the domains of non-waged labor, the practices and values of second life that emphasized public activities undermined the meanings and values that they had given to their own activities. For many women, transnational retirement was a mixture of liberation from, and continuation of, the gendered lifecourse. In the former cases, some women felt released from shigarami, the ties of social obligations that had bound them to reproductive roles and neighbors' watchful eyes in Japan. Some could take up public positions which were denied to them when they were younger. But even when they did so, the liberation from the feminized practices did not necessarily mean that the women wanted to join men's projects or their value production processes. Neither did it mean that they needed men—Japanese or otherwise—to enable them (compare Kelsky 2001). Instead, many women embraced the fact that they could be fully independent, or independent with the support of other women, in Malaysia.

At the same time, even when women seemed to have liberated themselves from the gendered lifecourse, the hegemonic gender structures and the vertical relationality associated with the capitalist system were somewhat reproduced in Malaysia. Although women were encouraged by men to take up public roles and to present themselves to others as equal partners, the women were simultaneously prevented from doing so, often either because of the circulation of signifiers in which few women could partake or simply because of the linguistic and transportation challenges they faced in Malaysia. Instead, many women were called in from the place of their domesticity in order to assist in the making of nakama for men in Malaysia. Despite their importance, women's affective labor of maintaining relations with neighbors through *idobata kaigi* or the circulation of everyday objects, was disregarded and deemed unimportant or unworthy in men's perception of a successful retirement. The silver backpackers' transnational movement highlighted the togetherness of people, but this sense of togetherness tended to be based on the male model of value production processes. In their retirement, the gendered hierarchy continued to constitute the basic terms of what were considered valuable activities within the discourse of second life.

Toward the end of the transnational retirement, however, the book revealed a partial shifting of gender relations in what seemed like a reverse of liberal feminist processes. Instead of men becoming the standard to which women became equal, here, *women* became the standard to which men were rendered equal, at least to some extent. At the end of their stays in Malaysia, some men borrowed women's assistance to rekindle ties with their family members back in Japan. In doing so, the men departed their capitalist, generational temporality to enter into the domains of intergenerational temporality. While neoliberalism and the associated concept of successful aging demand one to shape their own future (Takeyama 2016, 9), in deciding to return and revalue the spaces and sociality of home, the future was enacted together.

*   *   *

Japanese silver backpackers' stories could be read as a chapter in their long second lives or as a chapter in the socioeconomic history of aging in Japan. But even more, their stories could be read as elucidating the widespread consequences of gendered divisions of labor in capitalism, as told through the lens of a group of retirees who felt the effects of these ideologies on their intimate lives throughout their lifecourses, including in their retirements. The chapters in this book tracked the negotiations and ambiguities of their experiences as silver backpackers tried to attain a meaningful second life overseas. Post-work anxieties over their relationships with the state, spouses, and children gave rise to new inter-Asian transnational mobility at an older age. They negotiated their post-work personhood, relationality, and lives from the margins of their own aging temporality and spaces in the Global South. The renegotiation of regulatory categories such as family, friends, and spouses, once associated with work, emerged from these processes. After work, these categories were subject to such change that they could be reordered.

By focusing on gender and retirement, this ethnography pushes us to consider deep flaws in some of our key concepts, particularly surrounding the work/retirement or work/(second)life separation. This book ends with a reflection on post-work lives and a broader critique of the work–retirement or work–life dichotomies that are an analytic assumption both in scholarship on aging as well as in the popular imagination of work-life balance.

The story of silver backpackers calls into question what retirement is. The rapidly growing Malaysian economy seemed to have symbolized the future for retirees. By aligning themselves with the space and temporality of progress, the Japanese retirees were striving for temporal progress beyond their positions as elderly people in the period of so-called comfortable retirement. Silver backpackers in Malaysia were self-motivated to go beyond the conventional retirement lives in Japan. They self-sufficiently gathered information, and overall took the "business" of their retirements into their own hands. In doing so, they transformed a period of retirement into a "second life." Their quest for a sense of progress and the associated sense of rejuvenation and youthfulness that they experienced in Malaysia challenged the monolithic view of aging as decay. Their transnational retirement was less about the negotiation of retirement than it was about the negotiation of lifecourse. Instead of ending the productive lifecourse with one's retirement, and hence going "off stage," transnational retirement allowed the silver backpackers to resume movement on a productive lifecourse; it allowed them to continue to be "on stage."

At the same time, the place of retirement which many men relegated as off-stage was precisely the place which had been occupied by women as reproductive laborers. Many women started "on stage" with men in school and in companies, but they were pulled to the off stage, or to the domains of home, through various social and cultural structures after marriage. In that space, women accumulated their own values. Yet in men's retirement, activities at home are regarded as "boring," "inactive," and worse, "unproductive." People who "just sit at home drinking tea" are looked down upon. Some men tried to transition from retirement to second life with their wives, but in doing so, they failed to appreciate the women's own value production processes.

By gendering the second life discourses and practices, *After Work* offers an alternative feminist perspective on aging. The discourse of second life enables active, socially involved retirees on the one hand and reproduces discourses that have marginalized them on the other, including the oppressive ageist and gender structure inculcated during the high-growth era. Retirement and second life are created and policed by the capitalist system which also reproduces the devaluation of home. I do not question the seemingly unproblematic statement that the seniors should pursue purposeful activities in retirement. Rather, I argue that it is important to acknowledge the gendered nature of this ideology. It privileges forms of activities more regularly pursued by men over those which had already and always been pursued (largely) by women. The exaggerated emphasis on the dream-like qualities of second life or on companionate marriage ideals can obscure the broader processes of the marginalization of home and domestic activities that can affect communities beyond the aging population.

The book, then, challenges the conceptual boundaries between work and retirement or between work and (second) life. The Japanese government has been encouraging those who are currently in the workforce to achieve work-life balance (*waaku raifu barannsu*) so that people can accumulate the three skills discussed in Chapter 3—to be able to look after one's self (*jiko ryoku*), to have friends (*nakama ryoku*), and to be part of the local community (*chiiki ryoku*)—in preparation for retirement (Cabinet Office 2012a, 10, 24–25). But this book has shown that the existential crisis in later life was in part brought about by placing both one's lifecourse and one's relationship under an economic system which created an artificial divide between waged labor and non-waged labor. I am writing this conclusion in early 2023, when everything we thought was normal has been challenged through the coronavirus pandemic. Although the term, work-life balance has gained traction in recent years, the spread of work-from-home arrangements during the pandemic has revealed deep flaws in the supposed separation of work and home that underlies the concept of work-life balance. Scenes of work in the midst of everyday life have become very familiar. Discourses around work can no longer sustain the erasure of private lives and domestic experiences. Instead, we would do well to revalue their specific and underappreciated qualities (Mol 2016, 403).

What needs reworking in contemporary society then, is not a better balance between work and life. Rather, it is the very separation of these two domains. That is, we must acknowledge the value production processes which had been relegated to the feminine and domestic domain, and then meld the gendered domains so that we all appreciate "life" in its entirety. In other words, what is needed instead of a work-life balance is the revaluation of "life." Retired people are best positioned to nurture the non-work aspects of life. I hope the stories of silver backpackers can start a new conversation about the value of life in every stage of life, not just after work.

GLOSSARY

akogare—yearning
chiiki ryoku—the skill to be able to be a part of the local community
chouki ryokou—long-term travel
dankai no sedai—baby boomers
deban—a role
do-kokai kappuru—a couple united together by their common interests
gaishi-kei—employees of foreign companies
ganbaru—persevere
gojo—mutual support
henjin—weirdo
hikikomori—the socially withdrawn youth of Japan
hinichijo—extraordinary environment
ibasho—a space of belonging
idobata kaigi—a world of housewife gossip
ie—family, house, household, stem family, genealogy
ijuu—relocation
ikigai—what makes life worth living
ippan kaiin—ordinary members
ji-ei—self-employed
jiko ryoku—the skill to be able to look after one's self
jukunen rikon—later-life divorce
juunannsei—flexibility
kaicho—chairman
karoushi—death by overwork
katami ga semai—constricted shoulders
kazoku-mitai—like family
kigyou senshi—corporate warriors
kyaputen—captain
mottainai—a waste

muenbotoke—disconnected spirits
mura—village
nakama—a close community of people
nakama ryoku— the skill to be able to have friends
omiai—an arranged marriage
ryoku—skills
sapota—supporters
sarariiman—white collar salaried workers
seinen—youth
shinia—seniors
shirubaa bakku pakkaa—silver backpackers
shigarami—social obligation
shimanagashi—banishment
soto—outside, non-family members, outside home
sotsukon—graduation from marriage
uchi—inside, family, home
yakuin—officers
yakunitatsu—being useful

NOTES

Preface

1. Pseudonyms are used throughout the book where appropriate. For formal interviews and focus group interviews, I presented a consent form and asked my interlocutors to sign the document beforehand. For more impromptu participant observation, I constantly reminded interlocutors of my research projects so that they could make their own decision about the nature of our conversations. Some wrote or spoke to me afterward requesting that I exclude their conversation from my research notes. I deleted those notes.

2. All Japanese words and conversations are translated into English by the author.

3. The term *rokaru* or "the locals" cannot, of course, stand for the diverse inhabitants of Kuala Lumpur. Yet it was the term that my interlocutors used to refer to Malaysian people whom they encountered. Hence, I use the term "the locals" in this book simply as an analytic category to discuss the dynamics of encounters between Japanese retirees and Malaysian neighbors.

Introduction

1. My interlocutors' use of terms that have been adopted from English, for instance, *shiruba bakkupakka* (silver backpackers), *waifu* (wife), and *mentaru haamonii* (mental harmony) are consciously left in this book.

2. This vignette was originally included in a journal article, "Ageing with Bad-Boy Charm: An Affective Analysis of Japanese Retirement Migration in Malaysia" in *Japanese Review of Cultural Anthropology* (Shakuto 2017, 169).

3. The retirement (*teinen*) system in Japan was set up during the Meiji period (1868–1912) for the army and navy officers, and it was later expanded to apply to officers in public service, manufacturing sectors, and banks before the war (Sekizawa 2003, 22–28). After World War II, due to the oversupply of labor from returned soldiers, the retirement system spread rapidly among private companies to manage the workforce. By 1955, almost all companies had adopted the retirement system for their employees (Sekizawa 2003, 28).

4. The definition of "the elderly" itself varies when one compares it cross culturally and highlights its religious and social meanings. According to the United Nations, the definition of the elderly applies to those above the age of sixty-five. In Japan, the sixty-first year after birth is celebrated as the marker of maturity as it denotes the entry into the *kanreki* period when the traditional Chinese calendar of sixty years resets itself (Izuhara 2006, 162). Socially, the moment could be when one becomes a grandparent.

5. *Dankai no sedai* usually refers to those who were born between 1947 and 1949.

6. Japanese-style management system shifted to create labor conditions that flexibly adjust to fluctuating demand in the service economy and economic externalities (Takeyama 2016, 7). In 2001, more than 40 percent of working men and women aged fifteen to twenty-four years were

working either part-time or in short-term contracts with much lower incomes than full-time employees (Rebick and Takenaka 2006, 9).

7. Given the socially constructed nature of aging, in this book, I use the term "seniors" as at once both a fixed and a fluid category. My usage points both to the ways in which they are labelled as such, especially after retirement from the labor market, and to the fact that such individuals view it as a subjective state of being—and hence changeable.

8. Benson and O'Reilly (2009b, 611–13) further divided lifestyle migrants into three types, based on their motivations: "residential tourists" (seekers of coastal, relaxed lifestyles), "rural idyllic seekers" (seekers of rural, simple, countryside living and community), and "bourgeois bohemians" (seekers of spiritual and artistic lifestyles).

9. It can encompass the movement of people in a wide range of scales, from internal migrants, such as those who move from the colder U.S. and Canadian cities to warmer states like Florida (Bjelde and Sanders 2012) and to international migrants, such as those who move from the U.S. and Canada to Latin American countries. From North America to Mexico, see Morrison, et al. 2002; Croucher 2009; Lardiés-Bosque, et al. 2016. To Ecuador, see Hayes 2014; Miles 2015; Viteri 2015. To Panama, see Benson and O'Reilly 2018. To India, see Korpela 2020. From the U.K. and other North European countries to rural France, see Benson and Smith 2011; Benson 2012; Hoggart and Buller 1995. To Spain, see O'Reilly 2000; Casado-Díaz 2006; Oliver 2008. For Mediterranean regions, see Morrison, et al. 2002; King, et al. 2000; A. M. Williams, et al. 1997; Gustafson 2001; Åkerlund and Sandberg 2015.

10. More recently, scholars have paid attention to the movement of people from and within the Asian regions, including the internal migration between cities and international migration For instance, Chen and Bao 2020; Ono 2015a; Toyota and Thang 2017a; Thang, et al. 2012b; Kim 2016; Ho and Chiu 2020; Newendorp 2020.

11. The term neoliberalism is generally characterized by the post-1980s deregulation and privatization of public institutions (Berlant 2011, 192). Scholars such as Nikolas Rose have since erased analytic distinctions between the government of the state and the government of the self (Strakosch 2015, 36), arguing that the neoliberal state attempts to govern subjects "by reconstructing them as autonomous, economically productive, rational and competitive individuals" (Strakosch 2015, 37). Anthropologists have lent support to this view by providing ethnographies which show how the state and the self are closely intertwined in the neoliberal economy (Comaroff and Comaroff 2000; Greenhouse 2010; K. Z. Ho 2009; Eagleton-Pierce 2016). Carla Freeman (2014, 1), for instance, defines the key signpost of neoliberalism as the making of "the self as an entrepreneurial 'project' under constant renovation . . . and its perpetual quest for flexibility in the changing global marketplace." She observes that "in the contemporary neoliberal milieu every aspect of life is becoming subject to regimes of flexibility, quests, and commands for self-mastery and self-examination." The neoliberal society evidences the rise of liberal terms used in self-help manuals, such as "choice, responsibility, agreement and participation" which help to construct an image of an active and free subject (Strakosch 2015, 37–39).

12. The term "successful aging" was first introduced by two gerontologists, Rowe and Kahn, against the backdrop of the demographic crisis in the West in the late 1980s (Ramirez-Valles 2016, 17; Bülow and Holm 2016). Rowe and Kahn broadly set two requirements for successful aging: autonomy and social support (Ramirez-Valles 2016, 17). The first requirement encourages a sense of independence while the second encourages senior citizens to have social networks to fight decaying health. The literature on successful aging has proliferated in the last few decades. Gerontologists have since expanded this idea, arguing that older people must engage in "productive" activities (Ramirez-Valles 2016, 18). Anthropologists, who have been especially adept at illuminating how aging is constructed within wider socio-political structures (Fry 1984; Vesperi 1986; Lock 1993; Lynch and Danely 2013) started to critique the successful aging movement as a profoundly neoliberal ideal (Lamb 2014; Bury 1995). The successful aging paradigm "rests on

certain understandings of individualist, autonomous personhood, featuring a sense of individual control over one's own self and life" (Lamb 2017, xii). This might reflect a particular cultural conception of personhood.

13. The concept of successful aging has since had a wide appeal to senior citizens beyond North America. In Brazil, for example, individual health-promoting activities have become a central concern for the elderly (Brown 2013, 125). Likewise, in rapidly aging Singapore, many people above the age of seventy continue to work out of need or desire (Fischer 2015, 208; Kua 2014). Andrea Muehlebach (2012) offers a powerful critique of successful aging policies in Italy and calls a retiree who seeks self-fulfilment in community activities, "a moral neoliberal." According to her research in Italy, the neoliberal Italian state has relocated responsibilities for welfare and security to flexible and retrainable private individuals, such as retirees (Muehlebach 2012, 138). By volunteering their resources, retirees reenforce the neoliberal framework of the state by providing support in domains that should be the responsibility of the state (Muehlebach 2012, 140).

14. In an era in which global mobility is ever more accessible to a wider range of people, the enactment of neoliberal active subjecthood is increasingly performed across borders. Individuals from the Global North can move to the Global South to "escape the inconveniences of social structural transformations resulting from a severe economic crisis in developed societies" (Hayes and Pérez-Gañán 2017, 117). Hayes and Pérez-Gañán (2017) call it "geoarbitrage," which "is one way of fulfilling neoliberal cultural ideals of perfectly efficient markets, relocating lower-income older individuals from the Global North to geographic regions in the Global South where they can maximize the marginal utility of their consumer desires, reproducing the coloniality of inherited structural inequalities" (King, et al. 2021, 1212).

15. For the majority of Japanese retirees, there were limited interactions with local communities, and when there were, it was in a formal classroom setting, such as Malay language classes and the silver backpackers' excursions to the "local area" or the performance of Japan cultural activities at local schools.

16. Gustafson (2001, 391), who studied Swedish retirees in Spain, also observed that "the relatively privileged position of the winter residents made cultural adaptation an individual choice rather than a necessity."

17. In contrast to preceding generations, the baby boomers generation is marked by higher education, urbanisation, and consumption (Cabinet Office 2012b, 1).

18. In 2017, another acclaimed TV series produced a film, titled *Kazoku ha Tsuraiyo* (What a Wonderful Family!). Contrary to the upbeat title, the spousal relations in the drama fall apart when a husband asked his wife what she wanted for the fiftieth anniversary of their wedding. She asked for a divorce. The drama humorously chronicles the transformation in their relationship.

19. Cross-culturally, "the early sacrifices of motherhood are later rewarded with meaningful care [by others] in elderhood" (Livingston 2007, 166).

20. The other two miracles are: "a lower cost of living stretching one's pension," and "the ability of care services for one's own parents" (Sakamoto 2011). By going to Malaysia, the book advocates, one does not have to work during their retirement to supplement their pension. However, as I will show in this book, I found that the financial issue was less of a concern for my interlocutors who were from middle to upper-middle class backgrounds. Similarly, although it was true that many interlocutors still had living parents, very few of them came to Malaysia with them. Instead, when their aging parents needed care, the retirees were more likely to return to Japan to provide care there.

21. An increasing amount of scholarship has focused on geopolitical relations within Asia through intimate connections formed between Japanese and people from other Asian countries, such as Indonesian care workers and Japanese elderly (Switek 2016), Burmese aid workers and

Japanese NGOs (Watanabe 2019), and Chinese women marrying Japanese men through matchmaking agencies (Yamaura 2020). These scholars have demonstrated the everyday working of global capitalism and the remaking of Asia by providing nuanced ethnographies on intimate connections between "the local" and "the migrants" (Watanabe 2019, 64).

22. Feminist economic anthropologists have decentered related binaries, such as "productive and reproductive," "public and private" (M. Z. Rosaldo 1980), "market and family" (Ueno 2009), and "economic and affective" (Zelizer 2005; Yanagisako 2002). They classified the types of activities, roles, spaces, institutions, and attributes into gendered domains and argued that women have been incorporated into capitalist systems through their feminized labor practices.

23. Although one of LeBlanc's interlocutors viewed being a housewife as "only one of many roles that women might shoulder in a larger attempt to be a whole person," she also believed in "the importance of the rightness of a woman's role as 'traditional' housewife, dedicated first and foremost to maintenance of the home and family" (LeBlanc 1999, 47). It was this label which simultaneously constricted these women as well as bestowed them with collective political power. Hence LeBlanc argues that "housewife" seems to be the best word for conveying "what Japanese women understand they are saying about themselves when they call themselves shufu" (LeBlanc 1999, 30).

Chapter 1

1. The temporal signifiers arose in various sites including official state policies, schools, companies, neighborhoods, media and homes. For instance, postwar Prime Minister Katayama's campaign called for people to "work harder by bearing all present hardships with the idea of sacrificing the present for a better future" (Garon 1997, 164). One of the most symbolic aspects of the campaign was the use of clocks as symbols of rationality and efficiency (Garon 1997, 163). In 1947, the minister of education announced awards for citizens' public halls that had done the most to advance culture within their communities (Garon 1997, 164). The prize was a large community clock, which was considered essential to fostering a sense of respect for a time among the residents.

2. The Japanese state had always mobilized particular forms of gender, kinship, and emotional practices to advance its goals, from the Meiji Restoration to the introduction of capitalism in the 1920s to World War II and to the postwar high-growth era. The period before the Meiji Restoration also laid the foundations for many social and economic antecedents of contemporary practices. An edited volume by Nakane and Oishi (1990) provides a helpful analysis of some of these foundations.

3. In some cases, men married the daughter of the employer through omiai to become a legally recognized son-in-law and subsequently to succeed the company (Nakane 1970, 110).

4. For a scholarly work on single Japanese men who search for Filipina wives to achieve "maturity" in the eyes of their company, see Suzuki (2002).

5. Yet only girls had to attend the mandatory homemaking courses. This 1969 policy was only abolished in 1989 (Uno 1993, 306).

6. It was only in the late 1960s that the number of love marriages exceeded the number of arranged marriages (Tokuhiro 2010, 18). By 1996, the proportion of love marriages exceeded 85 percent (Tokuhiro 2010, 20).

7. From the 1890s to the 1920s, marriage was considered a practice of alliance-making between families, rather than between two persons. The Meiji Constitution of 1890 mandated the consent of parents for legal marriage (Tokuhiro 2010, 96). The love between the parties was antithetical to the ideal of filial piety and it was thus considered a disruptive, rebellious act against the family and the nation (Hendry 1981a, 16–24). During WWII, marriage continued to be arranged through omiai, and mate selection through love continued to be considered im-

moral, a sign of mental weakness (Hendry 1981, 24). After the war ended in 1945, the Allied Occupation enacted the new constitution enabling men and women to marry without the consent of their parents (Tokuhiro 2010, 18).

8. In addition to the tax system, even the Labor Standards Law that was intended to benefit women had the effect of restricting women from working to the same extent as men. Originally enacted to protect women from exploitation (Broadbent 2003, 95), the law placed limits on overtime and bans on night work. However, in doing so, it allowed employers to use these rules to exclude women from higher managerial positions (Broadbent 2003, 95). Moreover, the law was based on the assumption that it would protect women's reproductive functions when it was found that some women preferred to work at night so that their husbands could look after their children (Broadbent 2003, 95).

9. Unlike the Meiji Constitution which placed the emperor as granting limited rights to people, the post-World War II Constitution granted citizens inalienable rights (Mackie 2003, 128). The emperor renounced his own divinity in 1946 and the teaching of the Shinto religion was banned in schools (Hendry 1981, 27). The Imperial Rescript, which taught the virtues of loyalty to the emperor and filial piety, was withdrawn and replaced with moral education in the basic principles of democracy (Hendry 1981, 27).

10. A more detailed elaboration of the shifting Japanese aging policies was published in a journal article, "An independent and mutually supportive retirement as a moral ideal in contemporary Japan" in *The Australian Journal of Anthropology* (Shakuto 2018b).

11. The nineteenth-century ideology of "good wife, wise mother" was used repeatedly during World War II when men were conscripted and women remained at home. The family became the crucible of feminine duty as women supported the nation through thrift campaigns (Dales 2009, 14). Women were also called "the mothers of the nation" (*nihon no haha*) (Mackie 2003, 110–11) and the war-time slogan, *umeyo fuyaseyo* (produce and multiply), encouraged women to produce more children while also taking part in productive activities, such as farming, to support the household under the conditions of rationing, or as factory workers in the mines or the munitions industry (Mackie 2003, 113).

12. While the government may have coined the new system, "Japanese style welfare," it is important to note that the influence of religious moral values on a family-oriented welfare system was hardly unique to Japan. The Confucianism of the Japanese state and the Catholicism of the Italian state, both of which are frequently represented as "familist" welfare states (Trifiletti 2006, 177), make them apt for a comparison (Rebick and Takenaka 2006, 13). The Italian state has used the rhetoric of *gratuità* and *solidarietà*, which resonates with the country's deeply held Catholic traditions, to encourage unremunerated voluntary labor as the country's welfare schemes are dismantled (Muehlebach 2012; Muehlebach 2009, 504). Bettio (2006, 65) noted that the welfare safety nets for those who were unable to earn an independent living hardly existed in Italy as the family was expected to provide for them. Italy recorded the highest rate of young people living with their parents for all age groups and the lowest rate of female employment in the EU in 2003 (Bettio 2006, 61). It also recorded the lowest rate of divorce and single-parent households (Bettio 2006, 57).

13. It was common for elite sarariiman to be sent to other cities or even overseas to work in branch offices for a year or more. To avoid disruption to their children's education, most men went on these missions alone (*tanshin funin*) leaving behind women to look after their children in Japan. This was even more so for overseas transfers because of the stigma attached to children growing up overseas as becoming unfit for Japanese society (R. Goodman 1993). Many women felt the anxiety of raising a family alone. Ueno (1994, 236) cites the rising numbers baby killings among younger mothers who felt pressure from society in the 1970s.

14. From a young age, the Japanese school system lays an important training ground to inculcate the value of inter-dependence (Cave 2016). By sharing space and time together, the child

develops great familiarity and affinity with their classmates and the teacher (Duke 1986, 25–49). On the first day of elementary school, every child is allocated his or her *kumi* (class) with an assigned teacher (*tannin no sensei*). The teacher will teach different subjects to the same group of students for a year, but neither the class nor the teacher changes room for different subjects. Each class has thirty to forty students and each student is assigned a desk and sits at that same desk for all subjects for months at a time. Even lunch is had at the same desk in a smaller group of *han*, that is, a group of five or six students who sit near each other. Children are also encouraged by their peers and teachers to *ganbaru*, which is to persevere and overcome the difficulties that they face in their young lives (Duke 1986, 121–147).

15. The suicide of a young worker from Dentsu, one of the largest advertising companies in Japan in late 2016, sparked debates over karoushi and corporate exploitation.

16. In contrast with white-collar sarariiman who spent much time doing unpaid overtime, blue-collar male workers tended to have more discretionary time after working hours. Hence some of them spent more time at home doing housework and playing with children (Roberts 2014, 39).

17. The summary of this ethnographic vignette was published in "An independent and mutually supportive retirement as a moral ideal in contemporary Japan" in *The Australian Journal of Anthropology* (Shakuto 2018b, 188).

18. Similarly in a popular movie *The Lunchbox*, an Indian man on the verge of his retirement reconsidered his decision to meet his younger lover when he smelled the scent of his grandfather on himself.

19. In addition to financial reasons, in 2015, 40 percent of men responded that they felt ikigai while working.

20. The retirement age had been raised gradually, from fifty-five to sixty years in 1998, to sixty-one in 2013, and to sixty-two in 2016.

21. In 2021, the act was modified to mandate that employers provide a setting in which people can work up to the age of 70.

22. Costs, benefits, pensionable ages, and other provisions of pension schemes differ substantially across various population groups (Campbell 1992, 11). The largest program is the Employee Pension System (*Kosei Nenkin*), which covers most private and public employees (Campbell 1992, 11). Others, such as farmers, shopkeepers, and other self-employed workers, are on the National Pension System (*Kokumin Nenkin*), and only receive nominal amounts (Campbell 1992, 11–12).

23. Fewer women work in their old age. Glenda Roberts (1996, 126) writes that one of the reasons for this gender disparity is the younger generation's reluctance to have their mothers work outside the home as it is seen to reflect badly on the family.

24. The establishment of these universities was based on the Life-long Learning Promotion Act (1990).

25. Men who retired at the age of sixty in 2014 were on average expected to live for another 23.36 years, and women another 28.68 years (Ministry of Health, Labor, and Welfare of Japan 2015).

Interlude

1. This interlude was originally included in "Postwork Intimacy: Negotiating Romantic Partnerships Among Japanese Retired Couples in Malaysia," *American Ethnologist* (Shakuto 2019a).

Chapter 2

1. The 10th Malaysia Plan suggests promoting "differentiated strategies to cater for unique and distinctive travel patterns and needs such as for nature adventure (including ecotourism), cultural diversity, family fun, affordable luxury, and meetings, incentives, conferences and exhibitions" (10MP, 128).

2. According to Rudnyckyj (2019, 29), this push for Islamization reflected the critique by the Islamic opposition political party PAS against the then-ruling party UMNO (Mahathir's party) of catering to non-Malay population and foreign business interests. This has pushed UMNO to a deeper embrace of Islam.

3. These companies include Mitsubishi Corporation, Mitsui & Company Ltd., Itochu & Company Ltd., Sumitomo Corporation, Marubeni Corporation, and Nissho Iwai Corporation (Dauvergne 1997).

4. Furuoka (2007, 510), who studied the bilateral relationship between Japan and Malaysia during Mahthir's administration, shows that a loan of $127 million was provided to enable 1,400 Malaysians to study in Japan and a loan of $75 million was allocated for scholarships for 440 Malaysian engineering and science students in 1998 and 1999.

5. Applicants under this program were not allowed to work and were required to deposit 150,000 Malaysian ringgit in Malaysian banks (Ono 2015a, 618).

6. Other major nationalities include Bangladeshis (4,135), British (2,691), South Korean (2,378), and Singaporeans (1,459).

7. A popular movie, *Hula Girls*, was produced in 2006 to tell the stories of how this resort came about in 1966.

8. Yet Japanese retirees consistently ranked Malaysia as the most popular retirement destination (Yamada 2013; Ono 2015a, 617).

9. The average income of female employees didn't vary across the age group (National Tax Agency 2015, 18). It is possibly because many of them were employed part-time.

10. An older suburb of Taman Desa which was nearer to the city centre used to house many Japanese expatriate households, but when Mont Kiara was developed, expatriate families moved to Mont Kiara. Some retirees then started to move into Taman Desa to enjoy the cheaper rent. Even then, Mont Kiara was still the most popular area for retirees.

11. Around the world, it is not an uncommon practice to develop real estate to attract foreign direct investment through appeal to the "residential tourist" population (van Noorloos 2011). The land in the Global South has become the dream "global commodity" for retirees from the Global North to consume (McCarthy 2008; Viteri 2015).

12. Scholars have documented the displacement, segregation, and marginalization of local populations in locations including Costa Rica (Haas and Janoschka 2014; van Noorloos 2011), Mexico (Torres and Momsen 2005), and Panama (McWatters 2008; M. C. Benson 2013, 315; Spalding 2013).

13. There are no official records of the Japanese invasion into this part of Kuala Lumpur. Many sites of war atrocities and mass graves remain relatively unknown (Tay 2015, 221).

14. There were two important exceptions. One of them was a real estate agent who assisted mainly Japanese people in finding their homes. These Japanese in turn referred her to each other. Being the only "local" that Japanese people knew, this agent began to assume more than the role of a real estate agent as she was regularly called in by Japanese seniors seeking to settle administrative matters in government offices. Another person owned a beauty salon. She could speak Japanese so Japanese women referred her salon to each other. An avid ballroom dancer herself, the second agent began to be invited to the Japan Cultural Center's ballroom parties too.

15. For example, a social welfare publication published pictures of a woman in a white apron with a bank note to encourage people to save for the family (Garon 1997, 185).

16. A history of feminism in Japan stretches back at least to the 1870s when several prominent feminist activists were nurtured in the movement for democratization (*jiyu minken undo*) in the 1870s and 1880s (Mackie 2003, 1).

17. *Shufu no Tomo* (Housewife's Companion), a magazine that first appeared in 1917 and remained popular until 2008, also featured kakeibo, with tips on how to save and economize in the home (Garon 1997, 233). From the 1960s to the 1980s, more than half of households reported that they recorded the details of family finances in these account books (Garon 1997, 271–273).

18. The financial reliance on women was so complete that some men did not even know the ATM pin needed to access their earnings (Borovoy 2005, 105).

19. Although contemplating the significance of plastics for Japanese women is outside this book's scope, Joy Hendry, in her *Wrapping Culture* (1993), compares and contrasts the use of plastics in the U.K. and Japan. In the U.K., as one moves up the social class ladder, they use less plastic. But in Japan, she observes, people entertain guests with coffee, sugar, and milk wrapped in plastic. In Japan, in contrast to in the U.K., wrapping things in plastic is considered refined and polite. Perhaps cling wrap holds special cultural significance to Japanese people.

Chapter 3

1. Japanese songs included, for instance, "Amairo No Kamino Otome," "Makka na Taiyo," "Minato no Sindobatto," "Sotsugyou Shashin," and "Yesterday Once More."

2. This was in 2014. When I returned in 2015, the fee had been raised to MYR 70 per person.

3. I only knew two Malaysian people who joined other Japanese; one of them was an owner of a massage parlor which was frequented by Japanese residents because she spoke Japanese, and another was a partner of a Japanese male retiree.

4. This vignette was originally included in "Ageing with Bad-Boy Charm: An Affective Analysis of Japanese Retirement Migration in Malaysia," in *Japanese Review of Cultural Anthropology* (Shakuto 2017, 169).

5. The longer version of this vignette was originally included in "Ageing with Bad-Boy Charm" (Shakuto 2017, 167–168).

6. The analysis of the Cabinet Office report was first published in "An Independent and Mutually Supportive Retirement as a Moral Ideal in Contemporary Japan," in *Australian Journal of Anthropology* (Shakuto 2018b, 188–190).

7. The average monthly household income for Malaysian citizens living in Kuala Lumpur was MYR 7,620 (around USD 1,870) in 2014 (Department of Statistics Malaysia 2015a).

8. Both exceeded the average monthly pension which was around 177,970 yen (around USD 1,590) in the same year (Ministry of Internal Affairs and Communications of Japan 2016).

9. This story of Mich was originally included in "Ageing with Bad-Boy Charm" (Shakuto 2017, 164–66).

10. Across the globe, more and more single women are migrating overseas in their retirement (Gambold 2013). Migration has empowering effects on single women as it allows them to break from gender norms (Hayes 2021, 1228) and "age unencumbered by the past and the expectations others held for them in the future" (Gambold 2013, 194).

Chapter 4

1. This ethnographic vignette was originally included as a journal article, "Postwork Intimacy: Negotiating Romantic Partnerships Among Japanese Retired Couples in Malaysia" in *American Ethnologist* (Shakuto 2019a, 306)

2. Journalists offer a sensational view of older migrants, particularly men, who could not support themselves with their limited pensions in their home countries, searching for cheaper lifestyles and, in many cases, intimacy with younger women in their destinations. This view is particularly present in writings on retirement migration to Southeast Asia, especially Thailand. Scholars have provided a more nuanced analysis of the relationships between older male migrants and younger local women (Howard 2008; Lafferty and Maher 2020; Scuzzarello 2020).

3. Even though younger couples are said to desire a companionate relationship, Emma Cook (2014) observed that there was a gender difference. While both the young women and men whom she interviewed did look for their partners based on shared interests and hobbies, when it came to marriage, women tended to continue to seek companionship as an important aspect of their married lives while men tended to revert back to an older ideology of responsibility. She observed anxieties among young couples whose expectations of their marital relationships were not equally matched.

4. In 1983, housewives who faced impossible pressures to work and simultaneously care for others formed the Women's Committee for the Betterment of Ageing Society (WCBAS). They set out to mobilize women around the issues of the family's care burden. They critiqued the state's welfare policy that relied heavily on women's unpaid labor (Peng 2002).

Chapter 5

1. Scholars on Asian retirement migration tend to place family as the central focus of their investigations (Chen and Bao 2021; Sergeant and Ekerdt 2008; Sun 2021; Newendorp 2020). Many senior migrants from Asia moved to unite with children and relatives who lived in the migration destinations (Chen and Bao 2021; E. L.-E. Ho and Chiu 2020). In cases where the retirees left their children behind, scholars focused on how migrants maintained and reproduced intergenerational and familial relations from a distance (Chen and Bao 2021, 2773). In their study of seasonal retirement migration of Chinese people within China, for instance, Chen and Bao (2021, 2762) observed that retirement migrants seldom severed connections with family members after relocation. At the same time, mobilities inevitably subverted entrenched familial ties and social relations in the original countries (Chen and Bao 2021, 2762). This stimulates the transformation of family practices and relations among transnational retirees (Åkerlund and Sandberg 2015).

2. A summary of the reasons was published in "An Independent and Mutually Supportive Retirement as a Moral Ideal in Contemporary Japan," *Australian Journal of Anthropology* (Shakuto 2018b, 186–87).

3. Indeed, a growing number of young Japanese families were migrating to Malaysia at the time of my fieldwork, 2014–2016. For more about the lives of those who fled the threat of radiation after the Fukushima nuclear disaster, see Shakuto 2018a; Shakuto 2019b; Shakuto 2022.

4. This vignette was originally included in "Postwork Intimacy: Negotiating Romantic Partnerships Among Japanese Retired Couples in Malaysia" in *American Ethnologist* (Shakuto 2019a, 307).

5. Garcia (2016, 89) used a blog as a method in his study of underground music scenes in Paris. He kept a record of his observations on his blog site. In the article reflecting on this methodology, he notes that his blog can also be seen as "a trove of lost letters: missives sent to distant friends, local collaborators, myself, and an intimate public of strangers" (Garcia 2016, 89). Gar-

cia also notes that the blog can be used as a "primary source" for history, capturing the record of early twenty-first-century music scenes.

6. There was another speculative reason why this condominium complex had so many retired residents. It had become infamous among the Japanese after a young Japanese expatriate couple was electrocuted to death by a faulty water heater in 2013 (The Star Online 2013). Although the rest of the nation seemed to have quickly forgotten the incident, it stayed in the collective memory of the expatriate Japanese community. There was a large poster on a prominent wall of the Japan Cultural Club warning members to check their water heaters regularly. Every retiree I met told me the story of the dead couple upon noticing that I too lived in the Mont Kiara district. After the incident, the property value of the condominiums declined as fewer young expatriates were willing to stay there. Instead, retirees began to move into the same condominium in order to enjoy lower rents.

7. In her fieldwork in the Trobriands, Weiner (1992, x–xi) paid attention to banana leaf bundles, human hair strings, faded pieces of cloth, and old plaited mats to theorize social and political relationships between women and men. By showing that women's banana leaf wealth equaled men's kula wealth, Weiner brought women into the heart of the political process of reproduction.

8. The shorter version of this vignette was originally included in "Postwork Intimacy" (Shakuto 2019a, 308).

Chapter 6

1. Within two years of his return to prime ministership, Mahathir Mohamad was replaced by Muhyiddin Yassin in what was allegedly a "political coup" that occurred in early 2020.

2. During the corporate gift-giving practices, women as mothers and wives assisted their husbands in fulfilling their gift-giving obligations. The women were "responsible for selecting and sending appropriate gifts to other women in order to facilitate and soften relationships between men" (Daniels 2009, 390). Preferred gifts were perishable objects, such as food and drinks, or utilitarian objects that could be used up, such as cooking oils, washing powders, and cleaning detergents (Daniels 2009, 389; Rupp 2003, 59). In considering why perishable objects were preferred, Daniels (2009, 389) argues that it is because it is considered inappropriate to burden the superior with something enduring. Additionally, I suggest that it might also be because it was women who were behind the circulation of gifts. As managers of homes which are not always spacious, it is understandable why they preferred gifts that "do not leave a trace in the home" (Daniels 2009, 391).

3. This vignette was originally included in "Postwork Intimacy: Negotiating Romantic Partnerships Among Japanese Retired Couples in Malaysia" in *American Ethnologist* (Shakuto 2019a, 309).

4. The Tokyo Olympic Games 2020 was postponed to 2021 due to the Covid-19 pandemic.

REFERENCES

Abdul-Aziz, Abdul-Rashid , J. H. M. Tah, J. X. Lim, and Cheng-Lit Loh. 2015. "Government Initiatives to Attract Retired Migrants: An Analysis of Malaysia's My Second Home (MM2H) Programme." *Tourism Management Perspectives* 16 (October): 58–66. https://doi.org/10 .1016/j.tmp.2015.07.004.

Abdul-Aziz, Abdul-Rashid, Cheng-Lit Loh, and Mastura Jaafar. 2014. "Malaysia's My Second Home (MM2H) Programme: An Examination of Malaysia as a Destination for International Retirees." *Tourism Management* 40 (February): 203–12. https://doi.org/10.1016/j .tourman.2013.06.008.

Åkerlund, Ulrika, and Linda Sandberg. 2015. "Stories of Lifestyle Mobility: Representing Self and Place in the Search for the 'Good Life.'" *Social & Cultural Geography* 16 (3): 351–70. https://doi.org/10.1080/14649365.2014.987806.

Alexander, M. Jacqui, and Chandra Talpade Mohanty. 2012. *Feminist Genealogies, Colonial Legacies, Democratic Futures*. Thinking Gender. New York: Routledge. https://doi.org/10.4324 /9780203724200.

Alexy, Allison. 2020. *Intimate Disconnections: Divorce and the Romance of Independence in Contemporary Japan*. Chicago: University of Chicago Press.

Alexy, Allison, and Emma E. Cook. 2019. *Intimate Japan: Ethnographies of Closeness and Conflict*. Honolulu: University of Hawaii Press.

Allison, Anne. 1994. *Nightwork: Sexuality, Pleasure, and Corporate Masculinity in a Tokyo Hostess Club*. Chicago: University of Chicago Press.

———. 2013. *Precarious Japan*. Durham, NC: Duke University Press.

Anderson, Benedict. 2016. *Imagined Communities: Reflections on the Origin and Spread of Nationalism*. Revised edition. London: Verso.

Anderson, Clare. 2019. *Discourses of Ageing and Gender: The Impact of Public and Private Voices on the Identity of Ageing Women*. Houndsmills, UK: Palgrave Macmillan. https://doi.org/10 .1007/978-3-319-96740-0.

Arber, Sara. 2004. "Gender, Marital Status, and Ageing: Linking Material, Health, and Social Resources." *Journal of Aging Studies*, New Directions in Feminist Gerontology, 18 (1): 91–108. https://doi.org/10.1016/j.jaging.2003.09.007.

Arber, Sara, Lars Andersson, and Andreas Hoff. 2007. "Changing Approaches to Gender and Ageing: Introduction." *Current Sociology* 55 (2): 147–53. https://doi.org/10.1177/0011392107073298.

Arber, Sara, Kate Davidson, and Jay Ginn. 2003. *Gender and Ageing: Changing Roles and Relationships*. Maidenhead: McGraw-Hill Education (UK).

Arber, Sara, and Jay Ginn. 1995a. "Choice and Constraint in the Retirement of Older Married Women." In *Connecting Gender and Ageing: A Sociological Approach*, edited by Jay Ginn and Sara Arber, 69–86. Buckingham, UK: Open University Press.

———. 1995b. *Connecting Gender and Ageing: A Sociological Approach*. Buckingham, UK: Open University Press.

Ardener, Edwin. 1972. "Belief and the Problem of Women." In *The Interpretation of Ritual: Essays in Honour of A.I. Richards*, edited by J.S. La Fontaine. London: Tavistock.

Asahi Shimbun. 2014. "Growing Old with Dignity in Japan's Graying Society." *Asahi Shimbun*, August 5, 2014. http://ajw.asahi.com/article/views/vox/AJ201408050035. Accessed 11 April 2024.

Baksh, Rawwida, and Wendy Harcourt. 2015. *The Oxford Handbook of Transnational Feminist Movements*. Oxford Handbooks in Politics & International Relations. New York: Oxford University Press. https://doi.org/10.1093/oxfordhb/9780199943494.001.0001.

Baldassar, Loretta. 2001. *Visits Home: Migration Experiences Between Italy and Australia*. Victoria, AU: Melbourne University Press.

Ball, Christopher, and Shunsuke Nozawa. 2016. "Tearful Sojourns and Tribal Wives: Primitivism, Kinship, Suffering, and Salvation on Japanese and British Reality Television." *American Ethnologist* 43 (2): 243–57.

Bardsley, Jan. 2011. "The *Oyaji* Gets a Makeover: Guides for Japanese Salarymen in the New Millennium." In *Manners and Mischief: Gender, Power, and Etiquette in Japan*, edited by Jan Bardsley and Laura Miller, 114–35. Berkeley: University of California Press.

Barrett, Michele. 1989. *Women's Oppression Today: The Marxist/Feminist Encounter*. Revised edition. London: Verso.

Basic Law on Measures for the Aging Society, L. No.129. (1995).

Basu, Amrita, and C. Elizabeth McGrory. 1995. *The Challenge of Local Feminisms: Women's Movements in Global Perspective*. Social Change in Global Perspective. Boulder, CO: Westview Press.

Beauvoir, Simone de. 1972. *The Coming of Age*. New York: Putnam.

Benson, Michaela. 2012. "How Culturally Significant Imaginings are Translated into Lifestyle Migration." *Journal of Ethnic and Migration Studies* 38 (10): 1681–96. https://doi.org/10.1080/1369183X.2012.711067.

———. 2013. "Postcoloniality and Privilege in New Lifestyle Flows: The Case of North Americans in Panama." *Mobilities* 8 (3): 313–30. https://doi.org/10.1080/17450101.2013.810403.

———. 2015. "Class, Race, Privilege: Structuring the Lifestyle Migrant Experience in Boquete, Panama." *Journal of Latin American Geography* 14 (1): 19–37. https://doi.org/10.1353/lag.2015.0009.

Benson, Michaela, and Karen O'Reilly. 2009a. *Lifestyle Migration Expectations, Aspirations and Experiences*. Farnham, UK: Ashgate.

———. 2009b. "Migration and the Search for a Better Way of Life: A Critical Exploration of Lifestyle Migration." *Sociological Review* 57 (4): 608–25.

———. 2018. *Lifestyle Migration and Colonial Traces in Malaysia and Panama*. Migration, Diasporas and Citizenship. Houndsmills, UK: Palgrave Macmillan. https://doi.org/10.1057/978-1-137-51158-4.

Benson, Michaela, and Alexander Smith. 2011. *The British in Rural France: Lifestyle Migration and the Ongoing Quest for a Better Way of Life*. Manchester, UK: Manchester University Press.

Berlant, Lauren. 2011. *Cruel Optimism*. Durham, NC: Duke University Press.

Bettio, Francesca. 2006. "Strong in Tradition and yet Innovative: The Puzzles of the Italian Family." In *The Changing Japanese Family*, edited by Marcus Rebick and Ayumi Takenaka, 54–71. Abingdon, UK: Routledge.

Bjelde, Kristine E., and Gregory F. Sanders. 2012. "Change and Continuity: Experiences of Midwestern Snowbirds." *Journal of Applied Gerontology* 31 (3): 314–35. https://doi.org/10.1177/0733464810386223.

Blackburn, Kevin. 2009. "Recalling War Trauma of the Pacific War and the Japanese Occupation in the Oral History of Malaysia and Singapore." *Oral History Review* 36 (2): 231–52.

Bofulin, Martina, and Jamie Coates. 2017. "Bakugai! Explosive Shopping and Entangled Sino-Japanese Mobilities." *Anthropology News* 58 (1): 275–78. https://doi.org/10.1111/AN.314.

Bolognani, Marta. 2014. "The Emergence of Lifestyle Reasoning in Return Considerations among British Pakistanis." *International Migration* 52 (6): 31–42. https://doi.org/10.1111/imig.12153.

Bolzman, Claudio, Rosita Fibbi, and Marie Vial. 2006. "What to Do After Retirement? Elderly Migrants and the Question of Return." *Journal of Ethnic and Migration Studies* 32 (8): 1359–75.

Borovoy, Amy. 2005. *The Too-Good Wife: Alcohol, Codependency, and the Politics of Nurturance in Postwar Japan.* Berkeley: University of California Press.

———. 2010. "Japan as Mirror: Neoliberalism's Promise and Costs." In *Ethnographies of Neoliberalism*, edited by Carol Greenhouse, 60–76. Philadelphia: University of Pennsylvania Press.

Bourdieu, Pierre. 1984. *Distinction: A Social Critique of the Judgement of Taste.* London: Routledge and Kegan Paul.

Brinton, Mary C. 1993. *Women and the Economic Miracle: Gender and Work in Postwar Japan.* California Series on Social Choice and Political Economy 21. Berkeley: University of California Press.

Broadbent, Kaye. 2003. *Women's Employment in Japan: The Experience of Part-Time Workers.* ASAA Women in Asia Series. London: Routledge Curzon.

Brown, Diana. 2013. "'I Have to Stay Healthy': Elder Caregiving and the Third Age in a Brazilian Community." In *Transitions and Transformations: Cultural Perspectives on Aging and the Life Course*, edited by Caitrin Lynch and Jason Danley, 123–36. New York: Berghahn Books.

Browne, Colette V. 1998. *Women, Feminism, and Aging.* New York: Springer Pub Co.

Bui, Huong T, Hugh Wilkins, and Young-Sook Lee. 2014. "Liminal Experience of East Asian Backpackers." *Tourist Studies* 14 (2): 126–43. https://doi.org/10.1177/1468797614532179.

Bülow, Morten Hillgaard, and Marie-Louise Holm. 2016. "Queering 'Successful Ageing': Dementia and Alzheimer's Research." *Body & Society* 22 (3): 77–102.

Bury, Mike. 1995. "Ageing, Gender and Sociological Theory." In *Connecting Gender and Ageing: A Sociological Approach*, edited by Jay Ginn and Sara Arber, 15–29. Buckingham, UK: Open University Press.

Butcher, Melissa, and Selvaraj Velayutham. 2009. *Dissent and Cultural Resistance in Asia's Cities.* Abingdon, UK: Routledge.

Butler, Gareth, and Kevin Hannam. 2014. "Performing Expatriate Mobilities in Kuala Lumpur." *Mobilities* 9 (1): 1–20.

Cabinet Office. 2012a. "Discussion Report on the Measures for an Aging Society: Towards a Dignified Independence and Mutual Support (*Koureishakai Taisaku No Kihonteki Arikatatou Ni Kansuru Kentoukai Houkokusho: Songen Aru Jiritsu to Sasaeai Wo Mezashite*)." Tokyo: Cabinet Office. http://www8.cao.go.jp/kourei/kihon-kentoukai/pdf/report1-1.pdf. Accessed 11 April 2024.

———. 2012b. "Report on the Opinions Held by the Dankai Sedai." Tokyo: Cabinet Office. http://www8.cao.go.jp/kourei/ishiki/h24/kenkyu/gaiyo/pdf/kekka.pdf. Accessed 11 April 2024.

———. 2013. "Report on the Elderly Community Participation." Tokyo: Cabinet Office. http://www8.cao.go.jp/kourei/ishiki/h25/sougou/gaiyo/pdf/kekka1.pdf. Accessed 11 April 2024.

———. 2014. "Public Opinion regarding Women's Participation." Government Report. Tokyo: Cabinet Office. http://survey.gov-online.go.jp/h26/h26-joseikatsuyaku/gairyaku.pdf. Accessed 11 April 2024.

———. 2015. "Annual Report on the Aging Society." Tokyo: Cabinet Office. http://www8.cao.go.jp/kourei/whitepaper/w-2016/gaiyou/28pdf_indexg.html. Accessed 11 April 2024.

———. 2016. "White Paper on the Ageing Society." Tokyo: Cabinet Office. http://www8.cao.go.jp/kourei/whitepaper/w-2016/gaiyou/28pdf_indexg.html. Accessed 11 April 2024.

Calasanti, Toni. 2004. "New Directions in Feminist Gerontology: An Introduction." *Journal of Aging Studies*, New Directions in Feminist Gerontology, 18 (1): 1–8. https://doi.org/10.1016/j.jaging.2003.09.002.

Calasanti, Toni, and Neal King. 2017. "Successful Aging, Ageism, and the Maintenance of Age and Gender Relations." In *Successful Aging as a Contemporary Obsession: Global Perspectives*, edited by Sarah Lamb, 27–40. New Brunswick, NJ: Rutgers University Press.

Calasanti, Toni, and Kathleen Slevin. 2001. *Gender, Social Inequalities, and Aging*. NY: AltaMira Press.

Campbell, John Creighton. 1992. *How Policies Change: The Japanese Government and the Aging Society*. Princeton, NJ: Princeton University Press.

Carmel, Sara. 2019. "Health and Well-Being in Late Life: Gender Differences Worldwide." *Frontiers in Medicine* 6 (218): 1–11. https://doi.org/10.3389/fmed.2019.00218.

Carroll, Tessa. 2006. "Changing Language, Gender and Family Relations in Japan." In *The Changing Japanese Family*, edited by Marcus Rebick and Ayumi Takenaka, 109–26. Abingdon, UK: Routledge.

Casado-Díaz, María Angeles. 2006. "Retiring to Spain: An Analysis of Differences among North European Nationals." *Journal of Ethnic and Migration Studies* 32 (8): 1321–39. https://doi.org/10.1080/13691830600928714.

Cave, Peter. 2016. *Schooling Selves: Autonomy, Interdependence, and Reform in Japanese Junior High Education*. Chicago: University of Chicago Press.

Cerase, Francesco P. 1974. "Expectations and Reality: A Case Study of Return Migration from the United States to Southern Italy." *International Migration Review* 8 (2): 245–62. https://doi.org/10.2307/3002783.

Chen, Jingfu, and Jigang Bao. 2021. "Chinese 'Snowbirds' in Tropical Sanya: Retirement Migration and the Production of Translocal Families." *Journal of Ethnic and Migration Studies* 47 (12): 2760–77. https://doi.org/10.1080/1369183X.2020.1739377.

Chowdhury, Elora Halim, and Liz Philipose. 2016. *Dissident Friendships: Feminism, Imperialism, and Transnational Solidarity*. Dissident Feminisms. Urbana : University of Illinois Press.

Chu, Julie Y. 2010. *Cosmologies of Credit: Transnational Mobility and the Politics of Destination in China*. Durham, NC: Duke University Press.

Classen, Constance, David Howes, and Anthony Synnott. 1994. *Aroma: The Cultural History of Smell*. London: Routledge.

Coe, Cati. 2022. *Changes in Care: Aging, Migration, and Social Class in West Africa*. Global Perspectives on Aging. New Brunswick, NJ: Rutgers University Press,. https://doi.org/10.36019/9781978823280.

Cohen, Erik. 2003. "Backpacking: Diversity and Change." *Journal of Tourism and Cultural Change* 1 (2): 95–110. https://doi.org/10.1080/14766820308668162.

Cole, Jennifer, and Deborah Lynn Durham. 2007. *Generations and Globalization: Youth, Age, and Family in the New World Economy*. Bloomington: Indiana University Press.

Cole, Jennifer, and Lynn M Thomas. 2009. *Love in Africa*. Chicago: The University of Chicago Press.

Comaroff, Jean, and John Comaroff. 2000. "Millennial Capitalism: First Thoughts on a Second Coming." *Public Culture* 12 (2): 291–343.

Constable, Nicole. 2003. *Romance on a Global Stage: Pen Pals, Virtual Ethnography, and "Mail-Order" Marriages*. Berkeley: University of California Press.

Cook, Emma E. 2014. "Intimate Expectations and Practices: Freeter Relationships and Marriage in Contemporary Japan." *Asian Anthropology* 13 (1): 36–51. https://doi.org/10.1080/1683478X.2014.883120.

Creighton, Millie R. 1995. "Imaging the Other in Japanese Advertising Campaigns." In *Occidentalism: Images of the West*, 135–60. Oxford: Clarendon Press.

Croucher, Sheila L. 2009. *The Other Side of the Fence: American Migrants in Mexico*. Austin: University of Texas Press.

Dales, Laura. 2009. *Feminist Movements in Contemporary Japan*. Asian Studies Association of Australia Women in Asia Series. Abingdon, UK: Routledge.

Daniels, Inge. 2009. "The 'Social Death' of Unused Gifts: Surplus and Value in Contemporary Japan." *Journal of Material Culture* 14 (3): 385–408.

———. 2015. "Feeling at Home in Contemporary Japan: Space, Atmosphere and Intimacy." *Emotion, Space and Society* 15 (May): 47–55.

Dauvergne, Peter. 1997. *Shadows in the Forest: Japan and the Politics of Timber in Southeast Asia*. Cambridge, MA: MIT Press.

Davidoff, Leonore, and Catherine Hall. 2013. *Family Fortunes: Men and Women of the English Middle Class 1780–1850*. Abingdon, UK: Routledge.

Dekker, Rianne, and Godfried Engbersen. 2014. "How Social Media Transform Migrant Networks and Facilitate Migration." *Global Networks* 14 (4): 401–18. https://doi.org/10.1111/glob.12040.

Department of Statistics Malaysia. 2015a. "Report of Household Income and Basic Amenities Survey 2014." June 22, 2015. https://www.statistics.gov.my/index.php?r=column/cthemeBy Cat&cat=120&bul_id=aHhtTHVWNVYzTFBua2dSUlBRL1Rjdz09&menu_id=amVoW U54UTl0a21NWmdhMjFMMWcyZz09. Accessed 11 April 2024.

———. 2015b. "Report on Household Expenditure Survey 2014." November 16, 2015. https://www .statistics.gov.my/dosm/index.php?r=column/ctheme&menu_id=amVoWU54UTl0a21N WmdhMjFMMWcyZz09&bul_id=cGpPdWw3REhucFZPdXRpek1Jd3FZUT09. Accessed 11 April 2024.

Dore, Ronald Philip, and Ronald Dore. 2000. *Stock Market Capitalism: Welfare Capitalism: Japan and Germany Versus the Anglo-Saxons*. Oxford, UK: Oxford University Press.

Douglass, Mike. 2000. "The Singularities of International Migration of Women to Japan: Past, Present and Future." In *Japan and Global Migration: Foreign Workers and the Advent of a Multicultural Society*, 89–117. London: Routledge.

Duke, Benjamin C. 1986. *The Japanese School: Lessons for Industrial America*. New York: Praeger.

Eagleton-Pierce, Matthew. 2016. *Neoliberalism: The Key Concepts*. New York: Routledge.

Edelman, Lee. 2004. *No Future: Queer Theory and the Death Drive*. Series Q. Durham, NC: Duke University Press.

Edwards, Walter. 1989. *Modern Japan through its Weddings: Gender, Person, and Society in Ritual Portrayal*. Stanford, CA: Stanford University Press.

Farquhar, Judith, and Qicheng Zhang. 2012. *Ten Thousand Things: Nurturing Life in Contemporary Beijing*. New York: Zone Books.

———. 2017. "Nurturing Life in Contemporary Beijing." In *Successful Aging as a Contemporary Obsession: Global Perspectives*, edited by Sarah Lamb, 168–84. New York: Zone Books.

Ferries, Jonathan. 1996. "Obasuteya in Modern Japan: Ageing, Ageism and Government Policy." In *Case Studies on Human Rights in Japan*, edited by Roger Goodman and Ian Neary, 222–44. Richmond, UK: Routledge.

Fischer, Michael M. J. 2015. "Ethnography for Aging Societies: Dignity, Cultural Genres, and Singapore's Imagined Futures." *American Ethnologist* 42 (2): 207–29.

Freeman, Carla. 2014. *Entrepreneurial Selves: Neoliberal Respectability and the Making of a Caribbean Middle Class*. Next Wave: New Directions in Women's Studies. Durham, NC: Duke University Press.

Freeman, Elizabeth. 2010. *Time Binds: Queer Temporalities, Queer Histories*. Perverse Modernities. Durham, NC: Duke University Press.

Freixas, Anna, Bárbara Luque, and Amalia Reina. 2012. "Critical Feminist Gerontology: In the Back Room of Research." *Journal of Women & Aging* 24 (1): 44–58. https://doi.org/10.1080 /08952841.2012.638891.

Friedman, Sara L. 2005. "The Intimacy of State Power: Marriage, Liberation, and Socialist Subjects in Southeastern China." *American Ethnologist* 32 (2): 312–27.

Fry, Christine. 1984. *Aging in Culture and Society*. New York: Bergin & Garvey.

Furuoka, Fumitaka. 2007. "Malaysia-Japan Relations under the Mahathir Administration: Case Studies of the 'Look East' Policy and Japanese Investment in Malaysia." *Asian Survey* 47 (3): 505–19.

Gambold, Liesl. 2013. "Retirement Abroad as Women's Aging Strategy." *Anthropology & Aging* 34 (2): 184–98. https://doi.org/10.5195/aa.2013.19.

Gamburd, Michele Ruth. 2020. *Linked Lives: Elder Care, Migration, and Kinship in Sri Lanka.* Global Perspectives on Aging. New Brunswick, NJ: Rutgers University Press. https://doi.org/10.36019/9781978815346.

García, Héctor, and Francesc Miralles. 2017. *Ikigai: The Japanese Secret to a Long and Happy Life.* Illustrated edition. New York: Penguin Life.

Garcia, Luis-Manuel. 2016. "Withered Memories and the Ethnography of Hidden Things." *Continent.* 5 (1): 83–92.

Garner, J. Dianne. 1999. "Feminism and Feminist Gerontology." *Journal of Women & Aging* 11 (2–3): 3–12. https://doi.org/10.1300/J074v11n02_02.

Garon, Sheldon. 1997. *Molding Japanese Minds: The State in Everyday Life*. Princeton, NJ: Princeton University Press.

Geertz, Clifford. 1973. *The Interpretation of Cultures: Selected Essays*. New York: Basic Books.

Giddens, Anthony. 1991. *Modernity and Self-Identity: Self and Society in the Late Modern Age.* Cambridge, UK: Polity Press.

———. 1992. *The Transformation of Intimacy: Sexuality, Love, and Eroticism in Modern Societies.* Cambridge, UK: Polity Press.

Goldfarb, Kathryn. 2017. "Food, Affect, and Experiments in Care." In *Child's Play: Multi-Sensory Histories of Children and Childhood in Japan*, edited by Sabine Fruhstuck and Anne Walthall, 243–63. Oakland: University of California Press.

Goodman, Catherine, and Merril Silverstein. 2002. "Grandmothers Raising Grandchildren: Family Structure and Well-Being in Culturally Diverse Families." *Gerontologist* 42 (5): 676–89.

Goodman, Roger. 1993. *Japan's "International Youth": The Emergence of a New Class of Schoolchildren*. Reprint edition. Oxford, UK: Oxford University Press.

———. 1996. "On Introducing the UN Convention on the Rights of the Child into Japan." In *Case Studies on Human Rights in Japan*, edited by Roger Goodman and Ian Neary, 109–40. Richmond, UK: Routledge.

Greenberg, Jessica, and Andrea Muehlebach. 2007. "The Old World and Its New Economy: Notes on the 'Third Age' in Western Europe Today." In *Generations and Globalization: Youth, Age, and Family in the New World Economy*, edited by Jennifer Cole and Deborah Lynn Durham, 190–214. Bloomington: Indiana University Press.

Greenhouse, Carol, ed. 2010. *Ethnographies of Neoliberalism*. Philadelphia: University of Pennsylvania Press.

Grewal, Inderpal, and Caren Kaplan. 1994. *Scattered Hegemonies: Postmodernity and Transnational Feminist Practices*. Minneapolis: University of Minnesota Press.

Gunnarsson, Evy. 2002. "The Vulnerable Life Course: Poverty and Social Assistance among Middle-Aged and Older Women." *Ageing and Society* 22 (November): 709–28. http://dx.doi.org.virtual.anu.edu.au/10.1017/S0144686X02008978.

Gupta, Akhil, and James Ferguson. 1997. "Discipline and Practice: 'The Field' as Site, Method, and Location in Anthropology." In *Anthropological Locations: Boundaries and Grounds of a Field Science*, edited by Akhil Gupta and James Ferguson, 1–46. Berkeley: University of California Press.

Gustafson, Per. 2001. "Retirement Migration and Transnational Lifestyles." *Ageing & Society* 21 (04): 371–94.

Haas, Heiko, and Michael Janoschka. 2014. *Contested Spatialities, Lifestyle Migration and Residential Tourism.* Abingdon, UK: Routledge.

Hage, Ghassan. 2009. "Waiting Out the Crisis: On Stuckedness and Governmentality." In *Waiting*, edited by Ghassan Hage, 97–106. Carlton: Melbourne University Press.

Hamada, Tomoko. 2005. "The Anthropology of Japanese Corporate Management." In *Companion to the Anthropology of Japan*, edited by Jennifer Robertson, 125–52. Malden, MA: Blackwell Publishing Ltd.

Harms, Erik. 2010. *Saigon's Edge: On the Margins of Ho Chi Minh City.* Minneapolis: University of Minnesota Press.

———. 2016. *Luxury and Rubble: Civility and Dispossession in the New Saigon.* Oakland: University of California Press.

Hayes, Matthew. 2014. "'We Gained a Lot Over What We Would Have Had': The Geographic Arbitrage of North American Lifestyle Migrants to Cuenca, Ecuador." *Journal of Ethnic and Migration Studies* 40 (12): 1953–71. https://doi.org/10.1080/1369183X.2014.880335.

———. 2018. *Gringolandia: Lifestyle Migration under Late Capitalism.* Minneapolis: University of Minnesota Press. https://doi.org/10.5749/j.ctv6q52rv.

———. 2021. "'Sometimes You Gotta Get out of Your Comfort Zone': Retirement Migration and Active Ageing in Cuenca, Ecuador." *Ageing & Society* 41 (6): 1221–39. https://doi.org/10.1017/S0144686X20001154.

Hayes, Matthew, and Rocío Pérez-Gañán. 2017. "North-South Migrations and the Asymmetric Expulsions of Late Capitalism: Global Inequality, Arbitrage, and New Dynamics of North-South Transnationalism." *Migration Studies* 5 (1): 116–35. https://doi.org/10.1093/migration/mnw030.

Hendry, Joy. 1981a. *Marriage in Changing Japan: Community and Society.* London: Croom Helm.

———. 1981b. *Marriage in Changing Japan: Community and Society.* London: Croom Helm.

———. 1993. *Wrapping Culture: Politeness, Presentation, and Power in Japan and Other Societies.* Oxford, UK: Clarendon Press.

Hidaka, Tomoko. 2010. *Salaryman Masculinity: The Continuity of and Change in the Hegemonic Masculinity in Japan.* Leiden: Brill.

Hirayama, Junko, and Keiko Kashiwagi. 2004. "Communication Patterns of Married Couples: Association with Couples' Occupational Statuses and Marital Ideals." *Japanese Journal of Developmental Psychology* 15 (1): 89–100.

Hirayama, Yosuke. 2011. "Home Ownership, Family Change and Generational Differences." In *Home and Family in Japan*, edited by Richard Ronald and Allison Alexy, 152–73. Abingdon, UK: Routledge.

Hirsch, Jennifer S. 2003. *A Courtship after Marriage: Sexuality and Love in Mexican Transnational Families.* Berkeley: University of California Press.

Hirsch, Jennifer, and Holly Wardlow, eds. 2006. *Modern Loves: The Anthropology of Romantic Courtship & Companionate Marriage.* Ann Arbor: University of Michigan Press.

Ho, Elaine Lynn-Ee, and Tuen Yi Chiu. 2020. "Transnational Ageing and 'Care Technologies': Chinese Grandparenting Migrants in Singapore and Sydney." *Population, Space and Place* 26 (7): e2365. https://doi.org/10.1002/psp.2365.

Ho, Karen Zouwen. 2009. *Liquidated: An Ethnography of Wall Street.* Durham, NC: Duke University Press.

Hoang, Kimberly Kay. 2015. *Dealing in Desire: Asian Ascendancy, Western Decline, and the Hidden Currencies of Global Sex Work.* San Francisco: University of California Press.

Hochschild, Arlie Russell. 1978. *The Unexpected Community: Portrait of an Old Age Subculture.* Berkeley: University of California Press.

Hoey, Brian A. 2010. "Introduction: Locating Personhood and Place in the Commodity Landscape." *City & Society* 22 (2): 207–10.

Hoggart, Keith, and Henry Buller. 1995. "Retired British Home Owners in Rural France." *Ageing & Society* 15 (3): 325–53. https://doi.org/10.1017/S0144686X00002580.

Horiguchi, Sachiko. 2011. "Coping with Hikikomori: Socially Withdrawn Youth and the Japanese Family." In *Home and Family in Japan: Continuity and Transformation*, edited by Richard Ronald and Allison Alexy, 216–35. Abingdon, UK: Routledge.

Howard, Robert W. 2008. "Western Retirees in Thailand: Motives, Experiences, Wellbeing, Assimilation and Future Needs." *Ageing and Society* 28 (2): 145–63. http://dx.doi.org.virtual.anu.edu.au/10.1017/S0144686X07006290.

Humphrey, Caroline. 2008. "Reassembling Individual Subjects: Events and Decisions in Troubled Times." *Anthropological Theory* 8 (4): 357–80.

Ikeuchi, Suma. 2021. "Book Review of Intimate Disconnections: Divorce and the Romance of Independence in Contemporary Japan by Allison Alexy." *Journal of Asian Studies* 80 (2): 477–79. https://doi.org/10.1017/S0021911821000279.

Ingold, Tim. 2011. *Being Alive: Essays on Movement, Knowledge and Description*. London: Routledge.

Ivy, Marilyn. 1995. *Discourses of the Vanishing: Modernity, Phantasm, Japan*. Chicago: University of Chicago Press.

Iwabuchi, Koichi. 2002. *Recentering Globalization: Popular Culture and Japanese Transnationalism*. Durham, NC: Duke University Press.

Izuhara, Misa. 2006. "Changing Families and Policy Responses to an Ageing Japanese Society." In *The Changing Japanese Family*, edited by Marcus Rebick and Ayumi Takenaka, 161–76. Abingdon, UK: Routledge.

Japan Times. 2017. "Redefining the 'Elderly' Age." *Japan Times*, January 10, 2017. http://www.japantimes.co.jp/opinion/2017/01/10/editorials/redefining-elderly-age/#.WJAwE1V9670. Accessed 11 April 2024.

Jeffrey, Craig. 2010. *Timepass: Youth, Class, and the Politics of Waiting in India*. Stanford, CA: Stanford University Press.

Jenike, Brenda Robb. 2003. "Parent Care and Shifting Family Obligations in Urban Japan." In *Demographic Change and the Family in Japan's Aging Society*, edited by John Traphagan and John Knight, 177–201. Albany: State University of New York Press.

Kato, Akiko. 2009. "The Relationship Between Aged Parents and Cohabiting Unmarried Children: Results from the Tokorozawa Living Arrangement Study." *Journal of Intergenerational Relationships* 7 (1): 78–83.

Kavedzija, Iza. 2015. "Frail, Independent, Involved? Care and the Category of the Elderly in Japan." *Anthropology & Aging* 36 (1): 62–81. https://doi.org/10.5195/aa.2015.83.

———. 2019. *Making Meaningful Lives: Tales from an Aging Japan*. Philadelphia: University of Pennsylvania Press.

Kawashima, Kumiko. 2010. "Japanese Working Holiday Makers in Australia and their Relationship to the Japanese Labour Market: Before and After." *Asian Studies Review* 34 (3): 267–86. https://doi.org/10.1080/10357823.2010.508765.

———. 2014. "Uneven Cosmopolitanism: Japanese Working Holiday Makers in Australia and the 'Lost Decade.'" In *Internationalising Japan: Discourse and Practice*, edited by Jeremy Breaden, Stacey Steele, and Carolyn S. Stevens, 106–24. Abingdon, UK: Routledge.

Kelly, William W. 1993. "Finding a Place in Metropolitan Japan: Ideologies, Institutions, and Everyday Life." In *Postwar Japan as History*, edited by Andrew Gordon, 189–238. Berkeley: University of California Press.

Kelsky, Karen. 2001. *Women on the Verge: Japanese Women, Wester Dreams*. Durham, NC: Duke University Press.

Khong, Kim Hoong. 1987. "Malaysia-Japan Relations in the 1980s." *Asian Survey* 27 (10): 1095–1108. https://doi.org/10.2307/2644847.

Kim, Jieun. 2016. "Necrosociality: Isolated Death and Unclaimed Cremains in Japan." *Journal of the Royal Anthropological Institute* 22 (4): 843–63.

Kimoto, Kimiko. 2005. *Gender and Japanese Management*. English edition. Melbourne, AU: Trans Pacific Press.

King, Russell, Eralba Cela, and Tineke Fokkema. 2021. "New Frontiers in International Retirement Migration." *Ageing and Society* 41 (6): 1205–20. https://doi.org/10.1017/S014468 6X21000179.

———, Tony Warnes, and Allan M. Williams. 2000. *Sunset Lives: British Retirement Migration to the Mediterranean*. Oxford, UK: Bloomsbury Academic.

Kiyota, Takayuki. 2020. *Sayonara Oretachi*. Tokyo: Stand Books.

Kleist, Nauja, and Stef Jansen. 2016. "Introduction: Hope over Time—Crisis, Immobility and Future-Making." *History and Anthropology* 27 (4): 373–92. https://doi.org/10.1080 /02757206.2016.1207636.

Komashaku, Kimi. 1996. *Majo No Ronri*. Tokyo: Gakuyo Shobo.

Kondo, Dorinne K. 1990. *Crafting Selves: Power, Gender, and Discourses of Identity in a Japanese Workplace*. Chicago: University of Chicago Press.

Korpela, Mari. 2020. "Searching for a Countercultural Life Abroad: Neo-Nomadism, Lifestyle Mobility or Bohemian Lifestyle Migration?" *Journal of Ethnic and Migration Studies* 46 (15): 3352–69. https://doi.org/10.1080/1369183X.2019.1569505.

Krekula, Clary. 2007. "The Intersection of Age and Gender: Reworking Gender Theory and Social Gerontology." *Current Sociology* 55 (2): 155–71. https://doi.org/10.1177/001139 2107073299.

Kua, Ee Heok. 2014. *Ageing Baby Boomers*. Singapore: Write Editions.

Kurotani, Sawa. 2005. *Home Away from Home: Japanese Corporate Wives in the United States*. Durham, NC: Duke University Press.

Lafferty, Megan, and Kristen H. Maher. 2020. "Transnational Intimacy and Economic Precarity of Western Men in Northeast Thailand." *Journal of Ethnic and Migration Studies* 46 (8): 1629–46. https://doi.org/10.1080/1369183X.2020.1711571.

Lamb, Sarah. 2014. "Permanent Personhood or Meaningful Decline? Toward a Critical Anthropology of Successful Aging." *Journal of Aging Studies* 29 (April): 41–52.

———, ed. 2017. *Successful Aging as a Contemporary Obsession: Global Perspectives*. New Brunswick, NJ: Rutgers University Press.

Lardiés-Bosque, Raúl, Jennifer C. Guillén, and Verónica Montes-de-Oca. 2016. "Retirement Migration and Transnationalism in Northern Mexico." *Journal of Ethnic and Migration Studies* 42 (5): 816–33. https://doi.org/10.1080/1369183X.2015.1086632.

Laslett, Peter. 1989. *A Fresh Map of Life: The Emergence of the Third Age*. London: Weidenfeld and Nicolson.

Law, Lisa B. 2001. "Home Cooking: Filipino Women and Geographies of the Senses in Hong Kong." *Ecumene: A Journal of Cultural Geographies* 39 (9): 1625–45.

LeBlanc, Robin M. 1999. *Bicycle Citizens: The Political World of the Japanese Housewife*. Berkeley: University of California Press.

Lebra, Takie Sugiyama. 1975. "An Alternative Approach to Reciprocity." *American Anthropologist* 77 (3): 550–65.

———. 1976. *Japanese Patterns of Behavior*. Honolulu: University of Hawaii Press.

Lems, Annika, and Christine Moderbacher. 2016. "On Being Stuck in the Wrong Life: Home-Longing, Movement and the Pain of Existential Immobility." In *Bounded Mobilities: Ethnographic Perspectives on Social Hierarchies and Global Inequalities*, edited by Miriam Gutekunst et al., 113–28. Bielefeld, Germany: Transcript Verlag.

Lévi-Strauss, Claude. 1969. *The Elementary Structures of Kinship*. London: Eyre & Spottiswoode.

Lim, Adelyn. 2008. "Transnational Feminist Practices in Hong Kong: Mobilisation and Collective Action for Sex Workers' Rights." *Asia Pacific Journal of Anthropology* 9 (4): 319–31. https://doi.org/10.1080/14442210802449050.

Lim, Francis Khek Gee. 2008. "'Donkey Friends' in China: The Internet, Civil Society and the Emergence of the Chinese Backpacking Community." In *Asia on Tour*, edited by Tim Winter, Peggy Teo, and T.C. Chang. 291–301. Abingdon, UK: Routledge.

Lipset, David. 2004. "Modernity without Romance? Masculinity and Desire in Courtship Stories told by Young Papua New Guinean Men." *American Ethnologist* 31 (2): 205–24.

Livingston, Julie. 2007. "Maintaining Local Dependencies: Elderly Women and Global Rehabilitation Agendas in Southeastern Botswana." In *Generations and Globalization: Youth, Age, and Family in the New World Economy*, 164–89. Bloomington: Indiana University Press.

Lock, Margaret. 1993. *Encounters with Aging: Mythologies of Menopause in Japan and North America*. Berkeley: University of California Press.

———. 2002. "Medical Knowledge and Body Politics." In *Exotic No More: Anthropology on the Front Lines*, edited by Jeremy MacClancy, 190–208. Chicago: University of Chicago Press.

Long Stay Foundation. 2022. "Long Stay Foundation." (2024) https://www.longstay.or.jp /english/.

Long, Susan Orpett. 2005. *Final Days: Japanese Culture and Choice at the End of Life*. Honolulu: University of Hawaii Press.

———. 2014. "The Aging of the Japanese Family." In *Capturing Contemporary Japan*, edited by Satsuki Kawano, Glenda Roberts, and Susan Orpett Long, 183–201. Honolulu: University of Hawaii Press.

Lotherington, Ann Therese. 2019. "Feminist Theories and Later Life." In *Encyclopedia of Gerontology and Population Aging*, edited by Danan Gu and Matthew E. Dupre, 1–3. Cham, Switzerland: Springer International Publishing. https://doi.org/10.1007/978-3-319-69892-2_155-1.

Lynch, Caitrin. 2013. "Membership and Mattering: Agency and Work in a New England Factory." In *Transitions and Transformations: Cultural Perspectives on Aging and the Life Course*, edited by Caitrin Lynch and Jason Danely, 187–205. New York: Berghahn Books.

Lynch, Caitrin, and Jason Danely, eds. 2013. *Transitions and Transformations: Cultural Perspectives on Aging and the Life Course*. Life Course, Culture, and Aging: Global Transformations. New York: Berghahn Books.

Mackie, Vera C. 2003. *Feminism in Modern Japan: Citizenship, Embodiment, and Sexuality*. Contemporary Japanese Society. Cambridge, UK: Cambridge University Press.

Maoz, Darya. 2007. "Backpackers' Motivations: The Role of Culture and Nationality." *Annals of Tourism Research* 34 (1): 122–40. https://doi.org/10.1016/j.annals.2006.07.008.

Masquelier, Adeline. 2013. "Teatime: Boredom and the Temporalities of Young Men in Niger." *Africa: Journal of the International African Institute* 83 (3): 385–402.

Mathews, Gordon. 1996. *What Makes Life Worth Living?: How Japanese and Americans Make Sense of Their Worlds*. Berkeley: University of California Press.

———. 2002. "Can 'a Real Man' Live for His Family?: Ikigai and Masculinity in Today's Japan." In *Men and Masculinities in Contemporary Japan: Dislocating the Salaryman Doxa*, edited by James Robertson and Nobue Suzuki, 109–25. London: Routledge Curzon.

Mauss, Marcel. 2011. *The Gift: Forms and Functions of Exchange in Archaic Societies*, translated by Ian Cunnison. Mansfield Center, CT: Martino Fine Books.

Mayaram, Shail. 2009. *The Other Global City*. New York: Routledge.

McCarthy, James. 2008. "Rural Geography: Globalizing the Countryside." *Progress in Human Geography* 32 (1): 129–37. https://doi.org/10.1177/0309132507082559.

McCormack, Gavan. 1998. "Bubble and Swamp: MFP and the Australia-Japan Encounter, 1987–94." In *Australia in Asia: Episodes*, edited by Anthony Milner and Mary Quilty. 61–81. Melbourne, AU: Oxford University Press.

McKinnon, Susan, and Fenella Cannell, eds. 2013. *Vital Relations: Modernity and the Persistent Life of Kinship*. School for Advanced Research Advanced Seminar Series. Santa Fe, NM: School for Advanced Research Press.

McWatters, Mason R. 2008. *Residential Tourism: (De)Constructing Paradise*. Bristol, UK: Channel View Publications.

Miles, Ann. 2015. "Health Care Imaginaries and Retirement Migration to Cuenca, Ecuador." *Journal of Latin American Geography* 14 (1): 39–55.

Ministry of Economy of Malaysia. 2024. "Eighth Malaysia Plan, 2001–2005." Kuala Lumpur: Ministry of Economy of Malaysia. https://www.ekonomi.gov.my/en/economic-developments/development-plans/rmk/eight-malaysia-plan-2001-2005. Accessed 10 April 2024.

———. 2024. "Ninth Malaysia Plan, 2006–2010." Kuala Lumpur: Ministry of Economy of Malaysia. https://www.ekonomi.gov.my/en/economic-developments/development-plans/rmk/ninth-malaysia-plan-2006-2010. Accessed 10 April 2024.

———. 2024. "Tenth Malaysia Plan, 2011–2015." Kuala Lumpur: Ministry of Economy of Malaysia. https://www.ekonomi.gov.my/en/economic-developments/development-plans/rmk/tenth-malaysia-plan-10th-mp-2011-2015. Accessed 10 April 2024.

———. 2024. "Eleventh Malaysia Plan, 2016–2020." Kuala Lumpur: Ministry of Economy of Malaysia. https://www.ekonomi.gov.my/en/economic-developments/development-plans/rmk/previous-plans. Accessed 10 April 2024.

Ministry of Foreign Affairs of Japan. 2014. "Kaigai Zairyu Hojinsu Chosa Tokei 2014 (Annual Report of Statistics on Japanese Nationals Overseas 2014)." Tokyo: Ministry of Foreign Affairs of Japan. http://www.mofa.go.jp/mofaj/files/000049149.pdf. Accessed 8 April 2024.

Ministry of Heath, Labor, and Welfare of Japan. 2010. "Heikin Jumyo Hyo (Life Expectancy Graph)." 2010. http://www.office-onoduka.com/siru_nenkinseikatu/sn0702.html. Accessed 11 April 2024.

———. 2015. "Kanni Seimei Hyo (Simplified Life Graph) (2024)." http://www.e-stat.go.jp/SG1/estat/GL08020103.do?_toGL08020103_&listID=000001136655&requestSender=dsearch. Accessed 11 April 2024.

———. 2018. "Ninsampu Ni Taisuru Mentaru Herusu Kea No Tameno Hoken Iryo No Renkei Taisei Ni Kansuru Chosa Kenkyu Hokokusho." (Survey and Research on Health and Medical Cooperation System for Mental Health Care for Expectant and Nursing Mothers). Tokyo: Ministry of Health, Labor, and Welfare of Japan. https://www.mhlw.go.jp/content/11900000/000520478.pdf. Accessed 11 April 2024.

———. 2021. "Revision of the Child Care and Family Care Leave Law." Tokyo: Ministry of Health, Labor and Welfare of Japan. https://www.mhlw.go.jp/content/11900000/000851662.pdf. Accessed 11 April 2024.

———. 2022. "Summary of Statistics on Divorce." Tokyo: Ministry of Health, Labor and Welfare of Japan. https://www.mhlw.go.jp/toukei/saikin/hw/jinkou/tokusyu/rikon22/dl/suii.pdf. Accessed 8 April 2024.

Ministry of Internal Affairs and Communications of Japan. 2016. "Setai Zokusei Betsu no Kakei Shushi 2015 (Statistics on Family Expenditure 2015)." Tokyo: Ministry of Internal Affairs and Communications. http://www.stat.go.jp/data/kakei/sokuhou/nen/pdf/gk02.pdf. Accessed 11 April 2024.

Ministry of Tourism and Culture Malaysia. 2015. "MM2H Programme Statistics." Ministry of Tourism and Culture Malaysia. Kuala Lumpur: Ministry of Tourism and Culture Malaysia. http://www.mm2h.gov.my/index.php/en/home/programme/statistics. Accessed 11 April 2024.

Mizutani, Takehide. 2015. *Dasshutsu Roujin: Firipin Ijuu Ni Saigo No Jinsei Wo Kakeru Nihonjin Tachi (Seniors on Escape: Migration to the Philippines as a Last Hope in Life)*. Tokyo: Shogakukan.

Moeran, Brian. 1998. *Folk Art Potters of Japan: Beyond an Anthropology of Aesthetics*. Honolulu: University of Hawaii Press.

Mohanty, Chandra Talpade. 1984. "Under Western Eyes: Feminist Scholarship and Colonial Discourses." *Boundary 2* 12/13: 333–58. https://doi.org/10.2307/302821.

Mol, Annemarie. 2016. "Differences within: Feminism and Us." *HAU: Journal of Ethnographic Theory* 6 (3): 401–7. https://doi.org/10.14318/hau6.3.026.

Moore, Katrina L. 2010. "Sexuality and Sense of Self in Later Life: Japanese Men's and Women's Reflections on Sex and Aging." *Journal of Cross-Cultural Gerontology* 25 (2): 149–63.

———. 2013. "Transforming Identities through Dance: Amateur Noh Performers' Immersion in Leisure." *Japanese Studies* 33 (3): 263–77.

Moreton-Robinson, Aileen. 2000. *Talkin' up to the White Woman: Aboriginal Women and Feminism*. Brisbane, AU: Queensland University Press.

Morisaki, Kazue. 2016. *Karayuki-San: Ikokuni Urareta Shojo Tachi (Karayuki-san: Girls Sold to Foreign Countries)*. Tokyo: Asahi Bunko.

Morrison, William R., Robert Healy, and Ken S. Coates. 2002. "Tracking the Snowbirds: Seasonal Migration from Canada to the U.S.A. and Mexico." *American Review of Canadian Studies* 32 (3): 433–50. http://dx.doi.org.virtual.anu.edu.au/10.1080/02722010209481670.

Muehlebach, Andrea. 2009. "*Complexio Oppositorum*: Notes on the Left in Neoliberal Italy." *Public Culture* 21 (3): 495–515.

———. 2011. "On Affective Labor in Post-Fordist Italy." *Cultural Anthropology* 26 (1): 59–82.

———. 2012. *Moral Neoliberal: Welfare and Citizenship in Italy*. Chicago: University of Chicago Press.

Munn, Nancy D. 1986. *The Fame of Gawa: A Symbolic Study of Value Transformation in a Massim (Papua New Guinea) Society*. Lewis Henry Morgan Lectures 1976. Cambridge, UK: Cambridge University Press.

Murakami, Ryu. 2012. *55-Sai Kara No Harō Raifu (Life Guidance for the 55-Year-Olds and All Triers)*. Tokyo: Gentōsha.

Musharbash, Yasmine. 2007. "Boredom, Time, and Modernity: An Example from Aboriginal Australia." *American Anthropologist* 109 (2): 307–17.

Muzaini, Hamzah. 2006. "Backpacking Southeast Asia: Strategies of 'Looking Local.'" *Annals of Tourism Research* 33 (1): 144–61.

Myerhoff, Barbara G. 1978. *Number Our Days*. New York: Dutton.

Nadkarni, Asha, and Subhalakshmi Gooptu. 2021. "Transnational Feminism." In *Literary and Critical Theory*. Oxford Bibliographies. Oxford, UK: Oxford University Press.

Nagata, Satoko. 2013. *Mareishia de Rongusutei (Long Stay in Malaysia)*. Tokyo: Ikarosu.

Nagatomo, Jun. 2014. *Migration As Transnational Leisure: The Japanese Lifestyle Migrants in Australia*. Leiden: Brill.

Nakahara, Michiko. 2001. "'Comfort Women' in Malaysia." *Critical Asian Studies* 33 (4): 581–89. https://doi.org/10.1080/146727101760107442.

Nakane, Chie. 1970. *Japanese Society*. The Nature of Human Society Series. London: Weidenfeld & Nicolson.

Nakatani, Ayami. 2006. "The Emergence of 'Nurturing Fathers': Discourses and Practices of Fatherhood in Contemporary Japan." In *The Changing Japanese Family*, edited by Marcus Rebick and Ayumi Takenaka, 94–108. Abingdon, UK: Routledge.

National Tax Agency. 2015. "Minkan Kyuyo Jittai Toukei Chosa (Income Statistics) 2014." Tokyo: National Tax Agency. http://www.nta.go.jp/kohyo/tokei/kokuzeicho/minkan2014/pdf/001 .pdf. Accessed 12 April 2024.

Newendorp, Nicole DeJong. 2020. *Chinese Senior Migrants and the Globalization of Retirement.* Stanford, CA: Stanford University Press.

Nobuta, Sayoko. 2013. *Aijo To Iu Na No Shihai (Control in the Name of Affection).* Tokyo: Kairyusha.

Noorloos, Femke van. 2011. "A Transnational Networked Space: Tracing Residential Tourism and Its Multi-Local Implications in Costa Rica." *International Development Planning Review* 33 (4): 429–44. http://dx.doi.org.virtual.anu.edu.au/10.3828/idpr.2011.22.

Notle, Sharon H., and Sally Ann Hastings. 1991. "The Meiji State's Policy toward Women, 1890–1910." In *Recreating Japanese Women, 1600–1945*, edited by Gail Lee Bernstein, 151–75. Berkeley: University of California Press.

Ogasawara, Yuko. 1998. *Office Ladies and Salaried Men Power, Gender, and Work in Japanese Companies.* Berkeley: University of California Press.

Ogawa, Naohiro, Robert D Retherford, and Rikiya Matsukura. 2006. "Demographics of the Japanese Family: Entering Uncharted Territory." In *The Changing Japanese Family*, edited by Marcus Rebick and Ayumi Takenaka, 19–38. Abingdon, UK: Routledge.

Ohnuki-Tierney, Emiko. 1993. *Rice as Self: Japanese Identities through Time.* Princeton, NJ: Princeton University Press.

Oishi, Shinzaburo, and Chie Nakane, eds. 1990. *Tokugawa Japan: The Social and Economic Antecedents of Modern Japan.* Tokyo: University of Tokyo Press.

Okamoto, Junko. 2018. *Sekaiichi Kodoku Na Nihon No Ojisan (The World's Loneliest Japanese Men).* Tokyo: Kadokawa.

Oliver, Caroline. 2008. *Retirement Migration: Paradoxes of Ageing.* Routledge Research in Population and Migration 9. New York: Routledge.

Oliver, Caroline, and Karen O'Reilly. 2010. "A Bourdieusian Analysis of Class and Migration: Habitus and the Individualizing Process." *Sociology* 44 (1): 49–66. https://doi.org/10.1177/0038038509351627.

Ong, Aihwa. 2010. *Spirits of Resistance and Capitalist Discipline: Factory Women in Malaysia.* 2nd ed. Suny Series in the Anthropology of Work. Albany: State University of New York Press.

Ono, Mayumi. 2008. "Long-Stay Tourism and International Retirement Migration: Japanese Retirees in Malaysia." *Senri Ethnological Reports* 77: 151–62.

———. 2009. "Japanese Lifestyle Migration/Tourism in Southeast Asia." *Japanese Review of Cultural Anthropology* 10: 43–52.

———. 2012. "Nihonjin Koureisha No Kea Wo Motometa Kokusai Idou: Mareishia Ni Okeru Kokusai Taishoku Ijuu to Medikaru Tsurizumu No Doukou Kara (Searching for Care: International Retirement Migration and Medical Tourism among Elderly Japanese in Malaysia)." *Asia Taiheiyou Kenkyu* 18: 253–67.

———. 2015. "Commoditization of Lifestyle Migration: Japanese Retirees in Malaysia." *Mobilities* 10 (4): 609–27.

O'Reilly, Karen. 2000. *The British on the Costa Del Sol.* London: Taylor & Francis Group.

O'Reilly, Karen, and Michaela Benson. 2015. "Lifestyle Migration." In *Routledge Handbook of Cultural Gerontology*, 420–27. London: Routledge.

Osawa, Mari. 2002. "Twelve Million Full-Time Housewives: The Gender Consequences of Japan's Postwar Social Contract." In *Social Contracts under Stress: The Middle Classes of America, Europe, and Japan at the Turn of the Century*, edited by Oliver Zunz, Leonard Schoppa, and Nobuhiro Hiwatari, 255–77. New York: Russell Sage Foundation.

———. 2011. *Social Security in Contemporary Japan: A Comparative Analysis.* Routledge/University of Tokyo Series 2. Abingdon, UK: Routledge. https://doi.org/10.4324/9780203813669.

Osburg, John. 2013. *Anxious Wealth: Money and Morality among China's New Rich.* Stanford, CA: Stanford University Press.

Parkin, D. J. 1999. "Mementoes as Transitional Objects in Human Displacement." *Journal of Material Culture* 4 (3): 303–20.

Pearsall, Marilyn. 1997. *The Other within Us: Feminist Explorations of Women and Aging*. Boulder, CO: Routledge.

Peng, Ito. 2002. "Social Care in Crisis: Gender, Demography, and Welfare State Restructuring in Japan." *Social Politics: International Studies in Gender, State, & Society* 9 (3): 411–43.

Plath, David W. 1980. *Long Engagements: Maturity in Modern Japan*. Stanford, CA: Stanford University Press.

Pollard, Jane. 2013. "Gendering Capital: Financial Crisis, Financialization and (an Agenda for) Economic Geography." *Progress in Human Geography: London* 37 (3): 403–23.

Povinelli, Elizabeth A. 2006. *The Empire of Love: Toward a Theory of Intimacy, Genealogy, and Carnality*. Public Planet Books. Durham, NC: Duke University Press.

Ramirez-Valles, Jesus. 2016. *Queer Aging: The Gayby Boomers and a New Frontier for Gerontology*. New York: Oxford University Press.

Rebick, Marcus, and Ayumi Takenaka. 2006. "The Changing Japanese Family." In *The Changing Japanese Family*, edited by Marcus Rebick and Ayumi Takenaka, 3–17. Abingdon, UK: Routledge.

Riley, Pamela J. 1988. "Road Culture of International Long-Term Budget Travelers." *Annals of Tourism Research* 15 (3): 313–28. https://doi.org/10.1016/0160-7383(88)90025-4.

Robbins, Joel. 2010. "Anthropology, Pentecostalism, and the New Paul: Conversion, Event, and Social Transformation." *South Atlantic Quarterly* 109 (4): 633–52.

Roberts, Glenda. 1994. *Staying on the Line: Blue-Collar Women in Contemporary Japan*. Honolulu: University of Hawaii Press.

———. 1996. "Public Policy and the Old Age Revolution in Japan." *Journal of Aging & Social Policy* 8 (2–3): 115–32.

———. 2014. "Work and Life in Challenging Times: A Kansai Family across the Generations." In *Capturing Contemporary Japan*, edited by Satsuki Kawano, Glenda Roberts, and Susan Orpett, 27–59. Honolulu: University of Hawaii Press.

Rodriquez-Galan, Marta. 2013. "Grandmothering in Life-Course Perspective: A Study of Puerto Rican Grandmothers raising Grandchildren in the United States." In *Transitions and Transformations: Cultural Perspectives in Aging and the Life Course*, edited by Caitrin Lynch and Jason Danely, 137–50. New York: Berghahn Books.

Rohlen, Thomas P. 1973. "'Spiritual Education' in a Japanese Bank." *American Anthropologist* 75 (5): 1542–62.

Rosaldo, M. Z. 1980. "The Use and Abuse of Anthropology: Reflections on Feminism and Cross-Cultural Understanding." *Signs* 5 (3): 389–417.

Rosaldo, Renato. 1989. "Imperialist Nostalgia." *Representations* 26 (April): 107–22. https://doi.org/10.2307/2928525.

Rosenberger, Nancy Ross. 2001. *Gambling with Virtue: Japanese Women and the Search for Self in a Changing Nation*. Honolulu: University of Hawaii Press.

Rossi, Alice. 1985. *Gender and the Life Course*. New York: Routledge.

Roy, Ananya, and Aihwa Ong, eds. 2011. *Worlding Cities: Asian Experiments and the Art of Being Global*. Studies in Urban and Social Change. Malden, MA: Wiley-Blackwell.

Rubin, Gayle. 1997. "The Traffic in Women: Notes on the 'Political Economy' of Sex." In *The Second Wave: A Reader in Feminist Theory*, edited by Linda Nicholson, 27–62. New York: Routledge.

Rudnyckyj, Daromir. 2019. *Beyond Debt: Islamic Experiments in Global Finance*. Chicago: The University of Chicago Press.

Rupp, Katherine. 2003. *Gift-Giving in Japan: Cash, Connections, Cosmologies*. Stanford, CA: Stanford University Press.

Ryang, Sonia. 2006. *Love in Modern Japan: Its Estrangement from Self, Sex, and Society*. Anthropology of Asia Series. Milton Park, UK: Routledge.

Sacramento, Octávio. 2019. "For Love, Labour, and Lifestyle: European Men moving to Northeast Brazil." *Anthropological Forum*, March, 1–19. https://doi.org/10.1080/00664677.2019.1579704.

Sahlins, Marshall. 1972. *Stone Age Economics*. Chicago: Aldine-Atherton.

Sakamoto, Yasuhiko. 2011. *Gohoubi Jinsei Mareishia (Reward yourself by Living in Malaysia)*. Tokyo: Ikarosu.

Sakurai, Eiji. 2011. *Zouyo No Rekishigaku: Girei to Keizai No Aida (History of Gifts: Between Ritual and Economy)*. Tokyo: Chuko shinsho.

Sasagawa, Ayumi. 2006. "Mother-Rearing: The Social World of Mothers in a Japanese Suburb." In *The Changing Japanese Family*, edited by Marcus Rebick and Ayumi Takenaka, 129–46. Oxford, UK: Routledge.

Saso, Mary. 1990. *Women in the Japanese Workplace*. London: H. Shipman.

Schneider, David Murray. 1980. *American Kinship: A Cultural Account*. 2d ed. Chicago: University of Chicago Press.

Schulz, Carol. 1980. "Age, Sex and Death Anxiety in a Middle-Class American Community." In *Aging in Culture and Society: Comparative Viewpoints and Strategies*, edited by Christine Fry, 239–52. New York: Bergin & Garvey.

Schuster, Caroline E. 2015. *Social Collateral: Women and Microfinance in Paraguay's Smuggling Economy*. Oakland: University of California Press.

Scuzzarello, Sarah. 2020. "Practicing Privilege: How Settling in Thailand Enables Older Western Migrants to Enact Privilege over Local People." *Journal of Ethnic and Migration Studies* 46 (8): 1606–28. https://doi.org/10.1080/1369183X.2020.1711570.

Sekizawa, Mayumi. 2003. *Inkyo to Teinen: Oino Minzokugakuteki Kousatsu (Retirement: An Ethnographic Study of Aging)*. Kyoto: Rinsen Shoten.

Sennett, Richard, and Jonathan Cobb. 1977. *The Hidden Injuries of Class*. Cambridge, UK: Cambridge University Press.

Sergeant, Julie F., and David J. Ekerdt. 2008. "Motives for Residential Mobility in Later Life: Post-Move Perspectives of Elders and Family Members." *International Journal of Aging and Human Development* 66 (2): 131–54. https://doi.org/10.2190/AG.66.2.c.

Shakuto, Shiori. 2017. "Ageing with Bad-Boy Charm: An Affective Analysis of Japanese Retirement Migration in Malaysia." *Japanese Review of Cultural Anthropology* 18 (1): 159–72.

———. 2018a. "Japanese Radiation Refugees in Malaysia." *Anthropology News* 58 (4): 354–56.

———. 2018b. "An Independent and Mutually Supportive Retirement as a Moral Ideal in Contemporary Japan." *Australian Journal of Anthropology* 29 (2): 184–94.

———. 2019a. "Postwork Intimacy: Negotiating Romantic Partnerships among Japanese Retired Couples in Malaysia." *American Ethnologist* 46 (3): 302–12.

———. 2019b. "Radiation Migration: Motherhood and 3.11 Evacuees in Malaysia." *Teach 3.11* (website), posted March 11, 2019. https://www.teach311.org/2019/03/11/radiation-migration-motherhood-and-3-11-evacuees-in-malaysia/.

———. 2022. "'Radiation Refugees': The Role of Gender and Digital Communication in Japanese Women's Transnational Evacuation after Fukushima." *Journal of Immigrant & Refugee Studies* 20 (2): 177–89. https://doi.org/10.1080/15562948.2022.2042637.

Shea, Jeanne L. 2014. "Revolutionary Narratives of Self-Compassion among Older Women in Post-Mao Beijing." *Anthropology & Medicine* 21 (1): 8–26.

Simmons, Christina. 2009. *Making Marriage: Modern Women's Sexuality from the Progressive Era to World War II*. Oxford, UK: Oxford University Press.

———. 2015. "Companionate Marriage." In *The International Encyclopedia of Human Sexuality*, edited by Patricia Whelehan and Anne Bolin, 197–200. Hoboken, NJ: John Wiley & Sons.

Skolnick, Arlene S. 1991. *Embattled Paradise: The American Family in an Age of Uncertainty.* New York: Basic Books.

Sørensen, Anders. 2003. "Backpacker Ethnography." *Annals of Tourism Research* 30 (4): 847–67. https://doi.org/10.1016/S0160-7383(03)00063-X.

Spalding, Ana K. 2013. "Environmental Outcomes of Lifestyle Migration: Land Cover Change and Land Use Transitions in the Bocas del Toro Archipelago in Panama." *Journal of Latin American Geography* 12 (3): 179–202.

———. 2020. "Towards a Political Ecology of Lifestyle Migration: Local Perspectives on Socio-Ecological Change in Bocas del Toro, Panama." *Area* 52 (3): 539–46. https://doi.org/10.1111/area.12606.

Spreitzhofer, Guenter. 1998. "Research Notes and Reports." *Annals of Tourism Research* 25 (4): 979–83. https://doi.org/10.1016/S0160-7383(98)00048-6.

Star Online. 2013. "Japanese Couple Found Dead in Apartment Unit Bathroom." *Star Online*, September 10, 2013. http://www.thestar.com.my/news/nation/2013/09/10/japanese-couple -found-dead-in-apartment-unit-bathroom/. Accessed 12 April 2024.

Statistics Bureau, Ministry of Internal Affairs and Communications. 2016. "Employed Person by Age Group." Historical Data. Labour Force Survey. Statistics Bureau, Tokyo: Ministry of Internal Affairs and Communications. http://www.stat.go.jp/english/data/roudou/lngindex .htm. Accessed 12 April 2024.

Stoler, Ann L. 1989. "Making Empire Respectable: The Politics of Race and Sexual Morality in 20th-century Colonial Cultures." *American Ethnologist* 16 (4): 634–60.

———. 2002. *Carnal Knowledge and Imperial Power: Race and the Intimate in Colonial Rule.* Berkeley: University of California Press.

Stone, Lawrence. 1977. *The Family, Sex and Marriage in England, 1500–1800.* New York: Harper & Row.

Stout, Noelle M. 2014. *After Love: Queer Intimacy and Erotic Economies in Post-Soviet Cuba.* Durham, NC: Duke University Press.

Strakosch, Elizabeth. 2015. *Neoliberal Indigenous Policy: Settler Colonialism and the "post-Welfare" State.* Houndsmills, UK: Palgrave Macmillan.

Sun, Ken Chih-Yan. 2021. *Time and Migration: How Long-Term Taiwanese Migrants Negotiate Later Life.* Ithaca, NY: Cornell University Press.

Suzuki, Nobue. 2002. "Of Love and the Marriage Market: Masculinity Politics and Filipina-Japanese Marriages in Japan." In *Men and Masculinities in Contemporary Japan: Dislocating the Salaryman Doxa*, edited by James Roberson and Nobue Suzuki, 91–108. London: Routledge Curzon.

Switek, Beata. 2016. *Reluctant Intimacies Japanese Eldercare in Indonesian Hands.* New York: Berghahn Books.

Tabusa, Eiko. 2020. *Otoko Shakai Ga Shindoi (It's Hard to be in a Man's Society).* Tokyo: Takeshobo.

Tajima, Yoko. 1992. *Ai to Iu Na No Shihai (Control in the Name of Love).* Tokyo: Shincho Bunko.

Takeyama, Akiko. 2016. *Staged Seduction: Selling Dreams in a Tokyo Host Club.* Palo Alto, CA: Stanford University Press.

Tanaka, Toshiyuki. 2015. *Otokoga Tsuraiyo: Zetsubou No Jidai No Kibou No Danseigaku (It's Hard to be a Man: Hopeful Study of Masculinity in an Age of Despair).* Tokyo: Kadokawa.

Tay, Frances. 2015. "Remembering the Japanese Occupation Massacres: Mass Graves in Post-War Malaysia." In *Human Remains and Identification*, edited by Élisabeth Anstett and Jean-Marc Dreyfus. 221–238. Manchester, UK: Manchester University Press.

Thang, Leng Leng. 2001. *Generations in Touch: Linking the Old and Young in a Tokyo Neighborhood.* The Anthropology of Contemporary Issues. Ithaca, NY: Cornell University Press.

Thang, Leng Leng et al. 2011. "Being a Good Grandparent: Roles and Expectations in Intergenerational Relationships in Japan and Singapore." *Marriage & Family Review* 47 (8): 548–70.

Thang, Leng Leng, Sachiko Sone, and Mika Toyota. 2012. "Freedom Found? The Later-Life Transnational Migration of Japanese Women to Western Australia and Thailand." *Asian and Pacific Migration Journal* 21 (2): 239–62. https://doi.org/10.1177/011719681202100206.

Tokuhiro, Yoko. 2010. *Marriage in Contemporary Japan*. Routledge Contemporary Japan Series. Milton Park, UK: Routledge.

Torres, Rebecca Maria, and Janet D. Momsen. 2005. "Gringolandia: The Construction of a New Tourist Space in Mexico." *Annals of the Association of American Geographers* 95 (2): 314–35. https://doi.org/10.1111/j.1467-8306.2005.00462.x.

Toyota, Mika. 2006. "Ageing and Transnational Householding: Japanese Retirees in Southeast Asia." *International Development Planning Review* 28 (4): 515–31.

Toyota, Mika, and Leng Leng Thang. 2017. "Transnational Retirement Mobility as Processes of Identity Negotiation: The Case of Japanese in South-East Asia." *Identities* 24 (5): 557–72. https://doi.org/10.1080/1070289X.2017.1346509.

Traphagan, John. 2003. "Contesting Co-Residence: Women, in-Laws, and Health Care in Rural Japan." In *Demographic Change and the Family in Japan's Aging Society*, edited by John Knight, 203–28. Albany: State University of New York Press.

Trifiletti, Rossana. 2006. "Different Paths to Welfare: Family Transformations, the Production of Welfare, and Future Prospects for Social Care in Italy and Japan." In *The Changing Japanese Family*, edited by Marcus Rebick and Ayumi Takenaka, 177–203. Abingdon, UK: Routledge.

Tsing, Anna Lowenhaupt. 2012. "On Nonscalability: The Living World is not Amenable to Precision-Nested Scales." *Common Knowledge* 18 (3): 505–24.

Tsutsui, William M. 1998. *Manufacturing Ideology: Scientific Management in Twentieth-Century Japan*. Princeton, NJ: Princeton University Press.

Tusinski, Gabriel. 2016. "Fates Worse than Death: Destruction and Social Attachment in Timor-Leste." *Social Analysis* 60 (2): 13–30.

Twigg, Julia. 2004. "The Body, Gender, and Age: Feminist Insights in Social Gerontology." *Journal of Aging Studies*, New Directions in Feminist Gerontology, 18 (1): 59–73. https://doi.org/10.1016/j.jaging.2003.09.001.

Ueno, Chizuko. 1987. "The Position of Japanese Women Reconsidered." *Current Anthropology* 28 (4): 75–84.

———. 1994. *Kindai Kazoku No Seiritsu to Shuen (The Birth and the End of Modern Family)*. Tokyo: Iwanami Shoten.

———. 2007. *Ohitorisama No Rōgo (Old Age of a Single Person)*. Tokyo: Hōken.

———. 2009. *Kahuchousei to Shihonsei: Marukusu Shugi Feminizumu No Chihei (Patriarchal Capitalism: The Horizon of Marxist Feminism)*. Tokyo: Iwanami Gendai Bunko.

Ueno, Chizuko, and Eiko Tabusa. 2020. *Ueno Sensei, Feminizumu Ni Tsuite Oshietekudasai (Dr. Ueno, Please Tell us about Feminism)*. Tokyo: Daiwa Shobo.

Umegaki-Constantini, Hiroko. 2017. "Grandfathering in Contemporary Japan: Altruistic and Self-Serving Means to Happiness." In *Happiness and the Good Life in Japan*, edited by Wolfram Manzenreiter and Barbara Holthus, 86–105. London: Routledge.

Uno, Kathleen. 1993. "The Death of 'Good Wife, Wise Mother'?" In *Postwar Japan as History*, edited by Andrew Gordon, 293–24. Berkeley: University of California Press.

Upham, Frank. 1993. "Unplaced Person and Movements for Place." In *Postwar Japan as History*, edited by Andrew Gordon, 325–46. Berkeley: University of California Press.

Vesperi, Maria D. 1986. *City of Green Benches: Growing Old in a New Downtown*. The Anthropology of Contemporary Issues. Ithaca, NY: Cornell University Press.

Viteri, María Amelia. 2015. "Cultural Imaginaries in the Residential Migration to Cotacachi." *Journal of Latin American Geography* 14 (1): 119–38.

Vogel, Ezra F. 1979. *Japan as Number One: Lessons for America.* Cambridge, MA: Harvard University Press.

Vogt, Jay W. 1976. "Wandering: Youth and Travel Behavior." *Annals of Tourism Research* 4 (1): 25–41. https://doi.org/10.1016/0160-7383(76)90051-7.

Walsh, Katie. 2006. "British Expatriate Belongings: Mobile Homes and Transnational Homing." *Home Cultures* 3 (2): 123–44.

Watanabe, Chika. 2019. "Intimacy Beyond Love: The History and Politics of Inter-Asian Development Aid." *Anthropological Quarterly* 92 (1): 59–84. https://doi.org/10.1353/anq.2019.0002.

Weiner, Annette B. 1977. *Women of Value, Men of Renown: New Perspectives in Trobriand Exchange.* St. Lucia, AU: University of Queensland Press.

———. 1980. "Reproduction: A Replacement for Reciprocity." *American Ethnologist* 7 (1): 71–85.

———. 1992. *Inalienable Possessions: The Paradox of Keeping-While-Giving.* Berkeley: University of California Press.

Westerhausen, Klaus. 2002. *Beyond the Beach: An Ethnography of Modern Travellers in Asia.* Bangkok: White Lotus Press.

Weston, Kath. 1991. *Families We Choose: Lesbians, Gays, Kinship.* Between Men–between Women. New York: Columbia University Press.

White, Merry I. 1988. *The Japanese Overseas: Can They Go Home Again?* New York: Free Press.

Wilding, Raelene et al. 2022. "Practices of 'Digital Homing' and Gendered Reproduction among Older Sinhalese and Karen Migrants in Australia." *Journal of Immigrant & Refugee Studies* 20 (2): 220–32. https://doi.org/10.1080/15562948.2022.2046895.

Williams, Allan M., Russell King, and Tony Warnes. 1997. "A Place in the Sun: International Retirement Migration from Northern to Southern Europe." *European Urban and Regional Studies* 4 (2): 115–34. https://doi.org/10.1177/096977649700400202.

Williams, Bianca C. 2018. *The Pursuit of Happiness: Black Women, Diasporic Dreams, and the Politics of Emotional Transnationalism.* Durham, NC: Duke University Press.

Yamada, Chikako. 2013. "Achieving Dreams in One's Post-Retirement 'Second Life': A Study of Seniors' Migration from Japan to Canada." *Senri Ethnological Studies* 80 (January): 81–95.

Yamaura, Chigusa. 2020. *Marriage and Marriageability: The Practices of Matchmaking Between Men from Japan and Women from Northeast China.* Ithaca, NY: Cornell University Press.

Yanagisako, Sylvia. 2002. *Producing Culture and Capital: Family Firms in Italy.* Princeton, NJ: Princeton University Press.

Zelizer, Viviana A. 2005. *The Purchase of Intimacy.* Princeton, NJ: Princeton University Press.

Zoomers, Annelies. 2010. "Globalisation and the Foreignisation of Space: Seven Processes Driving the Current Global Land Grab." *Journal of Peasant Studies* 37 (2): 429–47. https://doi.org/10.1080/03066151003595325.

INDEX

aging: devaluation of home, 109–10, 162–63; gendered experience of, 9–10, 12–13, 15, 162; independence in, 75–79, 92; neoliberal policies, 5–7, 75–76, 79, 169n13; social construction of, 168n7; temporality of, 61–62, 74–75, 161–62; and work, 76–77. *See also* successful aging
Akiyama, Mr., 32
Alexy, Allison, 100, 176n9
Allison, Anne, 123, 127, 143–44
Amamiya, Karin, 34
Aoi, Mrs., xiii, 47, 65–66, 110–11, 132
Asia: geopolitical relations, xii, 169n21; intimate relations in, 169n21; Japanese soft power policy, 50; negative image of, 55–56; transnational retirement, 95, 168n10, 175n1, 175n2. *See also* Southeast Asia

baby boomers (*dankai no sedai*): care for aging parents, 119–20; characteristics of, 167n5, 169n17; educational attainment, 26; family relations of, 154; and gender norms, 3, 8; home ownership by, 123; and homosociality, 8–9; and Japanese-style productivity, 24, 170n1; lifecourse (*raihukosu*), 24–25; life expectancy, 120; and marriage, 25–27, 170n6, 170n7; retirement by, 9, 23
Bao, Jigang, 175n1
Bardsley, Jan, 38, 78
Beauvoir, Simone de, 10
belonging: and identity, 3; Japanese television, 52; and Japanese women, 133, 160; and non-waged labor, 160; and retired men, 38, 98, 145; retirement practices, 149; and transnational retirement, xii, 13; and voluntarism, 75; women's creation of, 11, 157; workplace relationships, 34, 75

Benson, Michaela, 6, 168n8
Borovoy, Amy, 154
Bourdieu, Pierre, 148

capitalism: division of labor, 3, 8, 23–24; feminist economic theories, 16, 170n22; feminized labor practices, 15–16, 170n22; gendered temporality of, 152–53; gender norms under, 3, 8, 24, 161; intimate relations in, 13, 170n21; productivist discourse, 82; regulatory forms, xii; and retirement, 16, 62; separation of waged/non-waged labor, 16, 163; upward mobility, 83
Chen, Jingfu, 175n1
Chizuko, Ueno, 10
Cook, Emma, 175n3

Dales, Laura, 27
Daniels, Inge, 176n2
Dauvergne, Peter, 49–50
division of labor: capitalist lifecourse, 35, 39, 161; gendered, xi, 8, 12, 23–24, 27, 34–35, 37, 43, 67–68, 85, 161; and geopolitical relations, 64, 67–68; and Japanese couples, 8, 99, 101, 103, 114–15, 133, 170n23; and middle class expectations, 34; state mechanisms for, 27
Dore, Ronald, 33

elderly: defining, 2, 42, 167n4; delinquent, 71, 81–84; family support for, 77; independence of, 75–79

family relations: absent fathers, 34, 101, 119, 123, 126–27, 137; care for aging parents, 2, 28–29, 119–21, 123, 153, 155, 169n20; care through absence, 123–26, 137–38, 159; communication with children, 124–26;

family relations (*continued*)
    death in, 134–38; eating together, 126–27,
    133, 138; filial piety ideology, 29, 120, 123,
    171n12; grandparents as caregivers, 5, 8,
    90–91, 133, 150–54, 156; and *ibasho*, 154;
    intergenerational co-residence, 28–29,
    119–20, 124; *nakama* (fictive kin), 119,
    126–28, 132–33, 136–38, 145, 153; parental
    leave, 90–91; retired *sarariiman*, 119, 154;
    sacrifices of motherhood, 90, 169n19;
    sarariiman sacrifice of, 30, 34, 37, 39;
    transfer of homes to children, 123–24, 137,
    143; transnational retirees, 119, 175n1;
    usefulness of seniors in, 123–24, 139–40,
    143; views on older women's vulnerability,
    86; women's affective care, 37–38, 96,
    109–13, 137–38, 153, 160. *See also* romantic
    partnerships
feminism: calls for spousal equality, 96; on
    capitalism, 16; on gendered aging
    experience, 8, 10, 12–13; on gifting
    practices, 142; Japanese, 64, 174n16;
    labeling of women, 104; on narratives and
    lived experience, 17; on productive and
    reproductive, 16, 170n22; on terms for
    spouses, 100–101
Ferries, Jonathan, 120
Freeman, Carla, 168n11
Freeman, Elizabeth, 25
Furuoka, Fumitaka, 173n4

Garcia, Hector, ix, xi, 6
Garcia, Luis-Manuel, 175n5
gender: affective costs of, 23–24; and aging, 10,
    12–13; in capitalism, 3, 8, 24; division of
    labor, xi, 8, 12, 24, 27–28, 34–35, 64, 67–68,
    85, 171n8; dominant discourse, 15, 17; in
    lifecourse (*raihukosu*), 23–25, 72;
    transgression of boundaries, 84–92, 105,
    174n10; views on retirement, 9–11, 14, 17, 35
geopolitical relations: gendered division of labor,
    64–65, 67–68; and intimate relations, 11–12,
    169n21; and Japanese retirees, xii, 64–65;
    material deprivation of Malaysia in, 64–66
Giddens, Anthony, 2, 153
gifting practices: in corporate culture, 141,
    145, 176n2; feminist economic theories, 142;
    generalized reciprocity, 142; as *ibasho*, 142,
    144–45, 153; silver backpackers, 141–45; and
    women, 176n2

Global South: environmental degradation,
    50, 60; postcolonialism in, 6–7, 169n14;
    retiree land consumption, 173n11;
    transnational retirement to, xii, 6, 161,
    169n14
Greenberg, Jessica, 76
Gustafson, Per, 169n16

Hasegawa, Martha, xiii, 103–6
Hayes, Matthew, 169n14
Hendry, Joy, 136, 174n19
Higashi, Mr., 144–145

ibasho: generation of roles, 143–45, 149, 153,
    157; gifting practices, 142, 144–45, 153; and
    grandchildren, 150, 154; impact of previous
    occupations, 148–49; men's dislocation
    from, 42, 83, 98, 127, 144; women's creation
    of, 150, 153, 157; women's dislocation from,
    150, 160; workplace relationships, 34
identity: after-work, 5, 14, 16, 41–42; ageless
    bad-boy seniors, 84; anxiety over, 16, 21;
    and belonging, 3; women's self, 37
ikigai, ix, xi, 7, 38, 143, 172n19
Ikigai (Garcia and Miralles), ix, 6
intergenerational relations: men's develop-
    ment of, 154, 161; by transnational
    migrants, 125–26, 175n1; women's
    temporality, 153, 156
intimate relations: under capitalism, 13,
    170n21; gendered division of labor, 161; and
    geopolitical relations, 11–12, 169n21;
    ittaikan (unity), 99–100; Japanese retirees,
    9–12, 16, 37, 105, 128, 159; men's romantic
    rhetoric, 93–95; by neighbors, 132–33. *See
    also* romantic partnerships
Ishida, Mrs., xiii, 35–36, 89–90, 110–11

Japan: aging policies, 5, 7, 71, 75–78, 163,
    169n12, 169n13, 171n10, 174n6; and
    Confucian ideologies, 29, 32–34, 76; division
    of labor in, 8, 27–28, 37, 171n8; ecological
    shadows, 50, 173n3; economic uncertainty
    in, 4–5, 121–23, 167n6; feminism in, 64,
    174n16; gender norms in, 27–28, 170n2,
    171n8; importance of inter-dependence, 31,
    171n14; lifecourse (*raihukosu*) in, 2, 4, 16, 24;
    life expectancy in, 2, 42, 120, 172n25;
    male-to-female wage gap in, 28; manage-
    ment systems in, 32, 167n6; Meiji Constitu-

tion of 1890, 170n7, 171n9; political economy, 11, 18, 24, 43, 75, 92; post-World War II Constitution, 28, 171n9; productivist discourse, 2, 16, 24, 62, 82, 121, 170n1; racial ideologies, 55–56, 65, 84, 96–98, 159; retirement system in, 2, 39–40, 167n3, 172n20, 172n22; television and imagined community, 52; temporality of, 81–82; welfare policies in, 28–29, 35, 71, 121–23, 171n10, 171n12, 175n4. *See also* Malaysia-Japan relations

Japan Cultural Center: activities at, 13–15, 57, 72–74, 79, 102; Art Club, 145–50; couple-hood in, 129–30; demographic bubbles in, 73, 174n3; fictive families in, 126–28, 133, 136–38, 145, 149; generalized reciprocity in, 142; intergenerational activities, 79; Karaoke Club, 100–101, 112, 127, 129–30; Language Club, 63, 91, 106–7, 113, 118, 127, 144–45; roles and ibasho, 144–45, 157

Japanese couples: division of labor, 8, 99, 101, 103, 114–15, 133, 170n23; divorce rate, 9, 169n18; equal partnership rhetoric, 103–6; exchange of name cards, 102, 102fig., 103; gendered value production processes, 96–97, 155, 160–62; hierarchy of practices, 106; *ittaikan* (unity), 99–100, 105, 110–11, 113; joint retirement project, 8, 11, 94, 96, 107, 109, 113–15; kinship terminology, 111–12; male responsibility ideology, 175n3; middle-class respectability, 47, 98–99, 159; public affection, 93–95, 101; second life discourse, 98, 109, 114–15, 159–60; and shared men's hobbies, 10–11, 44, 110–11; sotsukon relationships, 114–15; spousal companionship ideal, 95–99, 101–3, 109–13, 159–60, 175n3; spousal misrecognition, 9, 42; waifu terminology, 100–101, 111–12

Japanese men: absence from home, 33–34, 37–39, 119, 123, 126–27, 137, 172n16; after-work personhood, 3–5, 11, 14, 41–42, 67, 158, 161; aging body odor, 38–39; communication with children, 124–25; as delinquent elderly, 81–84; dislocation after retirement, 42, 83, 98, 127, 144; emotional experiences, 23–24, 30, 40–43; emotional support from wife, 37–38, 42, 96, 112–13; and *ibasho*, 34, 148–49; leisure activities, 71–72; lifecourse (*raihukosu*), 24–25, 34, 37, 42; marriage and maturity, 25, 170n4;

nakama (fictive kin), 126–28, 132–34, 136–38, 145, 153, 159; retirement projects, 14–15, 17, 152–53, 155; single, 94–95; social isolation, 38, 42; value production processes, 96–97, 155, 160, 162; views on retirement, 11, 37–41, 71–72; and younger local women, 97–98. *See also sarariiman* (salaried workers)

Japanese retirees: anxiety of wasted time, 124, 143–44, 151–52, 158–59, 161; bodily rejuvenation, 74–75; care through absence, 123–26; class structure, 78–79; cost of living, 39–40, 80, 169n20; cultural adaptation, 7, 169n16; disposal of possessions, 90–91, 151; double marginal-ization, 55–56; gendered experience of, ix, xii, 9, 14, 17–18, 115–16; and *ikigai*, xi, 6–7, 38, 143; increased longevity of, 2, 172n25; intimate relations, 9, 11–12, 37; migrant objects, 66–67; prospect of death, 134–36; reemployment of, 39–41, 172n19; second life discourse, 3, 12, 92, 159; self-improvement, 3, 36, 74, 78–79; sense of purpose, ix–xii, 6, 14, 35, 72, 133, 159, 162; social relations, 11, 16, 38–41, 127; spousal misrecognition, 9, 42; and temporality of progress, 61–62, 161–62; transnational mobility, 5, 16, 158–59; women's immobil-ity, 110–11, 116. *See also* silver backpackers

Japanese-style productivity: and baby boomers, 24, 170n1; chrononormativity, 25, 170n1; lifecourse (*raihukosu*), 2, 25, 83, 162; marriage in, 25, 170n3; productivity and redundancy chart, 40, 41fig.; and social welfare, 121–22; temporality of, 82, 158; total quality control, 33

Japanese women: affective care for husbands, 37–38, 42, 96, 109–10, 112–13, 137–38, 153, 160; as caregivers, 28–29, 90, 120–21, 150–51, 154–55, 171n13; constraints of social obligations, 35–36, 87, 89–90; cultivation of the home, 16–17, 64–65; and domestic work, x, 8, 10–11, 24, 27–30, 35, 67, 107–10, 152, 171n8, 175n4; education of, 26–27, 170n5; embedding in new environ-ment, 108–9, 150; emotional experiences, 23–24, 68; employment of, 27–28, 120–21, 171n8, 172n23; gender expectations, 27, 36, 67, 88–89, 159–60; good wife, wise mother discourse, 29, 64, 171n11; as household

Japanese women (*continued*)
  financial managers, 64–65, 101, 105, 174n15,
  174n17, 174n18; *ibasho* of, 150, 153, 157, 160;
  immobility in retirement, 110–11, 116; impact
  of marriage on, 29–30; intergenerational
  temporality, 152–53, 156, 161; and Japanese
  cling wrap, 17, 65–67, 174n19; keepers of
  friends and family, 133, 135–38; liberation
  from gender constraints, 12, 84–92, 105, 107,
  160, 174n10; lifecourse (*raihukosu*), 24, 34, 150;
  networks of, 36–37, 67–68, 131–33, 138, 160;
  omiai (arranged marriage), 26–27, 170n7;
  public recognition of, 103–7; quality
  consciousness, 64–66, 174n19; racial and
  gendered imaginaries, 65, 67; reproductive
  role, 38, 91–92, 112, 150, 152, 160, 162, 171n8;
  restricted social lives, 110–11; retirement
  activities of, 14–16, 65; sacrifices of
  motherhood, 90, 169n19; second life
  discourse, 9–10, 12, 35, 103–5; self-
  development, 36; as *shufu* (housewife), 8,
  18–19, 24, 64–65, 103, 170n23; social
  relations, 16, 35–38; on superiority of
  Japanese products, 64–67, 174n19;
  transnational retirement, 44–45, 84–92;
  travel by, 91–92; value production processes,
  17, 155, 162–63; views on retirement, 9–11,
  14, 35–37, 64, 67–68, 72, 84, 152; yogurt
  network of, 14–15, 129–33, 138
Japanese youth: compared with Malaysian
  youth, 61; and environmental disasters,
  122, 124; *hikikomori*, 143–44; marriage
  views, 100, 121, 123; and precarious
  economy, 76, 123–24; social dislocation,
  143–44; temporary employment, 4, 123,
  144, 167n6; transfer of family homes to,
  123–24, 137

Kahn, Robert Louis, 168n12
Katayama, Tetsu, 170n1
Kazuko, Morisaki, 104
Kelly, William W., 25
Kelsky, Karen, 88
Khadi, Mrs., 117–18
Kim, Jieun, 137
Kobayashi, Eisaku (Eddie), xiv, 37–38, 80–81
Komura, Mrs., 56–57, 135–37
Kosaka, Mr.: activities of, 21–22, 129;
  communication with children, 125;
  Malaysian retirement, 112; and prospective

migrants, 57–58, 128, 132, 142–43; return to
  Japan, xiii, 154
Kosaka, Mrs., xiii–xiv, 21–22, 112, 129–33,
  154
Kotaro, Sawaki, 1
Krekula, Clary, 15
Kuala Lumpur: environmental degradation,
  60; gentrification of, 59–60; medical
  tourism in, 47; Mont Kiara condominiums,
  58–59, 59fig., 60–61, 65, 129, 173n10, 176n6;
  Segambut Village, 58–59, 59fig., 60–61, 63;
  transnational retirement in, 8, 13, 47
Kurotani, Sawa, 66

labor: devaluation of women's, 15–16, 109–10,
  133; division between waged/non-waged,
  16, 163; male-to-female wage gap, 28; and
  seniors, 76–77; *shufu* (housewife), 8, 10–11,
  24, 28–30, 35, 67, 175n4; women's invisible,
  15, 121. *See also* division of labor;
  sarariiman (salaried workers)
Laslett, Peter, 41, 76
LeBlanc, Robin M., 19, 170n23
lifecourse (*raihukosu*): capitalist, 10, 12, 16, 37,
  42–43, 62, 83, 152–53; emotional consequences of, 43; flexibility in, 30; gendered
  experience of, 20, 23–25, 72, 150; marriage
  in, 25, 29–30, 170n3; middle-class ideals,
  25, 27, 34; normative, 21–23, 42, 81; and
  retirement, 2–3, 23, 72; sacrifice in, 30, 34;
  second life discourse, 78, 162; temporality
  of, 25, 34, 170n1; transnational retirement,
  4, 54
lifestyle migration: bourgeois bohemians,
  168n8; connections to destination, 46;
  defining, 6, 168n8; internal migrants,
  168n9; residential tourists, 45, 47, 168n8,
  173n11; rural idyllic seekers, 168n8;
  temporality of movement, 19; transnational
  retirement, 5–6, 19, 168n9
Livingston, Julie, 90
Long, Susan, 125, 137
Long Stay Foundation, 53–54

Machida, Ms., xiv, 130–31, 150
Mahathir Mohamad, 48, 50, 139, 173n2, 176n1
Malaysia: cost of living, 11, 80, 97, 169n20;
  health tourism in, 47–48; as Islamic
  finance center, 48, 173n2; Islamization, 48,
  50–51, 173n2; Japanese occupation of, 7, 49,

60–61, 173n13; Japanese popular culture in, 50, 56; MM2H program, 51, 54–57, 124–25, 144, 173n5; as moral nation, 47–48, 50–51, 95, 98–99; nation-building, 52–53, 56, 61, 63; negative image of, 55–56, 62–63; as the Other, 62; postcolonial landscape in, 46–47, 56, 60–61, 79, 173n13; promotion of Japanese development, 48–50; temporality of progress in, 61–62; tourism development, 47–48, 173n1

Malaysia-Japan relations: educational exchange programs, 50, 173n4; geopolitical relations, 47, 56, 64, 68; Japanese timber imports, 49–50, 56; look east policy, 48–50; postcolonial history, 49, 60–61; postwar aid programs, 49; shadow ecology, 50; soft power policy, 50; unequal race relations, 67

Malaysia My Second Home (MM2H) program, 51, 54–55, 57, 124–25, 144

Malaysian retirement: cultural adaptation, 9, 169n16; Japanese enclaves, 7–8, 11, 47, 58–59, 63, 72–73, 96–97, 129, 176n6; marginalization of local populations, 59–60, 173n12; nostalgic past in, 61–63; perceived inferiority of domestic products, 64–67; perceived material scarcity, 64–67; popularity of, 54, 173n8; postcolonial affect, 47, 56, 79–80; racial and gendered imaginaries, 11, 65, 97; respectability in, 47, 159; as *shimanagashi* (banishment), 44–46, 55, 64, 67; by single women, 87–89, 95, 129–30; temporality of progress in, 61–63, 68; transcendence of economic class, 79–80, 97; unequal spousal relations in, 67–68; as utopic landscape, 63, 96–97; women's domestic work in, 107–10; younger expatriates, 131–32. *See also* transnational retirement

marriage: alliance-making, 26, 170n7; and baby boomers, 25–26, 170n6; companionate, 95–96, 98, 101, 110, 163, 175n3; impact on women's lifecourses, 29–30; independence through, 124; love marriages, 26, 94, 170n6; *omiai* (arranged), 26–28, 93, 103, 170n7; reduction in rate of, 123–24, 152; state goals, 25, 170n2; women's views on, 121; and work, 25, 170n3, 170n4

masculinity, 96, 100, 159

Mauss, Marcel, 141

McCormack, Gavan, 53

Mich, xiv, 81–84, 130

Miralles, Francesc, ix, xi, 6

mobility: hypermobility, 81; transnational, 5, 16, 158–59; upward, 83; women's loss of, 110–11, 116

Moore, Katrina, 36

Mori, Mr., 21, 146–48

Muehlebach, Andrea, 76, 169n13

Mumeo, Oku, 64

Murakami, Ryu, 9, 41

Nakane, Chie, 149, 170n2

neoliberalism: aging policies, 5–7, 75–76, 169n12, 169n13; and flexibility, 168n11; geoarbitrage, 169n14; individualism in, 138, 176n9; self as entrepreneurial project, 168n11; self-responsibility, 77–79, 138; successful aging ideal, 7, 79, 158, 168n12, 169n13; and transnational retirement, 7, 169n14

Nishiguchi, Mr., 101, 112, 139–42

Nishiguchi, Mrs., xiv, 112, 134

Nobuta, Sayoko, 33

Obuse, Makoto, 78

Oishi, Shinzaburo, 170n2

Okada, Mr.: constraints on family, 21, 27–29, 113; return to Japan, 155

Okada, Mrs.: appearance of, 25–26; consideration of divorce, 114; constrainment of life, xiv, 21, 26–29, 155; employment of, 26–28; hopes for university education, 26–27; impact of marriage on, 29–30, 113; *omiai* (arranged marriage), 27; return to Japan, xiv, 155; as *shufu* (housewife), 27–28

Oliver, Caroline, 149

Ono, Mayumi, 56, 74

O'Reilly, Karen, 6, 149, 168n8

Orwell, George, 39

Otanis, ix–xi, 3, 13, 101, 103, 133

Paul (Toshihiko Yoshioka), xiv, 69–71, 145–49

Pérez-Gañán, Rocío, 169n14

postcolonialism: economic class, 79–80, 92; Malaysia-British relations, 48–49; Malaysia-Japan relations, 49, 60–61; and normative couplehood, 99; and transnational retirement, 6–8, 46–47, 52, 56 retirement: aging ideals, 77–79; and capitalism, 16; class structure in, 78–79; gendered views of, 9–11, 17; and post-work personhood, 3–4; self-responsibility, 77–78; by single women, 87–89, 95, 129–30, 174n10; as wasted time, 124, 143–44, 151, 158–59. *See also* transnational retirement

Roberts, Glenda, 172n23

romantic partnerships: devaluation of home in, 109–10; gender differences in, 113, 116, 159, 175n3; gendered power relations in, 96–97, 111–12, 116; *ittaikan* (unity), 99–100, 110–11, 113; kinship terminology, 111–12; male rhetoric of, 111–13; and masculinity, 96, 100, 159; public affection in, 93–94, 113, 159; sotsukon relationships, 114–15; spousal companionship ideal, 95–103, 116, 160; women and men's activities, 110–11

Rosaldo, Renato, 63

Rose, Nikolas, 168n11

Rowe, John, 168n12

Rudnyckyj, Daromir, 48, 173n2

Saito, Ms., xiv, 84–89, 130

sarariiman (salaried workers): as absent fathers, 33–34, 37–39, 127, 171n13, 172n16; affective lives of, 30–32; *bijinessman* (managers), 31, 37; blue-collar, 172n16; competitiveness of, 31–32; Confucian ideologies, 32–33; golfing, 31, 33, 37, 111; *ikigai* in, 172n19; inter-dependence among, 31, 33, 171n14; *karoushi* (death by over-work), 32, 172n15; lifecourse (*raihukosu*), 24–25, 30, 35; lifelong employment, 24, 34; long work hours of, 8, 32, 37, 143; productivist discourse, 30–33, 35, 40; sacrifice in, 30, 37; sense of dislocation after retirement, 42, 83, 98, 127, 144; transnational retirement, 72, 84

Schneider, David, 119

Schulz, Carol, 143

second life discourse: aging state, 92; devaluation of home in, 109–10, 162; gendered experience of, 9, 35, 153, 162; independence in, 114–15; Japanese couples, 3, 12, 92, 98, 109, 114–15, 159–60; *sarari-iman*, 42

self: aging discourse, 76–78, 163; multiplici-ties of, 37, 83; neoliberal, 77–79, 159, 168n11; reflexive process of, 3

seniors: as burden on economy, 122–23; curtailment of welfare services, 28–29, 35, 90; defining, 168n7; family care for, 2, 28–29, 77, 119–21, 169n20; ideal skills, 77–79; independence of, 75–79, 89, 92; Japanese policies, 71, 75–78, 174n6; life-long learning, 41–42, 172n24; lifestyle migration, 5–6, 168n8; self-responsibility, 77–79; successful aging, 6–7, 75–79, 168n12, 169n13; working, 76–77

Shigeta, Ichiro, 135–37

Shimizu, Mr., 93–95

shufu (housewife): aspirations for, 18–19, 24; good wife, wise mother discourse, 29, 64, 171n11; household financial management, 64–65, 174n15; public identity of, 19; and quality goods, 64–65

silver backpackers: affluent lifestyles, 7–8, 47, 51, 56–57, 80–81, 84, 173n5, 173n6; after-work personhood, xii, 1–3, 14, 158, 161; agelessness, 6, 73–75, 77, 79, 81, 84, 143, 152, 159; ambivalence of normative lifecourses, 4–5, 21–23; brain exercises, 70–71, 79; defining, 1, 167n1; as delinquent elderly, 71, 81–84; desire to be useful, 123–24, 139–40, 142–45, 150, 154, 157; emotional lives, 11–12, 14, 23; fictive families, 118–19, 126–28, 138; gender relations, 18, 156–57, 161; gifting practices, 141–45; imperialist nostalgia, 62–63; international travel, 57, 81, 158; leisure activities, 13–15, 19–22, 69–74, 79–81, 118; limited local interactions, 7, 18, 58, 63, 97, 169n15, 173n14; nicknames, 128, 149, 159; racial imaginaries, 65, 67; return to Japan, 141, 150–51, 153–57; roles and ibasho, 142–45, 157; self-improvement, 74, 78–79; spousal companionship, 95–96; temporality of progress, 61–62, 161–62; transfer of homes to children, 123–24, 137, 143; on wifeless men, 94–96, 114. *See also* Japanese retirees

social relations: flexibility in, 149–50; material signifiers of status, 149, 160; norms of reciprocity, 141; obligation to neighbors, 111, 151; retirement practices in, 149–50; *sarariiman*, 33–34; school system, 171n14; silver backpackers, 11–12, 16, 38–41, 127; women's, 16, 35, 150

Southeast Asia: backpacker tourism in, 4, 48, 97; financial crisis in, 51; health tourism in,

47; negative image of, 55; older men and young local women, 95; sex tourism in, 48; shadow ecology in, 50; as *shimanagashi* (banishment), 44–45; transnational retirement in, 54, 88, 97–99

Stoler, Ann, 98

successful aging: activities at home, 15–16; and autonomy, 168n12; and busyness, 6–7; gender stereotyping, 10; ideal skills for, 77–78; as neoliberal ideal, 7, 158, 168n12, 169n13; patriarchal discourses, 15; and social support, 168n12; transnational appeal, 7, 169n13

Sugawara, Michizane, 90

Suzuki, Nobue, 170n4

Tabusa, Eiko, 33, 120

Tachibana, Claire, 150–51

Takeyama, Akiko, 78

Tanaka, Toshiyuki, 30

Taro, Aso, 122

Thang, Leng Leng, 88

Tomizawa, Jun, 30

Toyota, Mika, 88

Toyotomi, Hisashi, 74

transnationalism, 12

transnational retirement: after Fukushima nuclear disaster, 124, 175n3; care services in, 5, 169n20; and emotional lives, 11; family relations, 119, 175n1; gender differences in, ix, xi, 67, 84, 160–61; gendered and racial privilege, 84; gentrification for, 59–60, 173n11; geopolitical relations, 52, 64–65; and international mobility, 5, 11, 16, 43, 81, 159, 161, 169n14; liberation from gender constraints, 10, 57, 72, 84–92, 105, 107, 174n10; marginalization of local populations, 59–60, 173n12; older men and young local women, 95, 97–98, 175n2; postcolonial relations, 7–8, 46–47,

52, 99; resort facilities, 53–54; by single women, 87–89, 129–30, 174n10; visa costs, 51, 54–55. *See also* Malaysian retirement

Uchida, Mr.: after-work personhood, 42; blogging by, 125–26; hosting of parties, 107–8, 133; lifecourse flexibility, 30; Malaysian retirement, 46, 56–58, 61–63, 128; and public recognition of wife, 106–9; reemployment hopes, 40–41; relations with children, 124–25; return to Japan, 155–57; roles and ibasho, 144–45; as *sarariiman*, 30–34; and temporality of progress, 63

Uchida, Mrs.: domestic work by, 107–8, 133; immobility, 110; Malaysian retirement, 46, 58, 63, 128; patchwork-making, 106–9; public recognition of, 106–9; return to Japan, 155–57

Ueno, Chizuko, 36, 96, 120, 171n13

Vogel, Ezra F., 24

Watase, Mr., 44–45, 64

Watase, Mrs., 44–46, 55, 64–65, 115

Weiner, Annette B., 142, 153, 176n7

Weston, Kath, 126

women: and aging as problem, 10; capitalist lifecourse, 10, 16, 169n19; feminized labor practices, 15–16, 18–19, 170n22; invisible labor, 15, 121; keepers of friends and family, 133, 137

Women's Committee for the Betterment of Ageing Society (WCBAS), 175n4

Yamamoto, Mr., ix–xi, 13, 40, 41fig., 101

Yamamoto, Mrs., ix–xi, 3–4, 13, 35, 133, 159

Yassin, Muhyiddin, 176n1

Yoshida, Ms., 88–89, 130

Yoshimoto, Mr., 118, 125

Yoshioka, Yasuko, 69

ACKNOWLEDGMENTS

Feminist practices encourage us to acknowledge the fluid and collaborative nature of interpretations as they are shaped by experiences during and long after the fieldwork. It has been more than ten years since I first conceived of this project, and the book has changed through numerous drafts thanks to the comments and feedback I received from countless people. The book matured, as I myself grew older, through the dialogues I had. Here, I would like to acknowledge some of these encounters.

I thank my interlocutors in Malaysia who generously shared their stories with me. My interlocutors were so kind to let a naïve postgraduate student in her mid-twenties spend time with them, and when asked, so patient to explain their lifeworlds with depth of reflections and wit. I managed to highlight only small aspects of their otherwise very rich lives. Thank you for allowing me to join your second lives.

Having good mentors is key to navigating life and happiness. I was nurtured by numerous mentors. I especially thank Francesca Merlan and Caroline Schuster who were supervisor and advisor, respectively, for the dissertation research on which this book is based. It was through them that I learned that there were many ways of being a feminist anthropologist. They encouraged me to find my own.

The research was conducted while I was at the Australian National University (ANU), which was an ideal place to pursue anthropological research. Scholars such as Philip Taylor, Trang Ta, Ashley Carruthers, Gavin MacCormack, Sverre Molland, Andrew Kipnis, Katherine Robinson, Alan Rumsey, and Nic Peterson all showed me the wonders of anthropology and its value in activism. The inclusive environment of the ANU also showed me the attraction and addictiveness of collaborative learning. Here I am thankful especially for the friendship and readership of Ben Hegarty, Charlotte van Tongeren, Stephanie Betz, Rosita Armytage, Zaime Bujor, Xeem Noor, Isabela

Burgher, Basilia Sethu, Hseidi Law, Gaik Khoo, Elizabeth Gimbad, Trixie Tangit, Le Hoang Anh Thu, and Aya Horne.

The writing of this book mainly took place during my postdoctoral fellowship at the Asia Research Institute, National University of Singapore, from 2018–2020. It was there that I met scholars who inspired me in both scholarship and teaching. Brenda S.A. Yeoh, Thang Leng Leng, Chris McMorran, Jonathan Rigg, Tim Bunnell, and Kuan Yee Han all showed me the values and practices of generosity in academia. I also thank my colleagues, especially Sylvia Ang, Courtney Fu, Xiaorong Fong, and Ning Ning Chen, for always being up to exchanging ideas in food courts around Singapore. Being in Singapore also allowed me to be in more frequent contact with people who shaped my interests in Malaysia. Colin Nicholas, Kamal Solheimi Fadzil, Jenita Engi, Karlye Tham, Sze Ning, Lili Li, Koong Hui Yein, Geng Qian Choo, and Lilian Chen Le Leng all advocate for the rights of indigenous people in Peninsular Malaysia with the Center for Orang Asli Concerns. They taught me the ethics of engagement in the field. They will always hold me to their highest ethical standards and for that I am grateful.

When I started my faculty position at the Tokyo College, an interdisciplinary institute at the University of Tokyo, I had the chance to translate the feminist and decolonizing movement into everyday scholarly action. The Japan that I experienced from Tokyo, and in conversation with people from different disciplines and backgrounds, was complexly constituted. My understanding was deepened by stimulating conversations I had with my colleagues and friends in Tokyo, such as Haneda Masashi, Michael Facius, Marcin Jarzebski, Flavia Baldari, Yoshie Udagawa, Wang Wenlu, Yuki Terada, Mino Takashi, Mayumi Fukunaga, Susumu Kitagawa, Yasuko Kitagawa, Ryosuke Hasegawa, Noriko Taniguchi, and Naomi Iwasaki. Together, the people and the environment made me think about feminism from the moment I opened my eyes in the morning to the moment I closed them at night.

Many scholars kindly read and commented on drafts of this book. I am especially grateful to Anne Allison, Amy Borovoy, Erik Harms, Kumiko Kawashima, Gordon Mathews, Chris McMorran, Glenda Roberts, Nancy Rosenberger, and Thang Leng Leng, who read the manuscript and provided invaluable advice throughout the writing process. Additionally, three external reviewers engaged with this work with so much thoughtfulness, patience, and generosity. I am very grateful for their time and wisdom in making the book as best as it can be.

The research was presented at various venues, including the University of Sydney's Department of Anthropology Seminar Series, the National

University of Singapore Department of Japanese Studies Seminar Series, the University of Melbourne Gender Studies Seminar Series, and the University of Malaya Gender Studies Seminar Series. I thank the audience of these seminars for their enthusiastic engagement with my work. As my interlocutors described their relationships with others as a "give and give relationship," the audiences gave and gave their kindness to me. I hope that I will be able to one day give and give myself to others too.

The security of tenure provided by the University of Sydney allowed me to devote myself to completing this book. I thank my anthropology colleagues Ryan Schram, Robbie Peters, Anjalee Cohen, Sophie Chao, Luis Angosto Ferrandez, Michael Edwards, Sonja van Wichelen, and Warwick Anderson for their collegiality and inspiration. I will never take for granted what the comfort of ibasho allows one to achieve.

The research was supported by awards and generous funding from various institutions: the Australian Government Postgraduate Award, the Australian National University PhD Japan Alumni Award, the Australian Government Endeavour Research Fellowship, the Cambridge University Evans Fellowship, the National University of Singapore Asia Research Institute Postdoctoral Fellowship, and the National University of Singapore Faculty of Arts and Social Sciences and Asia Research Institute Book Manuscript Workshop Grant. I am very grateful for the invaluable opportunities that were given to me to conduct this research and work with talented people, including Jes Ebrahim Izaidin, who provided research assistance. I hope this book in a small way contributes to people's wellbeing across time and space.

I express my deepest appreciation to the University of Pennsylvania Press team. Elisabeth Maselli, my editor, stayed with me as an assuring pillar throughout the publishing process. Noreen O'Connor-Abel and Michelle Hawkins expertly polished the manuscript. Melissa Hyde compiled an impressive index with a careful eye for details. Thank you for your encouragement and support in bringing this work to publication.

Writing a book has truly blurred the boundaries between work and life. I would like to express my heartfelt gratitude to my family. Otosan and Okasan, thank you for the strength you gave me. Your unwavering support has allowed me to pursue my passion at all stages. Ross-san, thank you for being the fellow traveler in life and company. You are the most loving reader and cheerleader all at once. I now have a book, and a dearest child, Kazu-chan, to cherish with you.

www.ingramcontent.com/pod-product-compliance
Lightning Source LLC
Chambersburg PA
CBHW030328270326
41926CB00010B/1546